D1055048

PENGUIN BOOKS
UNLEASHING NEPAL

Sujeev Shakya is CEO of beed management, a management consulting and financial advisory services firm based in Kathmandu. He has worked for over twenty years in Nepal including heading one of Nepal's largest business groups. He is a chartered accountant and holds a graduate diploma in international marketing from Boston University and certification in coaching from Columbia University. He was awarded the Hubert H. Humphrey Fellowship by the US Department of State in 2002.

Sujeev chairs the Nepal Economic Forum, an interface for private sector development. From 2000 to 2011, he wrote a popular column under the nom de plume Arthabeed in *Nepali Times* and currently writes a column for the *Kathmandu Post*. For more information please visit www.sujeevshakya.com.

UNLEASHING
Nepal

Sujeev Shakya

for John Server

[signature]

PENGUIN BOOKS

PENGUIN BOOKS

Penguin Books India Pvt Ltd, 11 Community Centre, Panchsheel Park,
New Delhi 110 017, India
Penguin Group (USA) Inc., 375 Hudson Street, New York, New York 10014, USA
Penguin Group (Canada), 90 Eglinton Avenue East, Suite 700, Toronto,
Ontario, M4P 2Y3, Canada (a division of Pearson Penguin Canada Inc.)
Penguin Books Ltd, 80 Strand, London WC2R 0RL, England
Penguin Ireland, 25 St Stephen's Green, Dublin 2, Ireland (a division of Penguin Books Ltd)
Penguin Group (Australia), 707 Collins Street, Melbourne, Victoria 3008, Australia
(a division of Pearson Australia Group Pty Ltd)
Penguin Group (NZ), 67 Apollo Drive, Rosedale, Auckland 0632, New Zealand
(a division of Pearson New Zealand Ltd)
Penguin Books (South Africa) (Pty) Ltd, Block D, Rosebank Office Park, 181 Jan Smuts
Avenue, Parktown North, Johannesburg 2193, South Africa

Penguin Books Ltd, Registered Offices: 80 Strand, London WC2R 0RL, England

First published by Penguin Books India 2009
This updated edition published 2013

Copyright © Sujeev Shakya 2009, 2013
Foreword copyright © Gurcharan Das 2009
Introduction copyright © Ashraf Ghani 2009

All rights reserved

10 9 8 7 6 5 4 3 2

ISBN 9780143421092

The views and opinions expressed in this book are the author's own and the facts are as
reported by him which have been verified to the extent possible, and the publishers are
not in any way liable for the same.

Typeset in Minion Regular by SÜRYA, New Delhi
Printed at Replika Press Pvt. Ltd, India

To all who believe in the possibility of a transformation of Nepal and the unleashing of its potential

CONTENTS

PART III: UNLEASHING NEPAL

FOREWORD

There could be no better time for Sujeev Shakya's inspiring book on Nepal. The decade-long Maoist insurgency is over; the king has stepped down without bloodshed; the many parties, groups and interests have come together to give Nepal a new Constitution. The founding fathers of the new republic will soon be making choices in the constituent assembly which will decide Nepal's future. They should read this book to guide them in creating institutions which will lead the new nation from poverty to prosperity—a difficult but exciting enterprise, of consequence not only to thirty million Nepalis but to the whole subcontinent.

Nepal faces two starkly different but equally viable paths to the future—the way of China and the way of India. These huge neighbours of Nepal have become, amazingly enough, the two fastest growing economies in the world and are lifting millions successfully into the middle class. China is clearly ahead, and if the race were to end today, China would be declared winner. It has delivered more material well-being, raised more people out of poverty than any nation in history. But it is an open question as to who will be the long-term winner.

When it comes to the two paths, I am reminded of a conversation with my mother a few years ago. She asked, what is the difference between China growing at a rate of 10 per cent and India at 8 per cent? I replied that the difference was, indeed, very significant. If we were to grow at 10 per cent we could save twenty years. This is almost a generation. We could lift a whole generation into the middle class twenty years sooner. She thought for a while and then said gently, 'We have waited 3000 years for this moment. Why don't we wait another twenty and do it the Indian way?'

My mother had understood that the cost of democracy is the price that the poor pay in the delay of their entry into the middle class. She did not elaborate the 'Indian way' but it must include taking a holiday on half a dozen New Years Days! It is easy to get mesmerized by China's amazing progress and feel frustrated by India's chaotic democracy, but I think she had expressed the sentiments of most Indians who will not trade off democracy for 2 per cent higher growth. This is the real choice before Nepal.

In referring to the 'Indian way', my mother also meant that a nation must be true to itself. Democracy comes easily to us in India because India has historically 'accumulated' its diverse groups who retain their distinctiveness while identifying themselves as Indian. I suspect Nepalis are also 'accumulators'. China, on the other hand, has 'assimilated' its people into a common, homogeneous Confucian society. China is a melting pot in which differences disappear while India and Nepal are like a salad bowl in which the constituents retain their identity. Hence, China has always been governed by a hierarchical, centralized state—a tradition that has carried into the present era of reform communism. China resembles a business corporation today. Each mayor and party secretary has objectives relating to investment, output and growth, which are aligned to national goals. Those who exceed their goals rise quickly. The main problem in running a country as a business is that many people get left out.

India and Nepal, on the other hand, can only manage themselves by accommodating vocal and varied interest groups in their salad bowls. This leads to a million negotiations daily in India and we call this system 'democracy'. It slows us down—we take five years to build a highway versus one in China. Those who are disgruntled go to court. But our politicians are forced to worry about abuses of human rights, whereas my search on Google on 'human rights abuses in China' yielded 47.8 million entries in thirteen seconds! Democracies have a safety valve—it allows the disgruntled to let off steam before slowly co-opting them. Nepal should consider this as it debates its future over the next few years in the constituent assembly.

Both China and India have adopted the capitalist road to prosperity. They did this after learning painfully in the second half of the twentieth century that central planning and state ownership of the means of production are inefficient and perpetuate poverty in the end. In China, Mao's communism resulted in tens of millions of deaths; in India, Nehru's socialism led to a corrupt bureaucratic nightmare called the 'licence raj'. Nepal too, as Sujeev Shakya describes, had the same dismal experience under the kings Mahendra and Birendra. Nepal's constituent assembly must not be tempted to go along this discredited statist path and it ought to make room for the entrepreneurial energies of its people

Ferocious competition is a feature of the free market and it can be corrosive. But competition is also an economic stimulant that promotes human welfare. The choice is not between the free market and central planning but in getting the right mix of regulation. No one wants state ownership of production where the absence of competition corrodes the character even more. The answer is not to seek moral perfection which inevitably leads to theocracy and dictatorship. Since it is in man's nature to want more, let us learn to live with human imperfection, and seek regulation that not only tames crooks in the market but also rewards dharma-like behaviour. Nepal thus has no choice but to depend on the market. But the market has to be regulated and this is a delicate art—too much regulation can kill the golden goose; too little brings out the crooks.

Although both of Nepal's neighbours have adopted the market for economic decision-making, China's rise has been induced by a purposeful state. India's is almost despite the state. It is being driven by the people—by its entrepreneurs who are stepping into the vacuum as the state is getting out of the way through a process of slow, incremental reforms. Capitalism, according to theory, ought to sit more comfortably in India's democracy. Despite its many flaws, India has the rule of law and it respects property rights. I have an American friend who has lost his entire investment in China because his partner, who is closely connected to the party, has stolen his company, and he has no recourse. Partly because of the rule of law India is spawning globally competitive companies, who are becoming the envy of the world. The rule of law helps entrepreneurs to enforce contracts. The rule of law may slow India but it also protects its people (and its environment, as NGOs have discovered).

Democracy also respects property rights. As both nations urbanize, peasants in India are able to sell or borrow (using their land as collateral) against their land. Chinese peasants, I am told, are often at the mercy of local party bosses, who are the ones accumulating wealth in China. A recent survey shows that 90 per cent of the 20,000 richest persons in China are related to government or party officials.

Nepal should not underestimate the value of freedom which it has recently gained. When General Reginald Dyer opened fire in 1919 in Jallianwala Bagh killing 379 people, Indians realized they could only have dignity when they were free from British rule. The massacre at Tiananmen Square in 1989, where 300 students were killed, was China's Jallianwala Bagh. Eventually, China may approach First World levels of prosperity and it might even morph into a gigantic version of Singapore, a benign dictatorship with high levels of social welfare but with strict curbs on dissent. It sounds like an attractive future, but I have a feeling that people will not be happy unless they have democratic freedoms—especially when they have met their material needs.

Nepal should also draw lessons from the failure of the state in India. Indians are painfully aware that they must reform their government bureaucracy, police and judiciary—institutions, paradoxically, they were so proud of a generation ago. Because the state is inefficient, millions of entrepreneurs have stepped into the vacuum. When government schools fail in India, people start private schools in the slums, and the result is 'slumdog millionaires'. The lesson for Nepal is that it is easy to let institutions decline.

I suspect Nepal will find its own path in the end. Even if it wishes, it will not be able to adopt either the India or the China path. They are the result of historical accident and a bit of luck. The Chinese were lucky to have had a Deng, who knew the names of high-performing technocrats, and he brought them on board when he began the reforms, and drove China to prosperity. India was fortunate in having a Jawaharlal Nehru, who nurtured the institutions of democracy. The best that Nepal can do, I expect, is to learn from the successes and failures of its neighbours. At a minimum, if it is smart, Nepal will hitch its economy, as Sujeev Shakya suggests, to its fast-growing neighbours and reap the benefits of integration.

GURCHARAN DAS

PREFACE TO THE
UPDATED EDITION

Since the first edition was published in September 2009, to the outside world it may seem that Nepal has not changed as the political rhetoric, thanks to the judgment tool provided by the media, is still the same. However, the Nepali society and its socio-economic parameters are changing dramatically which gives us hope for the unleashing of Nepal.

In this updated edition, attempts have been made to provide new information, incorporate feedback and comments and a fresh chapter has been added, which narrates the journey of the unleashing of Nepal's potential.

I would like to take the opportunity to thank the readers, who were very kind to provide feedback, and the many institutions that hosted me for talks. I would also like to extend a big thank you to the members of the beed team who allowed me to find time to continue the 'unleashing Nepal' campaign.

From a book, *Unleashing Nepal* has become an icon of hope for the future of Nepal, where more narratives of change can evolve and a country that has always been identified with the three Ms—mountains, massacres and Maoists—for the outside world can now graduate to the three Ss—smile, service and success.

ACKNOWLEDGEMENTS

This book was inspired by the hundreds of people I have met during my twenty-year career—cab drivers, fellow passengers, strangers in bars, students, audiences I have addressed, the regular readers of my column 'Economic Sense', who never tired of sending me feedback (though they knew me by my nom de plume 'Arthabeed'), the many people who called in to share their frustrations and hopes.

I am grateful to Gurcharan Das for his words of encouragement and for being so gracious as to write the foreword to this book. I am also grateful to Professor Ashraf Ghani for writing the Introduction. Particular thanks to Manjushree Thapa, who constantly provided me the inspiration, guidance and support to complete this book, and to the tirelessly energetic Kanak Dixit, who makes you feel that you are doing too few things in life. He motivated me to walk that extra mile.

This book would not have been possible had Mr Prabhakar Rana, former executive director of Soaltee Hotel Limited, not been a role model for me when I joined the company as an audit trainee twenty years ago. His vision, his global perspective and his selfless and tireless propagation of a new agenda for the business community, have all shaped my views profoundly. I am grateful for the interviews he granted me for this book and also for helping in structuring it.

Many thanks to earlier mentors, Amar Raj Singh and Gagan Singh, and to Siddhartha Rana, who encouraged my hobby of writing and gave me the latitude to learn and discuss economic policy, during the twelve years I worked with him.

I am grateful for the time and insight provided by Finance Minister Dr Baburam Bhattarai, former finance ministers Dr Ram Sharan Mahat and Madhukar Rana, former vice chairperson of the National Planning Commission, Dr Jagadish Pokhrel, and former ambassadors Dr Bhekh Bahadur Thapa and Dr Singha Bahadur Basnyat in the course of writing this book.

While I was writing for the *Nepali Times* between 2000 and 2011, Kunda Dixit, its publisher and editor, always ensured that the columns were impeccable. He deserves a big thank you for continuing to encourage the Arthabeed in me. I am also grateful to a host of people who I have been using as a sounding board, Dr Ksenya Khinchuk, director of the Humphrey programme at the Boston University, Judith Babbitts, former director of the Humphrey programme at the Institute of International Education (IIE), Peter Moran, executive director of the Fulbright programme in Nepal, Prashant Jha, Arun Anand, Gerald Leader, Aniruddha Bose and Piyush Mathur.

This book would not have been possible without Pranab Singh, who worked with me tirelessly on making the book a reality. The fun of writing this book with him, holing up in hotel rooms to beat the sixteen-hour power cuts, is a memory to treasure.

I have been fortunate to have a stellar commissioning editor in Latika Neelakantan at Penguin. She has not only been patient but also someone who really knew how to bring the best out in me. A big thank you!

Finally, this book would not have been possible if my wife Alpa and daughter Suyasha had not given me the space and allowed me to sacrifice precious family time in order to write.

INTRODUCTION

In a meeting with progressive elements of the private sector in Kathmandu in 2008, I asked what it was that these Nepali businessmen wanted. The response of one of the participants was telling: 'We want to be part of a large middle-class in a middle-class country, not wealthy in a very poor country.' The deep economic and political analysis in this book explains both why Nepal remains extremely poor and how economic opportunities can be capitalized to create widespread and equitable economic growth for the Nepali people and a true middle class. There is already a globalized segment of the private sector in Nepal, which has an unwavering commitment to the country, impressive capabilities which can allow it to compete in the world economy and a clear vision for economic development. Sujeev Shakya is one member of this capable, dedicated and internationalized segment of the Nepali private sector, which will be critical to forging a 'New Nepal' from the midst of the ongoing economic, political and social problems that beset the country. He has been involved with economics in Nepal over several decades, and as such is uniquely positioned to explain how Nepal came to be where it is today and where it might go in the future.

Sadly, across the market in Nepal, a corrupt, illegitimate segment of the private sector continues to prevent the growth of the legitimate economy, and makes life increasingly difficult for those seeking to operate businesses within the law. Money laundering is pervasive and illicit economic activity is habitual among certain individuals and groups. Faced with unpredictable extortion demands, economic actors find it difficult to understand the cost of business, and therefore engage in long-term planning. Such illegal activities have led to disenchantment with the market economy and the view that market creates winners and losers in a zero sum game of economic competition. A history of centralized, nepotistic power structures and chronic aid dependency have further exacerbated these problems and the current financial crisis has hit ordinary Nepalis, many of whom continue to live in abject poverty.

As Sujeev explains, these problems have come about because the Nepali state has not provided predictable and fair rules of the game for the operation of the market, which has isolated or driven away many of the economic actors necessary to transform Nepal into a modern, vibrant state based on a legitimate and open market economy. The viability and credibility of capitalism have been called into question, not least by the Maoists, but communism is not the answer to Nepal's problems. A balance has to be struck between the state and the market, and Sujeev's call for a movement towards a capitalist welfare economy is welcome: the visible hand of the state is necessary to set the appropriate regulatory mechanisms to keep the market functioning according to a set of rules, and to provide social safety nets for those who are left out of economic growth, particularly during the current downturn. In this respect, this book could not have come at a more important time.

Both in political and in economic terms, a point that Sujeev makes very well is that history has a tendency to repeat itself in Nepal, and that history has not always been positive. As the title of this book indicates, Nepal's potential can only be unleashed when the conditions are put in place to allow the future of the economy to truly overcome the problems of the present and the shackles of the past. Nepal has incredible economic potential—from social capital at the community level, which has supported effective management of forestry, hydroelectricity and education, to a dynamic regional context and considerable natural resources, to bureaucratic ability and a huge set of diaspora skills and income— which, as Sujeev explains, must be harnessed coherently to produce a series of visible benefits for the population, create a sense of positive momentum and lay the basis for medium- to long-term transformation of Nepal.

This book acts as an essential tool for learning and discussion as it maps these assets and explains coherently how they can be mobilized through identification of key economic areas and value chains that provide the potential for significant growth in Nepal over the coming years. It provides the substance for a serious discussion between politicians, the private sector and donors in Nepal, which has not yet taken place, as to how to generate economic development; transform money into capital through creating stakeholders in property rights and the rule of law; create jobs; imagine what desirable and credible economic goals look like; understand the sectors and instruments for growth; and highlight how resources will best be mobilized, with the productive zones of business expanded, while corrupt, inefficient private sector elements are concurrently minimized.

Another point made clearly to me in past discussions with the private sector in Kathmandu is that revolution has one 'r' too many: the Nepali economy needs change, but only slowly and constructively, to ensure predictability. Political instability in Nepal has too often undermined economic development and prevented positive rhetoric from being transformed into implementation. Sujeev rightly ends by focusing on young people, who must be given an economic stake in the future of Nepal, in support of economic security, not further reasons to use the skills they develop elsewhere in India, the Gulf or further afield. These are the future leaders and managers of Nepali business and politics, and without them the future will only further replicate the past.

Sujeev has for many years been a strong proponent of the idea that Nepal must join and compete in the globalized economy, and this book provides yet another clear call for stakeholders in Nepal, both inside and outside the country, to make this a reality. This is possible, as the success stories detailed here—from Bhatbhateni Supermarket to D2 Hawkeye (now Verisk Information Technologies) to Darbur Nepal—indicate clearly. Positive business ideas of this type must be understood, the relevant rules and incentives put in place and the space for innovation expanded so that the incredible desire for change and innovative nature of the Nepali people can be used productively for individual and collective benefit. This book leaves little doubt that the private sector will play a central role in Nepal's development, not only in terms of the direct effects it can have on poverty reduction, job creation and economic stability, but also because it will support the growth of a politically conscious middle-class, the growth of a responsible civil society that can hold the government to account, and finally allow the country to move away from its dependence on aid and towards a model of co-production with the international community that allows for inclusive economic growth. It is time for stakeholders from across the Nepali society to come together, work to generate the positive change that the Nepali people so desperately want and ensure the prosperity and stability that they so richly deserve.

ASHRAF GHANI
Chairman, Institute for State Effectiveness and
co-author of *The Framework: Fixing Failed States*

AUTHOR'S PROLOGUE

PAST DEBACLES, PRESENT
OPPORTUNITIES, FUTURE DREAMS

Nepal witnessed events of profound significance from 2006 to 2009. From Maoist guerrillas coming over ground and actually winning a mandate to form a government, to the ending of the 240-year-old institution of monarchy, every day was history in the making. With the constituent assembly starting the process of writing the Constitution of the Federal Democratic Republic of Nepal, many questions on fundamental economic rights were being asked by an ever more assertive citizenry. There was never a better time to shape the future of Nepal's economy.

Nepal had remained a closed nation for much of its history prior to the twentieth century. Until the opening of the economy in 1990, the only events of note involved the capture of business by the elites. Since Nepal is a poor country that receives a lot of financial aid, writings on the Nepali economy have largely been the work of non-Nepali consultants paid for by aid money, and have generally taken the form of critical post-mortem. *Unleashing Nepal* will view Nepal's economy and history differently because it will not just examine what went wrong but also go on to look at how Nepal can transform its economic future.

With a population of close to thirty million people, Nepal stands forty-third in the world in terms of population.[1] With more than half of those people under the age of twenty-six, we have a large pool of human capital. With India and China coming to the centre stage of global economy, even splinter effects of the rapid economic growth of China and India can transform Nepal. The book will, of course, examine history and in doing that, come to terms with past debacles of the Nepali economy, but it will also point to future growth opportunities and contain prescriptions for the transformation of Nepal.

If one is to explain both contemporary political culture and Nepal's low levels of economic growth, it is critical to understand Nepal's economic history and its many legacies. Some of these include: (a) the emphasis on land as the only link to political and economic power, (b) the importance of physical proximity to quarters of power via the government, corporation or NGO (c) protectionism (d) the rent-seeking mentality (e) the popular feeling about development as a culture imposed from outside Nepal and (f) the constant search by Nepalis for greener pastures outside the country.

Nepal became a sovereign state in 1772, after the annexation of the Kathmandu Valley by Prithvi Narayan Shah who founded the Shah dynasty. **Part One** of the book analyses events from 1772 to 1990 in order to explain how Nepal's poverty was caused first, by its isolation from the world during the Shah and Rana rule and later, in the twentieth century, due to the confused economic policies of three generations of Shah kings—Tribhuvan, Mahendra and Birendra. The political isolation of the early Nepali kingdoms fostered an economic system in which all economic activities were linked to land and the army, both very well exploited. The inefficient management of land and the revenues thereof resulted in dysfunctional political institutions. This close association of power with land and the army is still prevalent—the Maoists, after coming to power in September 2008, believe in clinging to power through control of land in the guise of land reforms, as well as through control over the army.

Part Two of the book examines the events of the past two decades between 1990—when a popular uprising commonly referred to as the Jana Andolan ended thirty years of a partyless political system of autocratic monarchy—and 2012, when Nepal became a republic in a bloodless transition. This section begins with the economic reforms initiated by an elected government in the early 1990s and the subsequent chaos, as political parties vied for power through intra- and inter-party feuds, sidelining economic concerns completely. The analysis over the past two decades, from 1990 to 2012, places the blame of squandering opportunities and resources equally on the private sector, the donor community and the government. While much has been written on the ineptitude of the government, little reading is available on the role of the private sector and the donor community in our economic debacles. From the late 1990s on, the masses, thus far ignored and disempowered, found hope in the Maoists, and a People's War that lasted ten years was waged against the state. The war stalled Nepal's progress, resulting in young people looking for greener pastures outside Nepal, just as their ancestors had, due to the absence of opportunities during the days of autocracy. This gave rise to the remittance economy, which will play a key role in Nepal's economic future.

Part Three of this book has been shaped by my desire to constantly dream—this time the dreams have been for unleashing Nepal's potential. As a management consultant and advisory services provider, I have been selling dreams to companies and organizations and coming up with innovative ideas to achieve those dreams. In the last four chapters of the book I attempt to uncover and make sense of the vast economic opportunities in Nepal, for students, professionals, entrepreneurs, policy makers, development workers and others across the social spectrum. Having started my own career as a trainee and working all the way to the top in one of the largest business groups in Nepal, I have always believed that if there is a place in the world where one can be successful, it is here in Nepal. In every sector one looks at, there are vast areas of opportunity. In tourism, there is the opportunity to take tourists from snow-capped peaks to tropical jungle in less than an hour's flight, to showcase the birthplace of the Buddha and to offer heritage walks, spiritual sojourns and adventure sports. Branding Nepali tea, coffee, herbs and handicrafts or creating niche brands like Swiss Chocolate, would provide endless prospects for small and medium businesses that can be networked to support a pan-Nepali brand. If water is the key natural resource that the world will focus on in this century, then Nepal is bestowed with a natural bounty of water that can be used for many purposes, including for clean hydroelectricity. If Nepal is to develop only half of its potential for hydropower and sell it to India, the export revenues would be more than what Saudi Arabia makes by selling oil. If households in villages can farm herbs that can be processed at home and then marketed, or just grow flowers for export to different parts of the world, rural households will flourish. The list of opportunities is endless.

ॐ

I have been a proponent of market-oriented reforms that help to build the private sector, creating investment as well as job opportunities for every citizen. I have had the privilege of being able to look at the private sector closely during twenty years of a corporate career that included dialogue with various multilateral and bilateral agencies. I have thus been able to observe issues from a very simple perspective—the perspective of a Nepali in business, informed by a basic common sense understanding of how things work and don't work. For example, why is Nepal a hydropower-rich but electricity-starved nation? It is not graphs and guff that people want, but a simple analysis of what went wrong in the past and what can be fixed for the future.

The first detailed analysis of the emergence and squandering of the promises of the Nepali economy was written by this author as an essay in a compendium called *State of Nepal*, in 2001.[2] Every time I saw photocopies of this essay—during meetings with development consultants in Nepal or in the binders in the World Bank offices in Washington DC or with the confused Fulbright scholar trying to figure out the Nepali economy by citing this essay—I felt the need to write a comprehensive, readable book on the Nepali economy. When readers told me that it was a very engaging and lucid account of how the 1990s' economic reforms brought about significant growth opportunities which were subsequently squandered, I felt pushed to take some time off to write a book that would explain the Nepali economy in an easy-to-read manner. Manjushree Thapa's influential and widely read book *Forget Kathmandu*,[3] which lucidly interprets Nepali history for a contemporary reader, made me wonder why there could not be a book analysing the Nepali economy just as accessibly.

The words economy and economics suggest tedious and dull reading to many, but if there's one thing eight years of writing an overwhelmingly popular column called 'Economic Sense'* has taught me, it is that economics explained in simple terms can interest anyone. The overwhelming response I received from ordinary people when I wrote about the economic and political issues that govern their lives, made me realize that people are really thirsting for this understanding. In reading *Unleashing Nepal*, readers may at times find strongly stated opinions, but it could be argued that such opinions bring out the truth, however unpalatable it may be. I have reason to believe that many readers will be able to relate to these opinions—be it my criticism of the prevalence of the impractical traditional calendar over the Gregorian calendar in Nepal, or asking why the exchange rate between Nepal and India is seldom reviewed. These fundamental questions have a bearing on the life of every Nepali who is trying to figure out the calendar in a new mobile phone or queuing up for an LPG cylinder for the kitchen or for petrol for the motorcycle—the prices of these essentials are directly correlated to the exchange rate between India and Nepal.

I want to see Nepal as a capitalist welfare state, a state that believes in private enterprise while also taking responsibility for the welfare of its citizens. The unleashing of Nepal's potential rests on these two pillars. I have generally been introduced at talk programmes as a corporate executive with a societal conscience and have had the rare opportunity to observe both the corporate world and the social sectors at close quarters. I have always believed in this balance between private enterprise and social welfare—the

---

*This column appeared under the pseudonym 'Arthabeed' in the *Nepali Times*, a weekly published from Kathmandu.

strategies I pursued in organizations looked not only at profits for the organization, but also at the larger impact on the population. This book attempts to scale up this balance to a national level. The prescriptions in this book are not based on the usual picture painted of Nepal—a poor landlocked country that has literally left everything to fate. I attempt to look at Nepal's potential boundaries—these might be called boundaries of opportunity—which extend beyond its political boundaries. The 300 million people living in north and northeast India, along with the 150 million people in Bangladesh, form Nepal's potential area of economic influence.

ભ

My interactions as a Hubert Humphrey fellow with fellows from over a hundred developing countries in the past six years, have made me believe that there is a lot of hope for Nepal. Nepal can indeed transform itself, as other countries we should benchmark Nepal against, have. Malaysia has the same population as Nepal (about thirty million) but far healthier economic indicators. South Korea transformed itself in a mere four decades, from a poor country with a GDP equal to Ghana to one of the most developed countries in Asia. This book is therefore, about hopes, dreams and aspirations for Nepal. People may agree or disagree with the prescriptions but the hope is that we will start discussing and debating not only politics but also Nepal's economic future, and not just at endless conferences and seminars but also in every classroom, home, workplace, in *chautaris** and meeting places of all kinds.

I have been influenced by Gurcharan Das' influential book *India Unbound*[4] where the author was able to examine not just the problems with the Indian economy but also the sparks that ignited

---

*Chautaris are places in Nepal's towns and villages where people assemble to socialize.

the transformation of that economy. In *Unleashing Nepal*, I have tried to take account of past hurdles and failures as well as of potentialities that could very well spark Nepal's economic transformation. Thomas Friedman remarks in his bestseller *The World is Flat*, that economic transformations do not have to take a lot of time: 'India only twenty years ago, before the triple convergence, was known as a country of snake charmers, poor people and Mother Teresa. Today its image has been recalibrated. Now it is also seen as a country of brainy people and computer wizards.'[5] This book is dedicated to such a hope for the transformation and unleashing of potential in Nepal.

PART I

THE PAST TILL THE 1990s

In the following two chapters, an attempt has been made to present relevant portions of Nepali history, along with political and social interventions which have impacted the Nepali economy. This journey through Nepal's past reaches a turning point in the restoration of multiparty democracy and the establishment of a constitutional monarchy in 1990. I will first provide a narrative of the events that created modern Nepal—the annexation of Kathmandu Valley by Prithvi Narayan Shah and the rule of the Shah kings and the Rana prime ministers thereafter. I also look at what was happening in the rest of the world during that time. This provides the historical basis for understanding the present condition of the Nepal economy, its isolation from the global economy and the reasons why Nepal remains one of the ten poorest countries in the world.

PART 1

THE PAST TILL THE 1990s

1

ISOLATION, ISOLATION
AND ISOLATION

When Prithvi Narayan Shah was crowned the king of Gorkha in 1743, he had already set his sights on Kathmandu Valley. His interest in the valley was not surprising, given the valley's affluence and power. The valley was home to the wealthiest kingdoms in the entire Mahabharata range. Situated on the primary trade route between South Asia and the northern kingdoms of Tibet and China, the three kingdoms of Bhaktapur, Lalitpur and Kathmandu benefited from an extensive trade network and a prosperous agricultural economy. The economic sway of these three kingdoms over the entire hill region is attested to by the fact that the entire monetary requirement of the region was met through coinage minted in these kingdoms.[1]

Prithvi Narayan Shah understood that Gorkha was not a wealthy nation. Had he heard of Adam Smith's definition of wealth as the annual produce of the land and the labour of a society, he would have agreed. Born in the same year, both Prithvi Narayan Shah and Adam Smith shared an interest in the wealth of nations. However, if Adam Smith's motivations are widely believed (rightly or wrongly) to have been philosophical and intellectual, Prithvi Narayan Shah's are generally seen as real and practical—he strove for personal enrichment. He had a modest upbringing, for a prince—eating sugarcane for a treat and keeping pigeons as a hobby. An annual clothing budget of six and a half rupees and pocket money counted in quarters—all in the coinage of the valley kingdoms, were his other, equally unimpressive royal privileges. This austere upbringing, coupled with a long standing family desire to capture the wealth of Kathmandu, undoubtedly inspired him to lead Gorkha on a warpath towards Kathmandu.

Twenty-five years and several wars later, when Prithvi Narayan Shah finally sat upon the throne of the Malla kings of Nepal in 1768, he declared Kathmandu the capital of his newly formed empire and, some say, brought the modern nation of Nepal into being. In taking over Kathmandu Valley, Prithvi Narayan Shah gained the advantage of a monopoly over the trade between India and Tibet. A mid-1600s treaty between Kathmandu and Tibet had established the route through the valley as the only trade link to be used by Tibet for trade with India. Nepal was also to mint silver coins for Tibet for which Tibet provided silver or paid in gold. As the sole entrepot for Tibet, Kathmandu Valley flourished not only as a trade hub but also as a value-adding manufacturer, most prominently through its artisans and craftsmen. Centuries of doing business with Tibet had also established the Newar merchant community as the primary link between Indian traders to the south, and the Tibetan traders to the north. The control of the Newar community over this trade route is demonstrated by reports that place the Newars as the single largest group of foreigners in Lhasa.[2]

Prithvi Narayan Shah ruled over a predominantly Newar population and was fortunate in that this community came to accept Gorkhali rule without putting up too much of a fight, though they initially had reasons to do so. The prolonged war and blockade instituted by the Gorkhali army had created a shortage of food supplies in the valley and had seriously disrupted trade, the Newar mainstay. With the Gorkhali conquest of Kathmandu however, Newar traders suddenly found themselves in the capital city of an expanding empire and at the central trade hub for the entire hill region. A Newar farmer who traditionally produced and traded mustard oil with Tibet, suddenly found previously restricted markets in the western regions of Nepal opening up for trade. The initial resentment of being conquered quickly vanished as the Newars starting capitalizing on these undeniable business advantages. This resurgence of trade within and beyond the borders of empire led to an economic boom. By capturing Kathmandu Valley, Prithvi Narayan Shah controlled the primary trading and financial hub of the entire hill region.

Having secured a firm financial base for his empire, Prithvi Narayan Shah quickly moved south and conquered the three Terai kingdoms of Makwanpur, Vijaypur and Chaudandi by 1774. It is without a doubt that the prosperity of these regions made them targets of conquest. These regions were not only the primary gateway for trade into India, but were also rich in resources. The vast forests that dominated the southern expanses of Nepal provided a lucrative base for the trade of resources like wax, honey, musk, herbs and timber. In addition to this, major commodities like paddy, oilseeds, cotton, jute, tobacco and sugarcane were produced in the region in sufficient quantities to export to cities as far off as Patna and Calcutta (present-day Kolkata).

Although a sense of nationalism and the cause of defending the Hindu nation from the occupation and subjugation of the British and the Muslims are commonly cited political and personal motives behind Prithvi Narayan Shah's conquest, the economic rationale of his action cannot be underestimated. Indeed, an economic analysis of his expansion indicates that continued success in both conquest and rule hinged on the acquisition of a strong financial base. Prithvi Narayan Shah was a visionary and an astute tactician; it is not without reason that he has been glorified as a nationalist hero and the unifier of the nation in every Nepali textbook. However, given his personality traits of vision and strategic acumen, it is hard and perhaps even dishonest not to add the incentives of wealth, power and glory to his drive. Without the income secured from Prithvi Narayan Shah's initial conquests, it is unlikely the Gorkhali empire would have been able to sustain its expansion until well after his death in 1775.

The Invisible Hand Versus the Visible Fist

A year after Prithvi Narayan Shah's death, Adam Smith would publish his magnum opus, *The Wealth of Nations*. In his book, Adam Smith presents the notion of the invisible hand as a natural force which guides free market capitalism through the competition for scarce resources—regulating it in the absence of state control. Smith believed that the greatest benefit to a society is brought about by individuals acting freely and in self interest in a competitive market—leading to specialization and diversification in the economy. However, even if Adam Smith were himself the personal advisor to the kings of Nepal on all matters economic, he would have found it an extremely arduous and painstaking job, if not an impossible one, to convert the late eighteenth-century feudal rule of Nepal into a free market economy. The difficulty of such a task lay in the stark contrast between conditions in Europe and Nepal. Although Europe was also largely dominated by some form of feudalism during the eighteenth century, it had established a number of semi-autonomous institutions of scientific research and education. Financial and monetary systems had already been institutionalized in order to manage extensive trade networks while the lack of a caste system allowed for mobility of labour between occupations. The mobility and flexibility in Europe's labour market is perhaps best illustrated by the rise of Napoleon from a common solider to Emperor of the French republic. Such a feat would have been unheard of and socially unacceptable in Nepal. Most importantly, the involvement of the individual in the economy and the general perception of the economy in Europe was fundamentally different from that in Nepal. The rise of trade and capitalism had allowed Europe to perceive the economy as a distinct entity in its own right, an entity in which the state itself is a player. However, in Nepal, the economy was perceived as belonging to the state. This perception was further supported by the Nepali government's land ownership system (which will be described below), limitations on private enterprise, and restrictions imposed on the work force. The Nepali economy was clearly ruled by the iron fisted and very visible hand of the state.

The lack of favourable social and institutional conditions in Nepal is not the sole reason for its failure to enter a capitalist economy—the nature of the leadership was also a cause. When *The Wealth of Nations* was published, it practically founded the science of economics, at a time when the words *economics* and *capitalism* were not even in common use. The American nation had just come into being in 1776 while Germany was about a century away from establishing itself as a nation. Nepal, however, lacked leaders like Thomas Jefferson and Benjamin Franklin, raised during the age of enlightenment and taught in the progressive scientific tradition that was establishing itself in the West. Thus, it is not surprising that ideas of free market capitalism and universal suffrage were even further off. Maximizing efficiency and productivity, the hallmarks of any capitalist society, were not central to the Nepali economy. Instead, the focus seemed to be on maximizing revenues and state control while maintaining the status quo, rather than creating the conditions necessary for economic growth and expansion. The caste system is a classic example of this erroneous focus. Taken as an economic system for the division of labour, the caste system shows an understanding of the importance of labour specialization. However, as a state instituted regime, it became a hierarchical social order that restricted labour migration and led to a stifling of the economy.

Before his death, Prithvi Narayan Shah was able to present a vision for the nation popularly known as the *Divya Upadesh*.[3] The dictated vision of Nepal's conquering king contains the seeds of a Nepali national identity, a strong affinity for the traditional Hindu caste system and a tacit acknowledgment of the diversity present in Nepal. His realization of the need for a strong administration and judiciary are apparent in his emphasis on a system that is fair and just. He not only outlined a code of conduct for his citizens, but also demanded austerity and conservatism from his own descendents and the nobility. Unfortunately, he was unable to institutionalize this code of conduct. Additionally, he made strong statements that advocate a protectionist monetary economy based on nationalistic principles. This economic protectionism and his strong warnings against the British played a significant role in Nepal's hostile stance towards the British and its adoption of isolationist policies.

The state of Nepal was structured by a feudal system that centralized the ownership of land with the state, which was synonymous with the king. The nobility and feudal lords of Nepal, unlike the feudal lords of England and Germany, thus could not assert any independent authority based on the ownership of land. All feudal lords in Nepal enjoyed their rights to hold land only at the discretion of the king. This traditional system of administration, called the *pajani* system, was carried forward by Prithvi Narayan Shah because he believed it would allow the king to be the defender of justice. Under the system, each feudal lord's performance with his land grant, vis-à-vis revenue collection, would be reviewed, leading to either renewal or termination dependent upon performance levels. This system of administration held true for everyone working for the government, from the nobility to soldiers.

In simple terms, the *pajani* system was meant to ensure that the right man was matched with the right job, thus ensuring the productivity of land as an asset and that all the nobility remained loyal to the crown. Its weakness was its overdependence on a single individual, the king, as the guarantor of justice, a responsibility which he did not always conduct according to the stated rules. This resulted in a tenuous system of land administration where, lacking any guarantee of continued rights to the land, nobles preferred to wage war or attend at court to impress the king, rather than develop a viable political relationship with the populations in their territories.

Sowing the Nepali Rent-seeking Mentality

There is a rich tradition in Nepal which encourages the aristocracy and rich land owners to do nothing but tend to the renting out of their land. Upper caste males of the Brahmin, Chhettri and some Newar castes frowned upon the idea of working. The belief was that work was meant for the lower castes and the only dignified service for those of the upper caste was religious activity (for the Brahmins) or military service (for the Chhettris). The pattern of elite members of society showing an aversion to work, remaining content with doing nothing other than collecting rent and being socially praised for such inactivity, is what I call here the rent-seeking mentality. It has its roots in Nepal's early history and is a disposition to economic activity that resurfaces in various forms to this day. Till date, we are yet to become a society that believes in the dignity of labour, and finds doing a task as respectable as ordering a task to be done.

With an agrarian economy lacking private enterprise and facing mounting administrative and military expenses, the Nepali state could only respond to a shortfall in funds by exploiting its primary asset, land. Prithvi Narayan Shah was quick to realize that lacking a strong cash economy and inheriting a weak government revenue and expenditure system, land remained his primary asset. He had to maximize the productivity of the land he owned as it was the only means of increasing state revenue. He therefore made land central to the feudal and economic structure of Nepal and controlled access to it through the *pajani* system, in which there was no guarantee of continued rights to the land. Below, we will describe the various land tenure systems and ownership modalities that were already in operation in Nepal, and explain how combined with *pajani*, they eventually weakened the empire.

Birtas were land grants given out by the state to individuals* with the individual retaining all rights to the produce of the land along with the rights to earn an income from litigations, administrative fees and taxes on the surrounding area. This system placed the *Birtawals*† as the effective rulers over the tracts of land which they were renting from the state in return for supplying troops, weapons and ammunition to the expanding empire. If *Birta* land grants were an effective way to rent out state-owned land to ensure productivity, the *Jagir* system was an ingenious way to continue the expansion of the empire while running the government at a deficit. Adapted from a system that was introduced by the Muslim rulers in India during the thirteenth century, *Jagirs*

---

*Only to Brahmins during Prithvi Narayan Shah's time, but to other castes as well by the time of his descendants.

†*Birta* land grant recipients.

were short-term land grants which were mostly given for military services in lieu of cash salaries. This greatly reduced the cash burden on a state that lacked a strong cash economy, ensured productivity in newly acquired lands and was a successful means of payment, as a large number of land-hungry hill men thought the promise of fertile land in the Terai was worth more than the risk of death in military service.

Besides *Birta* and *Jagir* systems of land grants, *Guthi* land grants were given to temples and monasteries for the benefit of the local community. *Rakam* land grants were given to craftsmen and skilled workers as payment for their labour. *Birta* and *Jagir* started to replace other forms of land ownership under Prithvi Narayan Shah's rule. For instance, *Kipat* land was part of a more traditional form of communal land ownership practiced in the Eastern regions of Nepal by Rai and Limbu ethnic groups. Large tracts of *Kipat* land were converted into *Birta* and *Jagir* lands to fund the expansion of the Nepali state. Although the land system adopted by the new state of Nepal facilitated its expansionary steps, in the long run it was to prove a disastrous and costly system for the state. Under this system, the direct relationship between the state and the peasantry was replaced and superseded by the *Birta* or *Jagir* tenant. Thus the administration of justice and the protection of the peasantry, which according to Prithvi Narayan's *Divya Upadesh* were the direct responsibility of the king and state, were never experienced in that way by the peasants. For the peasantry, the state effectively was replaced by the *Birtawal* or *Jagirdar*. The word *Jagirdar* is still popularly used to refer to someone who has a plump 'rent-seeking' job that includes working as a driver in an NGO.

To make matters worse, the one relationship the peasantry had left with the state was one of exploitation through taxes. The state did not tax *Birta* and *Jagir* grant holders as they were land grants given with a tax exemption and so the burden of paying taxes to the state fell on the underprivileged class of peasants who owned small tracts of land compared to the vast tracts owned by the *Birtawals* and *Jagirdars*. This required peasants to work on *Birta* and *Jagir* land paying a rental fee for the rights to cultivate that land. These rents were often preposterously high as both *Birtawals* and *Jagirdars* tried to maximize their income during their limited tenure on the land. The *pajani* system ensured that there was no guarantee of continued rights to the land. Since the bulk of *Birta* and *Jagir* owners were members of the nobility, they rarely presided over the lands they were granted. Being in Kathmandu made it easier to secure the blessing of the king and earn larger land grants. This meant that they had to contract out the actual administration of the land, further removing the peasantry from any direct contact with the state. This contractual hiring of administrators, called the *Ijara* system, was also deployed by the state to collect taxes from the peasantry. Till date, the system is perpetuated by political parties which use different village representatives to collect money and propagate the party ideology; this method stems from the same mindset that was operating at that time.

After Prithvi Narayan Shah's death in 1775, the expansion of the state continued but successive rulers were unable to institutionalize either a strong governance system or a progressive economic policy. The empire thus made little progress—the traditional feudal economic system that was prevalent in Gorkha and the surrounding regions continued. The financial pressures on the Nepali state were tremendous; in 1772, three years before Prithvi Narayan Shah's death, the annual cost of maintaining an army of around nine thousand strong was about Rs 450,000 while its revenues amount to at most Rs 300,000 for the same year.[4]

The nobility's dependence on *Birta* grants and *Jagir* assignments for their own individual affluence created a lot of competition between them. These systems also were in stark contrast to the political and administrative system of the British East India Company, which followed a more modern system of land ownership, taxation, and governance. The two systems came into conflict in the Terai, where local land-holders would get rights to land from both the British and Kathmandu and declare themselves and their land as belonging to either party, depending on what was convenient at any given time. The British were used to having clearly demarcated boundaries and found it difficult to adapt to the more ambiguous Nepali land system. Land rights under the Nepali land system also included rights to adjudicate law in, administer and tax these lands, further confusing the British East India Company's administration. These land disputes eventually led to the 1814–15 Anglo-Nepal war.

The End of Empire

Given Nepal's weak financial situation due to its extensive expansion efforts, it is surprising that Nepal entered into a war against the British East India Company. A heavy loss to the Chinese in the 1792 Sino-Nepal war had already considerably weakened the Gorkhali army and empire. Additionally, the Nepali army had been weakened by a prolonged but unsuccessful siege at Kangra which had ended in a clash with the Sikh ruler Ranjit Singh in 1809. In contrast, by 1813, the Company had expanded its control over most of India aside from the kingdoms of Punjab and Nepal. Its military and financial superiority to the newly formed Gorkhali empire was evident in its accomplishments. The Gorkhali empire's continued expansionary efforts despite these known facts and its eventual war with the British, point to the weak governance and lack of foresight of its ruling aristocracy.

Unlike the agrarian Nepali state, the British East India Company's military power was the result of a commercial enterprise that grew out of a monetary economy. The East India Company had been established through a royal charter as a joint stock company in the year 1600. It functioned as a commercial organization with state-granted monopolies over the trade of certain goods or forms of labour. It began trading in India in 1608, and by 1813, had commercial and political control over most of the Indian subcontinent, aside from Punjab and Nepal. However, much like Nepal, it was on the brink of bankruptcy, with its wars of expansion in India having drained its coffers. In an attempt to stave off bankruptcy, the company petitioned parliament, leading to the British Crown asserting its sovereignty over its Indian territories but extending the administrative rule of the Company within those territories, in 1813.

In effect, the Anglo-Nepal war was fought between the state of Nepal and a Company which had been hired to manage the administration of British territories in India. On the eve of the war, Nepal's annual state revenue was no more than approximately Rs 800,000. During the same time period, the annual revenues of the British government totalled sixteen million pounds. Thus, the much acclaimed historical David and Goliath battle between the two nations was more a case of Nepali recklessness than courage and more arrogance than foresight. By the end of the war in 1816, Nepal had lost considerable tracts of agriculturally productive lands in the Terai, Sikkim and a significant portion of territory west of the Mahakali River. For a kingdom that was so heavily dependent on land, the loss of over 64,000 square kilometres of territory was a significant blow to the national ego. Nonetheless, the fact that the Gorkhali empire eventually retained an area of over 136,000 square kilometres, having started with a kingdom of less than 250 square kilometres, is a good measure of its success.[5] Even so, given the economic value of the one-thirds of lands lost to the British, Nepal was crippled by this territorial and economic defeat. The defeat to the British, which was preceded by defeats at the hands of the Chinese and the Sikhs, effectively ended Nepal's expansionary attempts and its attempts to establish itself as a regional power. Forced to acknowledge its disadvantage in both military size and economic power in comparison with the two major powers in the region, from 1816 onwards, Nepal followed an increasingly isolationist policy.

Autocracy in Rana-dom

The fallout from the end of empire was that the nobility and feudal lords of Nepal all returned to Kathmandu from different parts of Nepal. No longer able to win honours and land grants through their military prowess, the feudal *pajani* system made it necessary for the nobles to cosy up to the royal family in order to secure their land rights and increase their wealth. The result was a chaotic power struggle between the various families of the nobility—most notably the Thapa, Pande and Basnet families. Court intrigue, political manoeuvring and assassinations became a regular occurrence in these turbulent times. This culminated in the 1846

Kot Massacre, orchestrated by Jung Bahadur Kunwar and his brothers, resulting in the massacre of over fifty high ranking and prominent members of the nobility and military. In one bloody night, within the precincts of the royal court, Jung Bahadur successfully eliminated all his enemies and propelled himself into the position of prime minister of Nepal. Jung Bahadur is, in many ways, Nepal's Napoleon. Coming from a minor aristocratic family, the Kunwars, Jung Bahadur made a name for himself through his sheer recklessness and daring character. He was a man who would do anything for the right price. By 1846, having moved up the aristocratic ladder, he successfully annihilated most of the aristocracy, reduced the king and queen to mere puppets and assumed absolute power over Nepal. To commemorate his accomplishment he took on the title of Rana. The name 'Rana' was adopted by all his kinsmen and marks the beginning of the Rana regime.

By eliminating the most prominent members of all the other aristocratic families and banishing their remaining family members to British India, Jung Bahadur was able to assert absolute control over the Nepali court. He also utilized the *pajani* system to ensure that all offices of responsibility and all land rights were offered to his own family and supporters. Jung Bahadur did not appoint himself as king, choosing instead to retain the monarchy as a symbolic institution and severely curtailing the movements and activities of the king and queen. Perceval Landon in his book *History of Nepal*, quotes the British Resident Surgeon, Dr Wright's take on these events:

> Jung Bahadur has been the undisputed ruler of the country. The old King is the prisoner in the palace. The present King is kept under the strictest surveillance and not allowed to exercise any power whatever. The heir apparent is also kept in a state of obscurity, being never permitted to take part in any public business or even appear in the *Darbars*.[6]

From the end of the Anglo-Nepal war in 1816 till the time of Jung Bahadur's ascendancy, little had changed in the way Nepal was governed. However, unlike his predecessors, whose relations with Britain were cool, Jung Bahadur realized the futility of trying to stand up against them. With the British annexation of the Sikh empire in 1849, early on in Jung Bahadur's career, he realized the ability of the British empire to humble the expansive kingdoms of the south. Although cautious, Jung Bahadur sought to befriend the British, a strategy which was to work in his favour. Unwilling to allow British and Indian traders into Nepal, he nonetheless saw the benefits of trading with them. He was keen on restoring the monopoly Nepal had once possessed on the trade between India and Tibet. Using the mistreatment of Nepali traders in Tibet as an excuse, Jung Bahadur launched an offensive against Tibet in 1855. Jung Bahadur's intelligence on the Chinese was undoubtedly facilitated by the British, who were gearing up for the second Opium War of 1856. Thus, the inability of the Chinese to assist Tibet, who had, in the past, thwarted Nepali expansion, was effectively insured. This eventually led to Nepal's 1856 treaty with Tibet which granted Nepal similar privileges in Tibet as it had enjoyed during the Malla reign in the 16th and 17th century and subsequently lost during the late 18th century, but with Nepal still remaining a tributary state to China. Importantly, this reinstated Nepal's trade relations with Tibet which had taken a serious hit since the 1792 Sino-Nepal war.

In pursuit of friendlier relations with Britain, Jung Bahadur became the first prince from the subcontinent to travel across what were then known as the 'black waters', to England. His voyage across the black waters, forbidden by the Hindu religion, required him to return, for purposes of purification, via Rameshwaram in southern India. Many people thereafter referred to Jung Bahadur as impure, since he had crossed oceans and started behaving like a westerner. In explaining the significance of Jung Bahadur's visit, scholar Sanjeev Upreti explains:

> [He] was represented as a possible agent of western modernity . . . [and] seen not merely as an ordinary Gurkha soldier, but . . . as a tactful, well mannered native ruler through whose medium western 'civilization' might enter Nepal.[7]

Jung Bahadur's voyage to Europe allowed him to see Britain at the height of its industrial revolution, possessing the most powerful navy in the world and in command of an empire that had expanded throughout the world. The technological and military supremacy of Britain reaffirmed Jung Bahadur's belief that the British could not be beaten through military means. Upon returning, some of the things he saw appear to have rubbed off on him—he went on to institute a number of reforms in an attempt to modernize the nation, such as keeping accounts for revenues collected by the state. Figures from this period show Nepal having revenues of slightly above Rs 1.4 million in 1851, which went up to Rs 9.6 million by the last year of Jung Bahadur's rule in 1877. Subsequent Rana rulers chose not to keep an account of revenues, although at the end of Rana rule in 1951, state revenue was recorded at Rs 29 million. Although Jung Bahadur saw the value of good account keeping and tried to institute it, he saw no reason to change the tradition of claiming all state revenues as his own personal income. Thus, the view of land as the property of the state and all income generated from the land as the income of the king, remained.

In 1857, the Sepoy Rebellion in India allowed Jung Bahadur to cement his alliance with the British. He rode into India as the head of an army that assisted the British in suppressing the rebellion. This firmly established Nepal as an ally to the British empire and led to its eventual acknowledgement of Nepal as an independent and sovereign nation state. Jung Bahadur also promulgated and supported the active recruitment of Gurkhas* into the British Army. This was a tradition that had started as early as 1815 with the formation of King George the First's Own Gurkha Rifles by General David Ochterlony—who commanded the East Indian Army that was sent against Nepal. This concession on the recruitment of Gurkhas into the British army from Nepal, granted to the British as part of the peace treaty, led a Nepali general, Balbhadra Kunwar, to leave the country in disgust and go fight for the Sikh king Ranjit Singh in Lahore, which is the origin of the popular local Nepali

---

*In the official records of the British army, the soldiers were referred to as *Gurkhas*, while in India they are called *Gorkhas*. The word refers to inhabitants of the Gorkhali kingdom.

title for mercenaries who join foreign armies—*Lahure*. It also established a long standing trend of Nepali workers leaving Nepal in search of a better future.

To Greener Pastures, Ver. 1.0

Working and migrating to India features prominently in Nepali history and is closely related to the stagnation of the national economy. Nepali interests were hampered and economic revenues affected when in 1904, the British opened a new route into Tibet that passed from Siliguri through Sikkim and all the way up to Lhasa. This effectively made the trade route through Kathmandu redundant due to the closer proximity of the new route to Calcutta (now Kolkata) and the shorter travel time required to reach Lhasa. As a result, a considerable number of Newar families involved in the trade business with Tibet shifted to Kalimpong. This Newar migration came at the tail end of a much more voluminous Nepali migration into the neighbouring regions of Darjeeling and Assam to work in the newly established tea estates and agricultural land from the 1850s onwards.

The migration of a large number of Nepali people from the eastern hills and plains of Nepal into British controlled areas of Darjeeling and Assam evinces the opportunities they saw across the border. Simultaneously, it highlights the limited opportunities and the lack of hope that people felt in Nepal. The oppressive social hierarchy of the caste system and the totalitarian rule of upper caste Hindus made it impossible for the lower castes to branch out into fields of work other than what their caste designation allowed them. Within such a confining social structure, these lower castes could not even escape via entrepreneurial spirit as they were forbidden from partaking in a business or occupation beyond their caste. The discouragement of business through state intervention, the lack of capital access and limited mobility due to a lack of investment in transportation infrastructure, made Nepal a nation cut off from the progress and social transformation in evidence elsewhere. In such a dire situation, people's desire to migrate in the hopes of a better future, is understandable.

One of the primary lures of migrating to Darjeeling and Assam was the availability of land for the taking. Coming from a country in which the state hoarded all its land and allowed only limited land ownership among its people, the story of land being given out by the government to farmers in India must undoubtedly have been an astounding and magical tale of hope for Nepali farmers. For farmers who had never owned the land they tilled, this was an opportunity beyond their wildest dreams. As previously mentioned, in Nepal, the burden of taxes on land was borne by the peasants who often were forced to farm land belonging to big land owners in order to survive. Nepal's unwillingness to modernize, its insistence on maintaining a bigger than necessary army, its exclusionary land ownership system and its inability to establish a sound economic and monetary policy were just some of the causes that led to the stagnation of the Nepali economy, forcing its people to go abroad seeking better opportunities.

The Decline and Fall of the Ranas

For all of Jung Bahadur's audacity and daring, including his trip to England, he remained a child of tradition and was unable to push Nepal along a path of modernity. A classic example of how tradition held back reform and technology is when Jung Bahadur brought back a water pump to irrigate the fields of Kaski. A white man was needed to operate the pump, but since this would religiously and culturally 'pollute' the water, the pump became useless for all practical purposes.[8] To make matters worse, Jung Bahadur established the 1854 *Muluki Ain*—a civil code based on caste and class—and effectively re-instituted the caste system in Nepal, eliminating any chance of creating something like the Protestant revolution that was one of the cornerstones of the rise of capitalism and of the industrial revolution, in Europe. The fact that the *Muluki Ain* is yet to undergo a comprehensive makeover after more than a century and a half of its existence demonstrates the challenges of bringing Nepal to a contemporary frame of mind.

The Ranas' close relationship with the British in India was crucial to their control over Nepal. It legitimized and facilitated their rule by muffling any dissent against their regime in the south. The Ranas' power also depended on their military might, and so they maintained a strong standing army that was of considerable expense to the state. Although the army was to become a source of considerable revenue for the Ranas during the two world wars, they believed that they could maintain a stronger grip over Nepal and rule for much longer if they kept it isolated from the world and did not expose the people of Nepal to the changes that were going on in the broader world. This strategy was to prove effective for the Ranas, but it was not to last. The industrialization of India and the eventual fall of the British Raj in India meant that the tide of change that had swept through India would inevitably reach the Nepali kingdom as well.

The Rana regime was also an example of a lack of ambition. In the early 1900s, Nepal already had hydroelectricity and a ropeway, but the use of both remained limited to building palaces. The opportunity technology afforded for economic growth and an increase in state and concurrently, personal income, went unheeded by the Rana regime. The Ranas also focused on amassing personal wealth and assets in Kathmandu Valley, thereby alienating themselves from the rest of Nepal, as Nepal and Kathmandu became synonymous. The people outside Kathmandu Valley referred to Kathmandu as Nepal and this perception of a Kathmandu-centric Nepal would not change for decades to come.

The modernization projects they carried out were aimed primarily at impressing the British with their capacity to be western and modern. Although Prime Minister Juddha Shumsher (1932–45) did make a few progressive moves, such as printing currency notes, constructing factories and instituting a pension system to quell the growing resentment against the Rana regime, the power of the conservative elite did not allow him or his successors, Padma Shumsher and Mohan Shumsher, to go the full distance. Thus, modernization can safely be said to have entered Nepal early, but softly. Neither the rulers nor the people seemed to have much interest in it. They seem to have seen no great accomplishment worth deriving from it. The conservatism of the government and an overly strong emphasis on security seem to have been the primary culprits in the aforementioned lack of ambition.

Institution of *Chakari*

Dr Ram Sharan Mahat in his book, *In Defense of Democracy* summarizes what he calls the Rana Shogunate, 'The Rana political system was undisguised military despotism with absolute total control over all aspects of public life.'[9] The Ranas institutionalized the *chakari* system to control political dissent. The *chakari* system required the concerned nobles to formally and publicly attend the Rana courts for specified hours each day in order for them to remain in close proximity to the Ranas. This effectively controlled the movement and activities of potential troublemakers and conspirators. Furthermore, the practice of night time curfew rendered night time visits and activities impossible.[10] The *chakari* system continues in Nepal and is a feature of political life till date. It makes proximity to people in power and hobnobbing with them more important than the performance of administrative duties.

The Ranas had for long tried to restrict education among the Nepali people. They saw in more widespread education, the seeds of their own downfall. Although they did establish a limited number of schools in Nepal, these were primarily meant to prevent Nepali youths from going to study in India. They also were tools for state propaganda and an attempt to ensure the loyalty of the educated class. This attempt had limited success, as education in India was considered of much higher quality. As long as the British remained in India, the Rana regime remained strong in Nepal, but with a growing class of Nepali citizens studying and growing up in India due to educational restrictions in Nepal, a new class of Nepali citizens was forming. They were mostly upper class and upper caste landowning Hindus and the children of those who had loyally served in the Rana bureaucracy. It was this class of citizens that both assisted the Indian National Congress in its fight for independence and eventually fought against the Rana regime in the 1940s. Anti-Rana sentiments were sometimes fostered within the Rana family itself, most particularly among lower ranking Ranas who were not benefiting from the rule they were publicly associated with.

Although anti-Rana movements started in Nepal as early as the 1920s, the most comprehensive attempt to challenge the regime came from the Nepali Congress, constituted by the exiled children of Rana bureaucrats—India-educated and heavily influenced by Nehru and Gandhi. The Nepali Congress grew out of one of the earliest anti-Rana movements, which was led by the Praja Parisad, a political party. A few members of the Praja Parisad were executed by the Rana rulers on charges of treason. The anger of the Nepali public about the execution only strengthened the opposition against the Rana regime. Surviving members of the Praja Parisad escaped to India and went on to establish the Nepali Congress in India, with the goal of establishing democracy in Nepal. Although initially propounding a non-violent movement following the way of Gandhi, the Nepali Congress was to take up an armed struggle against the Rana regime from 1947 onwards. In this, they were supported by King Tribhuvan, who had been crowned as the tenth Shah king of Nepal in 1911 at the age of five and had been actively involved in the Praja Parisad. He was strongly opposed to the regime of the Rana prime ministers and wished to restore the Shah dynasty to its previous glory.

In April 1950, the National Congress led by B.P. Koirala and the Rana dissidents, led by Suvarna Shumsher and Mahabir Shumsher, joined forces. This gave King Tribhuvan the impetus he needed to use pro-democratic forces to push his anti-Rana crusade, the eventual aim of which was to legitimize his own powers. This quest was further facilitated by an independent India which by policy, supported the pro-democratic forces in Nepal. By 1951, as a result of these developments, the regime of the Rana prime ministers had fallen in Nepal, while Tibet had been annexed by the Chinese. King Tribhuvan had declared that a democratic government leading to a constituent assembly was to be established in Nepal. Under India's tutelage, an interim constitution was drawn up and plans for a constituent assembly leading to the establishment of a formal constitution were drafted. These years formed the first few years of Nepal's entrance upon the world stage and its first attempts at modernization towards an industrial society.

2

MIXED ECONOMY OF THE
1950s—CONFUSED RESULTS

What followed immediately upon the fall of the Rana regime in 1950 was a foretaste of Nepal's continually stymied attempts to modernize, industrialize and democratize in the coming half century. Between 1951 and 1959, Nepal went through a series of short-lived governments based on an interim constitution entitled the Interim Government of Nepal Act, 1951. This act was to be in effect until a constituent assembly was elected. Although this act ended the Rana regime, it also made way for the authoritarian rule of King Tribhuvan by granting the king supreme executive, legislative and judicial powers. The interim constitution was a drastic change, at least in wording, from anything the Government of Nepal had ever attempted or stated in a document. For instance, for the first time in Nepali history, it categorically stated that the objective of the government was to promote the welfare of the people of Nepal by securing social, economic and political justice. While this was a heartening development in terms of political ideals, economically, Nepal remained isolated from contemporary developments. At a time when the post-war and post-colonial economies in the then developing regions of South and Southeast Asia started to enter larger trans-national networks of trade and commerce, Nepal still had trade relations with only China and India. It also had few industries, practically an entire population working on the farms and no monetary policy of its own, which meant that the fate of prices and the demand and supply of commodities was completely linked to India. Only 2 per cent of Nepal's entire adult population was literate, less than 1 per cent was engaged in modern industrial occupations, and 85 per cent of all employment and income was based on traditional agricultural practices.[1] There were less than 5000 children in school, 200 doctors, 376 kilometres of metalled road and a currency that did not have any global value. The newly established government of 1951 faced daunting challenges such as these, as it attempted to usher into Nepal the same economic and social changes that were taking place in the rest of South and Southeast Asia.

The Currency Curry

The first few governments in the early 1950s quickly realized that because the Indian Rupee dominated trade and commerce, Nepal had no control over its own monetary policy and consequently, no control over its foreign currency holdings. The Indian Rupee was by far the most prevalent medium of exchange throughout the country. The Nepali Rupee remained in use only in Kathmandu and the surrounding hill areas, while the other parts of Nepal, especially the western and far western regions, continued to use the Indian Rupee. All of Nepal's foreign exchange earnings went to the Central Bank of India, which in return, provided all the foreign currency needs of the country. The existence of a dual currency system in the nation significantly restricted capital accumulation as people did not know which currency to save and which to spend. Government spending during these early years was curtailed as the transactions done in Indian Rupees never formed part of revenue streams for the government.

Responding to the needs of governance and development, the government instituted the Nepal Rastra Bank as the central bank of the nation under the Nepal Rastra Bank Act, 1955. As the central bank of the nation, it was charged with the responsibility of supervising all commercial banks and guiding the monetary policy of the nation. It also set out to regulate the issuance of paper money, mobilize capital, and develop the banking system in the country. Through the efforts of the central bank, a concerted effort was made to circulate the Nepali currency throughout the country as the primary medium of exchange. The Nepali Rupee also entered the international currency market through a fixed exchange rate between Nepali and Indian currency in April 1960. Prior to this, the Nepali and Indian currencies were traded at market value with the value of 100 Indian Rupees fluctuating between seventy-one and 177 Nepali Rupees between 1932 and 1955.

The argument given by the Rastra Bank for the fixed exchange rate was that it helped lower the fluctuation in the price level of Indian products. This was stated as important because the majority of items imported into Nepal and used by the poor came from India. This argument, that a fixed exchange rate controls inflation, is standard for any fixed exchange rate system. However, the fixed exchange rate, which still persists in Nepal, also prevents the central bank from having any control over the nation's monetary policy (which it was set up to guide), even though a strong monetary policy remains the primary means to ensure macro-economic stability. The fixed exchange rate policy of the Rastra Bank also makes it necessary for it to differentiate the Indian currency, as a freely convertible currency, from other currencies which are non-convertible within Nepal. The non-convertibility of other currencies allows the Rastra Bank to maintain a reserve of foreign currencies. Since 1960, the exchange rate has only been adjusted seven times. The last adjustment in February 1993 set the rate to 1.6 Nepali Rupees to an Indian Rupee and it has remained that until now, in 2012. It is shocking that an exchange rate set over twenty years ago, before the civil war, before the remittance economy, and before the Indian economic boom—still remains unchanged. If anything, it is a testament to the Nepali aversion to change that has been endemic since the 1810s.

The Banaras Connection

The construction of Nepal post the 1950s has perhaps been influenced by Banaras a lot. The houses of people in Biratnagar who went to Banaras for education emulated whatever they saw there lock, stock and barrel. The Nepali Congress developed a lexicon influenced by the ancient city, where every senior leader was addressed as Babu. The heady mix of religion and politics perhaps finds its foundation in Banaras as the control of religious trusts involving temples and control of political parties can be discussed in the same breath. Perhaps Nepal also emulated the filth and dirt of the city where citizens are always crying hoarse for their rights but don't want to begin the discourse on responsibility. The anti-English tirade, which included the creation of Sanskritized versions of words and meanings, having licence plates in Devnagari, and considering English as an enemy rather than a tool for facilitation have kept both Banaras and Nepal far away from globalization.

Foreign Aid Begins

The 1950s were also the time the first trickle of foreign aid started to flow into the country. The first aid grant of USD 2000 was provided by the United States to a tottering Rana regime that fell within a month of receiving the aid grant. The source of the money, the Marshall Plan* to fight the rise of communism, was an indication of the direction and intention with which foreign aid was to flood the nation in successive decades. Nepal's two neighbours, despite themselves being aid recipients and decades away from experiencing the prosperity of the 1990s, also got into the aid act, starting with India in 1952 and China in 1956. Both countries showed a keen interest in assisting in infrastructure development projects which remained beyond the financing capabilities of the Nepali government. Indeed, till the mid-1960s, Nepal was entirely dependent on foreign aid to carry out all its development projects.

---

*US plan to reconstruct western Europe and thwart communist expansion.

It is slightly ironic, that a country which had remained isolated and detached from the world for over a century should, upon re-entering the world stage, immediately lapse into a state of acute dependency. However, such was the case with Nepal and this dependency only grew with time. The average aid to GDP ratio of a mere 2 per cent in the 1960s grew to around 10 per cent by the 1990s. The government's revenues were perennially lower than its expenditure thereby requiring the government to borrow from aid agencies and obtain grants to meet the gap between revenue and expenditure. Being seen as a country chronically dependent on foreign aid has had serious economic implications for Nepal. Foreign aid has played a considerable role in shaping many of the socio-cultural changes that Nepal has witnessed since the 1950s. It has played a part in introducing Nepal to the world, in influencing its international relations and in shaping the fate of democracy and governance in Nepal. The tremendous impact of foreign aid on every aspect of Nepal's society, politics and economy will be discussed in detail in Chapter 5, but we can state here, that it is far from certain that all the billions of dollars of aid money in cash and cash equivalents like equipment, technology and training, have had the desired results of peace, prosperity and development in Nepal.

Flirting with Democracy

Nepal's entry on to the world stage during King Tribhuvan's rule in the 1950s was marked with considerable hope and aspiration for the future of the nation. However, King Tribhuvan, often referred to as the 'father of democracy', in Nepal, was a bit of an opportunist whose constant interference in the democratic process often impeded that process. For instance, in 1951, King Tribhuvan favoured as the first prime minister, Matrika Prasad Koirala, who was supposedly backed by the Indian government, over his younger brother B.P. Koirala, who was leading the Nepali Congress Party at that time. Still, the first cabinet under M.P. Koirala was created in a very inclusive way by today's definition, with five ministers coming from five different communities, namely M.P. Koirala, Narada Muni Thulung, Tripurawar Singh, Suryanath Das Yadav and

Mahavir Shumsher Rana. Thereafter, in the last sixty years in Nepal, the government has only paid lip service to this policy of inclusion.

King Tribhuvan thereby privileged Indian patronage over popular democratic norms. After the fall of the government led by M.P. Koirala (due to internal squabbles in the Congress), King Tribhuvan played a role in splitting the Congress, following which M.P. Koirala headed a new breakaway party—the Nepal Praja Parisad. King Tribhuvan then reappointed M.P. Koirala to the post of prime minister in 1954, despite the obvious lack of support from the main Congress Party.

King Tribhuvan's short post-Rana stint is also marked by the successful rise of the royal family back into its position of power, filling in the power vacuum left by the Rana prime ministers. The royals showed an increasing willingness to assert their executive power and reinstate their control over the army. In short, the power vacuum created during the period of the interim constitution allowed for the Shah royal family to re-consolidate its power base. King Tribhuvan died in 1955 without having held the constituent assembly he had promised the Nepali people. His son, Mahendra, ascended the throne that very year and proved to be a man of vision as well as of action.

In 1959, under the leadership of King Mahendra, Nepal's first election was held, paving the way for a Nepali Congress victory, with the Congress taking seventy-four of the 109 seats. This set the stage for B.P. Koirala to be the first popularly elected leader of the Nepali people. Kamal Mani Dixit, an intellectual and writer, recalls that during the 1950s, after seven years of confusion, the Nepali people were fed up with the inaction and lack of resilience of the government. But with the elections, he says that there was a renewed air of hope and excitement—his own aspiration at the time was '*Sachi nai aba desh banla jasto thiyo*' (It looked like people would actually prosper now).

It is worth mentioning the framework of the interim constitution within which the Koirala government had to work. The constitution decreed two legislative houses, an Upper and a Lower House. The 109-seat Lower House was elected by universal suffrage and the thirty-six-seat Upper House was composed of eighteen members handpicked by the king and eighteen elected from the Lower House. The leader of the majority in the Lower House was elected prime minister, but was second in line to the king who could act and dismiss the prime minister without consulting the Lower House. Additionally, the king had complete control over the army and foreign affairs, and could invoke emergency powers suspending all or part of the constitution. Thus the constitution was, in effect, only as democratic as its king. Given such a political backdrop, the achievements of the Koirala government were reasonable. It was able to abolish the *Birta* land system, that granted state land to select individuals for purposes of administration, thus releasing more land for the ownership of common Nepalis. It revised the lopsided trade arrangements that favoured India unduly and signed a new Trade and Transit Treaty with India in 1960. It was also successful in securing Nepal's territorial jurisdiction over waterways and in introducing Nepal into the United Nations.

During the Koirala government and even before it, since the early 1950s, the difficulty of carrying out major development work without skilled human resources, capital and a proper long-term plan of action, had become apparent. For this reason, five-year plans were instituted in order to facilitate development, with a major focus on transportation and communication. The lack of roads in a formidable terrain may have assisted the Rana regime's isolationist policy, but proved to be a serious challenge to the progressive Koirala government's attempts to ensure economic growth. The legacy of years of isolation, an administrative structure that had changed little since medieval times and the shortage of people with the capability and capacity to manage development projects, proved even bigger hurdles. As a result, the First Five-Year Plan's budget remained severely underutilized and none of the targets was met. For instance, out of 1450 km of roads planned during the First Five-Year Plan, only 565 km were built and of a development budget of Rs 576 million, the government was able to utilize only Rs 383 million. Sadly, this underutilization of budgets and the inability to fulfil development plans is a trend that continues to this day.

The 1950s were also marked by strong tensions between India and Nepal, with India trying to assert its dominance over all things

Nepali. The primary objective of the Indian government was to keep Nepal completely under its own economic umbrella and integrate it completely into the Indian economy. Facing an expansionist China to its north, which had only recently annexed Tibet and was embroiled in territorial disputes with India, India was not willing to allow Chinese influence to cross the Himalayan range into its backyard. Thus, it adopted a position as the dominant local power in the Himalayan kingdoms of Nepal, Bhutan and Sikkim. This was to eventually lead to the annexation of Sikkim and the imposition of Indian foreign and defence policies within Bhutan. This Indian position was to be a constant bone of contention for Nepal and assisted in the fostering of strong anti-Indian sentiments in Nepal.

The increasingly liberal bent of the Koirala government—especially typified in the Second Five-Year Plan—was giving the jitters to the army, former aristocrats, and landowners (all three of which were mostly the same class and caste of people). Given King Mahendra's self-professed lack of belief in democracy and his tendency to transform his beliefs into action, it was hardly a surprise that on 15 December 1960, the king, with the support of the army, exercised his executive powers to dismiss the government and assume full power. Thus ended Nepal's first flirtation with democracy, following which the country became entrenched in three decades of what is popularly known as Panchayat rule, instituted by King Mahendra. The Panchayat system was a partyless, centralized democratic system controlled by palace officials, with sovereign powers vested in the king. The three-tier Panchayat system was comprised of Village and Town Panchayats ruled by a local autocracy, District Panchayats ruled by the king's appointees and the National Panchayat, an appointed parliament.

The Panchayat System: Back to Autocracy

The Panchayat system successfully tamed its opposition when the king ordered the arrest of the deposed Prime Minister B.P. Koirala in 1960 and held him in prison for eight years. By the time Koirala was released, the Nepali Congress party had splintered into three groups—leaving Koirala no option but to go to India to muster support against the autocratic rule of the king. However, India's defeat at the hands of the Chinese in 1962 went in the king's favour, with the Indian government unwilling to alienate Nepal for fear of pushing it into the Chinese sphere of influence. It also confirmed King Mahendra's belief that getting too close to any one nation could seriously threaten the sovereignty of Nepal. Thus, unlike his father who was a staunch supporter of India, King Mahendra chose to maintain an equidistant relationship with India and China. King Mahendra's cool stance towards the Indians also served him in terms of popular sentiment, by allowing him to act as a saviour of Nepali sovereignty from Indian hegemony.

Nepal's quest for membership to the United Nations during the rule of Prime Minister Mohan Shumsher Rana in the 1950s, had been unsuccessful due to cold war competition between the Soviet Union and United States. Prabhakar Rana, who briefly worked at the Foreign Ministry at that time, recalls that in 1956, Nepal seized the opportunity to oppose both the Suez War and the invasion of Hungary, so that it could be seen as a neutral country. This stance of neutrality facilitated its entry into the United Nations. Nepal's neutral position also made Hrishikesh Shah, the first Nepali ambassador to the United Nations, quite popular in the international community. He stood a very good chance of becoming the UN Secretary General in a year when the seat was reserved for Asia, when even India would not have opposed his candidacy. That honour eventually went to U Thant from Burma, because Hrishikesh Shah was called back to Nepal by King Mahendra, exactly when Nepal had the opportunity to be on the global centre-stage. The days of autocracy were returning.

King Mahendra proclaimed that Panchayat rule was based on the spirit of democracy and Nepal's classical tradition of local governance. A loyal army, a business community protected by the protectionist policies of the state and feudal powers who opposed the land reforms of the Congress, became the main proponents of Panchayat rule. They claimed that historically, each caste group in Nepal had its own panchayat (literally: a council of elders) which functioned as the local governance unit. The 1960s Panchayat system, in their justification, merely scaled this local level unit up to the regional and national level, with the national-level Panchayat functioning as a council of ministers who advised the king. The king, in this system, remained the source of all power and authority. Further, as a modernization effort of a kind—King Mahendra sought to organize people into classes—peasants, labourers, students, women, former military personnel and college graduates—as a substitute to the traditional caste system. These classes were instituted as part of the political system as a replacement for trade and labour unions with ideological and political leanings. The Panchayat constitution not only explicated the irrelevance of political parties within the Panchayat system, but also banned them outright as illegal. Although King Mahendra claimed that the Panchayat system was a political expression of Nepali cultural identity, its similarity to the panchayat system in India suggests that its roots lay outside Nepal.

The royalist vision of the Panchayat system as an embodiment of Nepali identity and of the king as the divine representation of God on earth, is a vision that assumes and accepts an inherently hierarchical and unequal society. While in comparison to the autocratic Rana regime, Panchayat rule was significantly more progressive and oriented towards development, it also retained some of the autocratic and ultimately detrimental features of the Rana regime, including direct access to the royal treasury for the king, without any legitimate account keeping. It allowed for the fickle creation of laws at the whim of the king and maintained the system of *chakari* which required, as a surveillance measure, that palace officials and other concerned nobles attend the court formally and publicly at specified times. Further, the mixed economy model that King Mahendra adopted only helped to prolong and accentuate Nepal's nepotistic *chakari*-based tradition, since the centralized power structure based in Kathmandu meant that the getting of jobs and the securing of contracts were all a matter of knowing the right people in the right place.

Dr Bhekh Bahadur Thapa, only the second Nepali citizen to earn a PhD in economics, was the Secretary of Planning in the 1960s. He says that given the limited opportunities in Nepal, there was no other option for Nepali traders but to attempt to expand their reach to include the consumers of UP, Bihar and Bengal, in India. This prompted the Nepal government to charge a lower duty on imports than India did, thereby giving incentives to people to import consumable goods into Nepal and sell them in the aforementioned markets of India. In one example, the government encouraged industries that manufactured household steel utensils to set up operations in Nepal. They would import steel paying lower duties for it than India would and thereby make finished products at a lower cost than factories in India did. India had a major problem with this, as cheaper goods from Nepal were affecting its own domestic industry, which imported raw materials paying a very high duty and therefore had to price goods uncompetitively as compared to the imports from Nepal. Dr Bhekh Bahadur Thapa recalls a conversation with Indian Commerce Secretary K.B. Lal, who accused Nepal of trying to subvert Indian economic structures. Dr Thapa challenged Lal stating, 'I have a solution for you—if you fear Nepal's liberal policies, then why not make India more liberal?'

Although the Panchayat government sought to maintain its distance from India, it survived with the support of the Nehru government which had been weakened by its defeat in the 1962 Sino-Indian war, and thus needed to cultivate Nepal's support before China did. Ironically, King Mahendra was considerably influenced by the then prime minister of India, Jawaharlal Nehru and his support for Fabian socialism. Like Nehru, King Mahendra saw the public sector as the primary means of achieving long-lasting economic development. The loss of faith in capitalism caused by the Great Depression in the United States and the seemingly potent powers of communism on the rise in the USSR, had increased the appeal of the mixed economic model. However, with the benefit of hindsight, many believe that Fabian socialism and the mixed economy model adopted by Nehru for India and Mahendra for Nepal, have failed. While Nehru's staunch belief in liberalism, tolerance and democracy set the foundations for a robust Indian democracy, advocates of minimal state control are of the view that his economic policies hampered growth by allowing excessive state interference in industry and thus impairing productivity, quality and profitability. Nepal, under King Mahendra's autocratic quasi-democracy, lost out on both fronts— neither was a robust democracy allowed to develop nor was a vibrant economy allowed to flourish.

Mixed Economy or Failed Concoction?

Proponents of the mixed economic model claimed that utilizing the *best* of both capitalism and communism, this model would allow the state to take the lead in industrializing the nation. In reality and practice, the mixed economy for both India and Nepal turned out to be anything but the perfect balance between capitalism and communism. The problem with the mixed economic system lay not in the conceptualization but in the implementation. One of the primary problems inherent in the system as observed in both India and Nepal was the high levels of corruption it invited due to the heavy reliance on politicians and bureaucrats within the system. The individual politicians and bureaucrats quickly lost their ability to see the difference between serving their interests and those of the state, as they themselves were the state. This hegemony of the bureaucracy, due to its extensive and invasive rules and regulations, discouraged entrepreneurs from engaging with the state. The state was seen as an autocratic, nepotistic, unfriendly and extortive mafia where all employees worked not for the benefit of the nation but for their own individual benefit. Bribery and commissions grew to be an accepted part of this system and were necessary for carrying out tasks as mundane as paying electricity bills and getting a driving licence.

The private sector in Nepal took its first steps in 1951 when a new Companies Act was implemented for private limited companies. Previously, the Nepal Companies Act of 1936 only provided for the incorporation of industrial enterprises on a joint stock principle with limited liabilities. The first such firm, Biratnagar Jute Mills, was established in 1936, in a collaborative venture between Indian and Nepali entrepreneurs. By the mid-1960s, over ninety private companies had been established but they remained ineffective in scaling up due to a heavy reliance on the import of resources and too many restrictions on business. Following the Fabian economic model advocated by Nehru, King Mahendra's government gave little attention to facilitating the growth of these private companies and instead focused its efforts on the establishment and expansion of existing and new public companies.

A fundamental flaw in King Mahendra's regime was its perception of the role of government towards its people. The Panchayat government saw the nation through the traditional eyes of the Shah kings and saw the activities carried out by the government for its people as a gift from the monarch to his loyal subjects. Everything in the nation belonged to the crown and all acts of governance were acts of philanthropy carried out by the owner of those lands. The prevalence of this attitude is confirmed by an analysis of most big private sector investments that occurred during the Panchayat era. All businesses ran on nepotism and required the special blessing of the royal family in order to effectively start up and function. This was typified in the use of language in particular. The king and royal family members were addressed in a grammatical form that could not be used for common citizens. It contained a lot of Urdu usage and an exclusive vocabulary to describe food, eating, sleeping and other daily activities. As knowledge of this language was a major advantage in gaining proximity to the power centres around the palace, it functioned as a means of excluding people who were unfamiliar with it. On top of it all, most major businesses started during this time were owned by members of the royal family. For instance, hotels Soaltee and Annapurna were established in the early 1960s by the king's brothers as the premier hotels in the country. Both hotels benefited from a growing tourism sector, royal patronage, and a government which saw its best interest in ensuring the success of these two hotels.

The case of the Salt Trading Corporation demonstrates how the royal family interfered in various ways with the operation of business enterprises. The company was established in 1963 without royal intervention, as a public–private venture between existing private salt traders who were licensed by the government to import salt, but the company was formed with the special approval of the government. Kamal Mani Dixit, one of the company's initial promoters, recalls how the price of salt used to fluctuate based on market demand for it, especially when people from the hills came to the market to buy salt. As salt is an essential commodity, the government decided to regulate the salt trade through the Salt Trading Corporation. However, when the Salt Trading Corporation wanted to get into manufacturing vanaspati ghee, it was not granted a licence. Instead, it had to buy a licence for manufacturing vanaspati ghee from Deepak Singh, King Mahendra's son-in-law, paying him in Salt Trading Corporation shares. This is one example of how difficult it was to do business without getting members of the royal family quite closely involved.

Another of the many controversial decisions taken by King Mahendra during his regime was to provide people from Manang (popularly known as Mananges) preferential treatment—they were allowed to import goods into Nepal with a reduced duty. This was argued to be a continuation of the facility given to the Mananges by the former Rana rulers of Nepal. The Ranas, fearing an ethnic revolt from this strong ethnic group, had granted them permission to trade outside Nepal. This had allowed the Mananges to trade from Tibet to colonial India, Burma, Thailand and Laos. Dr Bhekh Bahadur Thapa, Secretary of Planning during the Panchayat era, explains that King Mahendra had decided to give Mananges preferential treatment because of their entrepreneurial spirit and their traditional occupation as nomadic traders. The preferential policy allowed anyone from Manang to obtain a passport without a hassle during a time when obtaining a passport was a difficult task. The benefits given to the Mananges were misused by many non-Mananges, including Marwari and Newar business people, who used Mananges as carriers for their goods, which they could now pass through customs at a reduced duty fee. This facilitated the establishment of Nepal as a centre for smuggling goods into India. Smuggling became big business and continued even into the 1990s—for instance, more than twenty-five million umbrellas were imported annually into Nepal during a time when the entire population of the country was less than the number of umbrellas it was importing. Since every Nepali does not have an umbrella collection, it is obvious that these umbrellas were being smuggled across the border into India. The high import duties in India coupled with restrictions on foreign exchange made Kathmandu and the border towns of Dhulabari in the east of Nepal among the biggest shopping attractions for Indians. The carrying of goods across the border in collusion with customs and border authorities on both sides of the border became a highly lucrative business for many people.

With smuggling becoming the most profitable business in Nepal, actual production and manufacturing came to be of only peripheral importance, especially once the state started to monopolize such industries. Stories of losses in efficiency and productivity, due to a business atmosphere structured to favour a particular business group or an industry, are common knowledge in Nepal. One such example is Hetauda Cotton Textile Mills which was a state-owned enterprise set up with Chinese assistance. The mill functioned as the sole producer of cotton textile in the central region of Nepal for decades, without any competition, due to the protectionist policies of the state. However, this lack of competition and the guarantee of survival meant that the company did not have to worry about efficiency or quality. It was quite simply the only large-scale producer of cotton textile produced on the sole machine that could produce cloth of a certain length. This allowed it to dictate the terms on which it provided its products, regardless of considerations of quality or price. In a competitive market, the company would not have been able to survive without developing quality products and minimizing costs.

The Education Mishap

A grave shortcoming of the entire Panchayat era was its educational policy. A New National Education Plan was launched in 1972 with the objective of focusing on job-oriented vocational education. However, the plan later on became a tool to produce people loyal to the Panchayat regime. Community-owned schools were nationalized and cosmetic changes were brought about by aping the US educational system—colleges were now called 'campuses', and there were 'internal assessments' of students, suggesting a mild degree of autonomy. Although the government was successful in establishing new schools and expanding the coverage of schools throughout the nation, the quality of education remained poor. The increasing number of schools could not be followed up with an increase in the number of teachers, leading to an acute shortage of teachers, with most teachers barely qualified to teach. In the early 1980s, around 60 per cent of all primary school teachers and 35 per cent of all secondary school teachers were untrained.[2]

Further, the imposition of King Mahendra's 'one country, one language' policy throughout the nation, promoting the Nepali language above all others, had a significantly detrimental effect. Not only was it seen as a sign of state-sponsored caste-based repression, but it also deterred the development of an English curriculum. At the higher education level, Nepal's first university, Tribhuvan University, was established in 1959. However, given the lack of quality at the primary and secondary level, it is hardly a surprise that very few students made it past the School Leaving Certificate (SLC) exams which acted as an iron gate to higher education. Education remained the exclusive domain of the urban elite, with a further stratum being created through the distinction between the English boarding school and the Nepali government school. The mastery of English that was offered at the former type of institution, combined with a standard of education that the government schools were unable to match, encouraged anyone with the means to either send their children to one of the English boarding schools or abroad, to India. The lack of human resources was acutely felt by the government, which led to it sponsoring a large number of its finest and brightest minds to go and study abroad in the universities of Europe, America and India.

Tourism of the 1950s—A Success Story

The only success story from the 1950s that endures, is the growth of the tourism sector. When Sir Edmund Hillary and Tenzing Norgay Sherpa climbed Mount Everest in 1953, Nepal arrived on the global tourism map as a forbidden Shangri-la, mystical and adventurous. Prabhakar Rana, a member of the first Tourism Master Plan Committee and the first General Manager of Soaltee Hotel, says that credit has to be given to Boris Lissanevitch, who started the Royal Hotel and brought in the first batch of tourists in 1955. Boris convinced King Mahendra of the potential of Nepali tourism, at a time when the Nepali people wondered why tourists would come to an underdeveloped country like theirs. This resulted in King Mahendra's visit to Switzerland and the arrival in Nepal of people like Tony Hagen, who became the first foreigner to trek throughout Nepal and conduct an extensive geological survey. This also set the stage for allowing Nepali entrepreneurs to enter the tourism business. With tourists being brought over by international groups like American Express and spending considerable amounts of money, tourism quickly became a thriving business. Even Air India started to include Nepal in its brochures, to attract tourists to India from the US and Europe. The Department of Tourism was established in 1957 and a Tourism Act enacted in 1964.

It is worth noting that two of Nepal's oldest and most prestigious hotels, Soaltee Hotel and Annapurna Hotel, were established in 1960 and 1965 respectively. Both hotels were established by the brothers of King Mahendra. Further, the expansion in the 1970s of the Royal Nepal Airlines Corporation locally and internationally, attracted a considerable number of tourists to a previously closed Shangri-la. Airplane and helicopter services to areas of Nepal previously completely untouched by modernity, further lured tourists in droves. The establishment of Casino Nepal in 1968, the promotion of Nepal's role in the Hindu world and the attraction of shopping the world's delights in Bishal Bazaar that began in the mid-1970s, when Indians faced many foreign exchange restrictions at home, also contributed to a dramatic rise in the number of Indian tourists.

In 1972, a vision document called the Tourism Master Plan was prepared, which emphasized investments in tourism by both the public and the private sector, with a view to creating more jobs and more revenue for the government. Though a good plan, it was never updated. During Dr Harka Gurung's tenure in 1977–78 as tourism minister, the big debate over the quality versus the quantity of tourists began and perhaps a lot of potential thereby lost. With the arrival of the hippies in the 1970s, Nepal started receiving a lot of backpacker tourists who came in search of instant nirvana in a country where marijuana and other drugs were not yet illegal. They outnumbered the high-end tourists who were brought in by leading international tour operations. Prabhakar Rana says that though many objected to the poor quality of the budget tourists in Nepal, these hippies were without a doubt the primary marketing tool for Nepal, providing the best publicity for the destination at a time when the government could not afford advertisements.

The opening up of the hotel sector for foreign investment and management allowed the Oberoi and Sheraton groups to enter Nepal, thereby providing wonderful training opportunities; this made hospitality services one of the key job opportunities for Nepali people in Nepal and abroad. The government started Royal Nepal Airlines in 1966 and by 1990 had a fleet of four jets, eleven Twin Otters, two Pilatus Porters and three Avros flying 600,000 passengers a year. Tourism grew in the 1980s at an annual rate of 10 per cent and by the 1990s, Nepal received close to 300,000 tourists, the tourism industry had a share of 4 per cent of GDP, while foreign exchange earnings from the sector were close to USD 50 million.

Transportation: Roads to Prosperity

The Panchayat government was also successful in developing the infrastructure of the country, which did facilitate the growth of business even into the 1990s. Before the Panchayat government fell, it had successfully developed its road network from a mere 276 km in the early 1950s to 7330 km by 1990. Although significant tracts of the country still remained inaccessible by motorized transport, the achievements, given Nepal's terrain, are remarkable. Without a doubt the development of these roads contributed significantly to the growth of the private sector. However, Kanak Mani Dixit, Editor of the magazine *Himal Southasian*, points out that the roads that were built during that era were logically defective, since both the roads out of Kathmandu linked the eastern parts of the country by going through the western cities of Hetauda or Narayangarh.

Undoubtedly though, the roads did bring about entrepreneurship. A good example is the story of Nepal Transport Service, the first private commercial passenger bus service in Nepal. Established in March 1959, to take advantage of the opening of the Tribhuvan Highway in 1956, the company was established by two former traders, Lupau Ratna Tuladhar and Karuna Ratna Tuladhar, along the Lhasa–Kathmandu–Calcutta trade route. However, with the closing up of Tibet, the opening of the 190-km stretch of dirt road between Kathmandu and the rest of the world provided them their next business opportunity. Although the company eventually closed shop in 1966, its brief life highlights the entrepreneurial spirit and the opportunities that modernization was capable of forming and creating. However, the story also highlights a major flaw with all businesses in: firms do not grow out of being family businesses and do not embrace the corporate culture of separating ownership and management, entrusting the management to professional people and letting the business take advantage of the competencies it has developed.

King Birendra: Failed Attempts at Change

King Birendra was crowned the king of Nepal in 1972 after the death of his father, King Mahendra. He followed the non-aligned policy of his father and went a step further in declaring Nepal a zone of peace. This was partly to protect Nepal from a situation like that of the Kingdom of Sikkim which, in 1974 was annexed into an Indian Union that feared a Chinese invasion in the politically unstable Kingdom of Sikkim. It was also an attempt to counter the anti-royal fervour that was gripping India and the Indian government after the abolition of the Privy Purse in 1971. A decade later, in the 1980s, the sending of Indian peacekeepers into Sri Lanka and the imperialistic model of a Big Brother that India was adopting in the region, caused increasing concern in Nepal. Simultaneously, the rise of the Gorkhaland movement in 1986 and the growing clamour for a separate state in the Darjeeling region was of growing concern to India. The Indian government did not want to deal with a separatist insurgency in its backyard when it was trying to establish itself as a regional power. The attempts of King Birendra's regime from 1972 to 1990 were not so much a product of anti-Indian sentiment as of a growing concern in Nepal about its own sovereignty in the face of a liberalizing and expanding Indian influence in the region, especially when Rajiv Gandhi was the prime minister from 1984 to 1989. The dominance of India in Nepal was constantly felt. When Dr Bhekh Bahadur Thapa, then Ambassador to the United States, discussed the possibility of American investments in Nepal during King Birendra's visit to United States in 1984; American companies were reluctant to invest. They advised the Nepali government to focus on India, indicating that making a deal in water resources with India would be the best scenario for Nepal.

Although he inherited an autocratic regime from his father, King Birendra was of a considerably more liberal bent. He instituted a number of economic reforms including the Industrial Enterprises Act of 1974, which shifted the government's emphasis from the public to the private sector as the primary medium for economic growth. Birendra was influenced by the Americans. Recalls Prabhakar Rana, Chairman Emeritus, Soaltee Hotel Limited and a relative of the royal family: 'He tried to decentralize the nation and, in those days when communication and travel was difficult, he decided to take the power away from Kathmandu for two months each year by operating out of one of the development regions. This was quite unlike his father who used to only tour around and never stick around.' While this was a great idea, it started becoming an expensive hobby when ministers and government officials had to shuttle between Kathmandu and those cities, along with the flowering of the business of *chakari* built around such visits. More people wanted to be seen at the palaces or king's retreat as part of the *chakari* mode of royal surveillance.

King Birendra's regime also instituted the Social Services National Coordination Council (SSNCC) in 1975, which attempted to bring the growing number of NGOs and INGOs under a single umbrella. Headed by Queen Aishwariya, the Council had six committees, generally headed by individuals close to the royal family. Membership to the Council was a privilege granted to the elite, and all NGOs were required to be registered with the Council so that the state could monitor the people who formed NGOs, their objectives, and their activities. By 1990, there were 219 NGOs registered with SSNCC. The Council was converted to a foreign aid coordination body after the 1990 constitution came into effect, wherein all NGOs that received foreign aid or grants had to be registered with the SSNCC.

Despite its liberal bent, King Birendra's regime also carried forward many traditional forms of royal patronage and business. A striking example of this was the establishment of the King Mahendra Trust for Nature Conservation in 1982, the Lumbini Development Trust in 1985 and the Pashupati Development Trust in 1987. All these trusts, established under specific acts, were set up with the stated objective of protecting, preserving and conserving their specified areas of interest. The establishment of these organizations and their laudable objectives speak well of King Birendra's regime. However, the lack of regulation, transparency or accountability in these organizations, especially during the royal regimes, significantly undercut their benefits. Not only were funds not flowing to the organizations' desired objectives, but quite often, the organization was being used to channel money for activities that were in no way related to and sometimes even contrary to its stated objectives.

With a growing population that found itself unemployed and unable to find employment, King Birendra's regime came under increasing pressure to liberalize. By 1979, in response to widespread student protests, he held a referendum in which the Panchayat system won by a narrow margin against the multi-party system, allegedly by rigging. After the referendum, the royal establishment had shifted its focus to power retention. An all-powerful Panchayat Policy, Enquiry and Investment Committee formed in 1980 reported directly to the king. This committee could take action against anyone they perceived as acting against the 'interest of the nation' and the action of the committee could not be questioned in any court of law. Dr Ram Sharan Mahat says, 'The Panchayat Policy's rationale rested on three founding ideals, viz. nationalism, economic development and indigenous character based on tradition and religion. The concept of nationalism was based on the shallow concept of one language, one crown and one country.' The creation of this all-powerful body fuelled a growing sense of dissent against the regime.

∞

Panchayat rule began and ended with politics in the forefront while the economic agenda remained second. Prabhakar Rana, Chairman Emeritus, Soaltee Hotel Limited says, 'The sad part of the Panchayat period was that it did not utilize and develop its own resources like hydropower but went with a begging bowl to other countries. It was a tremendous loss of face for Nepal and Nepalis.' Between 1960 and 1990, Nepal's GDP grew at an average of a merely 1.5 per cent per annum from USD 0.6 billion to USD 3.6 billion. During the same period Singapore's GDP grew from USD 0.6 billion to USD 36 billion and Thailand's from USD 2.76 billion to USD 85 billion. Malaysia's GDP grew from USD 2.5 billion in 1963 to USD 44 billion in 1990. The growing population in Nepal was faced with limited employment opportunities and was already clamouring for change. They wanted to capture the promise of a growing economy and follow the dream of becoming another Switzerland. These many dissatisfactions were to reach their culmination in a widespread popular agitation called the Jana Andolan in 1990, following which King Birendra agreed to step down and allow for the establishment of a constitutional monarchy and multiparty democratic system, paving the way for Nepal's second stint with democracy.

PART II

PRESENT CONTINUOUS— 1990 TILL 2012

The two decades from the Jana Andolan of 1990 to 2012, which saw the historic ending of the institution of monarchy in Nepal, were undeniably the most eventful years in Nepal's history. The introduction of multiparty democracy in 1990 resulted in a new constitution, the first elected government in over thirty years and the initiation of economic reforms. The Nepali state was transformed from a partyless Panchayat system headed by an absolute monarch into a state with a constitutional monarchy and parliamentary democracy. Sadly for the Nepali people and nation, the resulting opportunities were squandered. Intra-party and inter-party feuds among the political parties dominated these years. Nepal reverted to absolute monarchy briefly via a royal coup, between 2005 and 2006. In April 2006, the king gave in to another popular people's uprising, which is often called Jana Andolan II, after its 1990 avatar. The institution of monarchy was buried as history in August 2008, by the newly elected constituent assembly. The Maoists, who had fought a bitter battle with the state from 1996 to 2006, joined mainstream politics along with other political parties and won the highest number of seats in the constituent assembly elections of June 2008. The Maoists formed the first coalition government of the Federal Democratic Republic of Nepal in September 2008 and the process of constitution writing began, for the first time in Nepal's history. However, the constituent assembly, despite two extensions, failed to deliver a constitution. This led to the dissolution of the constituent assembly. In December 2012, elections to another constituent assembly were announced.

The next five chapters are a narrative of the economic roller coaster ride of the two decades since economic reforms began in the early 1990s. They are also thematic discussions on the way three key players in the economy—the government, the private sector and the development sector—have failed to deliver results in almost every arena. The opportunities created by the 1990s reforms were squandered equally by all three sectors, but some of the failures of these years have deep roots in a political culture that was shaped during the Rana regime, the Panchayat era and many decades of foreign aid dependence. These roots need examining and so the chapters that follow often reach back into history to understand recently prominent issues like Nepal's governance woes, its energy muddle, the role of foreign aid and the state of education.

I will also examine in considerable depth, two events of the past two decades and their unprecedented impact on every aspect on Nepali life but in particular, on the economy. One: the violent conflict between Maoist guerrillas and the state that lasted ten years and has left scars that are deep and must be addressed. Two: the large-scale migration that was in large part the effect of this conflict and resulted in substantial remittances from Nepalis working in other countries. These remittances managed to keep Nepal's battered economy afloat and will play a crucial role in Nepal's economic future.

3

THE PEOPLE'S MOVEMENT OF 1990: EMERGENCE AND SQUANDER

If the 1990 Jana Andolan, a people's movement for democracy, represented the spirit of the time, the first budget speech of 1991, presented by the finance minister presented the monetized expression of that spirit. The changes demanded in the Jana Andolan were to be brought about through the budgetary allocation of resources by the first elected government in over three decades. This belief in the political power of the budget was in itself a statement about the changing times. The Nepali public no longer trusted individuals to deliver their country from poverty, but instead placed their trust in the institution of democracy. The public presentation of the budget displayed the nation-building project transparently while reflecting the aspirations of the Nepali people who had voted in the new government. The fall of the Berlin Wall and the collapse of the USSR reinforced this belief in the triumph of democracy and liberal market capitalism over socialist or authoritarian institutions. Riding the airwaves via their newly acquired television sets, Nepali people witnessed scenes of change at home and abroad.

Indian Embargo, Nepali Democracy

The fall of the Panchayat government in 1990 provided considerable insight into the geopolitical location and role of the Nepali state. In March 1989, before the Jana Andolan, a trade embargo had been placed on Nepal by the Indian prime minister, Rajiv Gandhi. The reason given by an increasingly irate Indian government, however, was the Nepali government's unwillingness to sign a single treaty covering trade and transit agreements between India and Nepal. In truth, New Delhi was infuriated with its smaller neighbour's agreement for the purchase of arms from the Chinese government, which directly violated a secret treaty of 1965 between India and Nepal. The 1965 treaty required that Nepal purchase its arms from India whenever possible and when this was not possible, to inform India of purchase of arms from other countries as well as transport such arms through India. King Birendra's government had pushed the equidistance card too far and New Delhi made it all too apparent how dependent the Nepali economy was upon India. If this political scenario provided the foundation for the 1990 Jana Andolan, a youthful proletariat opposed to the traditional feudal structures of Nepal was the immediate catalyst of the popular movement.

The Indian embargo provided the ideal opportunity for Nepal's democratic forces to unite and accuse the Panchayat government of its ineptitude and inability to rule. This, together with the government's rampant corruption, restriction of freedoms and most importantly, its inability to meet the basic needs of the neediest, made the democratic movement unstoppable. During the height of the embargo, India closed down thirteen of its fifteen transit points into Nepal and severely limited the flow of goods from India to Nepal. Critically, it cut off the supply of petroleum to Nepal, which led to petroleum prices soaring from Rs 8 a litre to Rs 80 a litre in the grey market, causing an acute energy shortage. This had a direct impact on industries as well as on the average citizen through limitations on the transfer and transportation of goods and raw materials. However, the embargo did bring about two realizations—the importance of being energy independent and the need to tap into the extensive hydropower resources present within the country. The direct effect of the trade embargo was the opening up of space for the political parties to manoeuvre and initiate an anti-government and pro-democratic movement, which the Indian government tacitly supported.

The first Jana Andolan which brought about the fall of the Panchayat government and the establishment of an interim government under the leadership of the Nepali Congress leader Krishna Prasad Bhattarai. Following this, on 1 July 1990, New Delhi lifted the year-long trade embargo in recognition of a democratic Nepal. With the establishment of a democratic government formed of political leaders who had been nurtured in India, Nepal's flirtation with China also ended. Nepal was effectively entrenched in within the Indian sphere of influence and India in turn, became more willing to cooperate with a neighbour that acknowledged it as the 'big brother' in the region.

Economic Liberalization Follows Democracy

For the first time in 1990, the Nepali people felt like they were part of a global family clamouring for change. Colour televisions started receiving satellite images, hoardings of international products and services dotted the streets, restaurant chains started opening, department stores mushroomed, shop fronts started getting an international look, old buildings gave way to new structures and the latest models of cars started plying the streets. Expectations were high and politicians, during the first election post-1990, promised even more—they promised to turn Nepal into the Switzerland of Asia. An economic boom like that seen in the countries known as the 'Asian tigers', namely South Korea, Singapore, Taiwan and Hong Kong, was anticipated—it was expected that a sea of opportunities would flood the nation. Liberalization of markets, unrestricted expansion of trade networks, and industrialization were all expected to follow from an unshackled and reinvigorated private sector. The dividends from economic growth would facilitate the development and modernization of rural Nepal. The Nepali Congress, the leader of the democratic movement, had also shifted gears, abandoning the Fabian socialist model, advocated under B.P. Koirala, in favour of a more progressive liberal market economy during the election of 1991. Sure enough, in keeping with the spirit of the time, the Nepali Congress won a majority of 110 seats in the 205-seat parliament.

Following a comprehensive victory in the 1991 election, the Nepali Congress government formed under Girija Prasad Koirala forged closer links with India and looked towards liberalizing the economy to encourage private sector-led economic growth. With this objective in mind, the government instituted some sweeping reforms. It set forth the Industrial Policy 1992 as a programme statement, and passed the Foreign Investment and One-Window Enterprises Act 1992, the Industrial Enterprise Act 1992, and the Foreign Investment and Technology Transfer Act 1992. These Acts were initiated with the objective of making it easier to do business in Nepal by removing hurdles to starting businesses and encouraging investment by both foreign and local investors. The government wanted to change its role from being a 'process stopper' to a 'process facilitator', where they would treat businesses like businesses treat their customers.

The government also loosened its stranglehold over foreign currency exchange by incorporating free convertibility into the current account. This allowed individuals the freedom of converting and holding foreign currencies in special accounts without requiring explicit permission from the government. Import-licensing requirements were also abolished except for a few commodities, reducing the hassle of obtaining permits for securing foreign currency and importing foreign goods. Further, with reduction in the restrictions placed upon foreign banks, commercial banks were encouraged to open, operate and expand. The subsequent boom in the banking sector allowed for a considerable increase in savings while simultaneously increasing access to capital. Taxation laws were reformed, import tariffs reduced drastically, income tax rates cut significantly and tax sops for investments announced.

A private sector can only develop to meet the needs of the market if it is allowed to enter any market where it sees a gap and an opportunity to create profit. If the private sector is to be an engine for growth, it must be allowed to ply its wares anywhere and test the waters of all available markets. Towards this end, the government instituted the Privatization Policy 1991 which was followed by the formation of a separate privatization cell in the Ministry of Finance. This eventually led to the endorsement by parliament of the Privatization Act 1994 that June. The preamble of the Act read, 'To mitigate the financial administrative burden to the Government, and to usher in all round economic development of the country by broadening the participation of the private sector in the operation of such enterprises, it is expedient in the national interest to privatize such enterprises and to make arrangements thereof.'

The government believed that given the opportunity, the private sector could enter any sector and turn it into a profitable, national revenue-generating and economically self-sustaining industrial behemoth. The government opened up sectors that had for decades remained the exclusive domain of the state. Most significantly, it opened up the skies for private airlines to enter the domestic market, it opened up the financial sector for the rapid growth of banks, finance, and insurance companies, and it opened up the energy sector, allowing for private sector involvement in the generation of hydroelectricity and other forms of energy.

Following the Keynesian economic model advocated by the World Bank and International Monetary Fund, the next logical step for the government was to reform the capital market with the establishment of the Securities Board and the Nepal Stock Exchange which opened for trading in January 1994. The establishment of the Stock Exchange was expected to create opportunities for the common Nepali to invest in companies and be able to enjoy a share of the profits. The stock market was seen as a primary resource in ensuring the prosperity of not just a select few industrialists but the growing middle class as well. With Rs 70 million worth of shares being transacted during just the first six months of the year, public offerings of stocks became a viable way for companies to raise capital to finance their expansion activities. It wasn't just the private sector that was upbeat; the donor community in Nepal was also eager to see Nepal as an ideal example of the success of the democratic liberal market economy and thus lined up to get a cut of the action. From infrastructure to education, from health to hydropower, the donor community was willing to inject the necessary capital into Nepal to create a major economic boom.

1993–94: Dream Run for the Nepal Economy

Sure enough, the economy seemed to surge forward to match the policy leap towards a liberal market economy. The fiscal year of 1993–94 turned out to be a dream year for the economy, registering a 7.9 per cent increase in GDP. The agricultural sector alone recorded an unprecedented 7.6 per cent growth rate and tourism had forged ahead to contribute 4 per cent of the GDP. In manufacturing, the carpet industry had established itself as a major foreign exchange earner, accounting for half of all of Nepal's exports. This fuelled a near tripling of the value of exports in 1994 to Rs 19.3 billion, compared to the total of Rs 7.3 billion in 1991. The garment industry followed in the footsteps of the carpet industry and carpets and garments combined accounted for 80 per cent of Nepal's total exports.[1]

For that one year, Nepal was a model child for development economists and their development theories at the big financial institutions. Confirming predictions made using the Lewis model—the booming carpet and garment industry in the urban sector resulted in a relocation of labour from the rural agricultural sector to the modern industrial sector. Simultaneously, the increase in development expenditure by the government and a real estate boom in cities created, in turn, a boom in the construction industry, which absorbed even more unskilled workers into its industrial machine. There were also concerted government efforts to reach rural populations and this resulted in the spread of modern agricultural practices, new equipment and materials. An agricultural boom occurred in rural Nepal through a combination of encouraging government policies as well as an increase in entrepreneurial activities that saw in the boom, a good future for business. The development of road networks and trade routes further assisted in bringing excess production from rural to urban areas. Without a doubt, the Nepali economy was expanding; transactions were increasing and goods and services were in higher demand.

In addition to the urbanization and modernization process, a socio-cultural upheaval was in the making in urban Nepal. Traditional norms and values were increasingly challenged and often found wanting. A new culture of consumerism, desire and pleasure developed among the general population after the pessimistic and fatalistic years of the autocratic Rana and Shah regimes. New urban lifestyles included eating out, partying and keeping up with global trends. Catering to these new desires, an industry of restaurants, bars, clubs and trendy stores sprang up. Concurrently, the alcohol and cigarette industries in Nepal experienced a major boom, with the establishment of Surya Tobacco as the premiere Nepali cigarette brand and a host of internationally acclaimed beers and spirits introducing their brand into the Nepali market. The budding advertising industry, as the primary promoter of this new lifestyle, successfully utilized the commercialized airwaves of radio and television channels to disseminate the new religion of consumerism.

The children of the 1990s heralded a new age of youth in Nepal. They formed the first generation of children who were driven by the consumer culture that had finally made its way to Nepal. These children grew up not knowing a world without televisions or cell-phones, not being able to imagine a world unhooked to the web and with no remembered experience of the bureaucratic lethargy of the government owned Nepal Bank. These youths form the biggest consumer group to ever inhabit this country. Growing up under the spell of Bollywood and Hollywood while being nurtured by a traditional Nepal, they function as negotiators between the values of old and new. On the side of tradition stand the values of family, moderation, conservatism, and community, while on the newer side of things stand consumerism, individuality, and progress.

Bankers Have a Field Day

The reform of the financial sector through the liberalization of the banking system during the early 1990s has been a success story that endures to this day in Nepal. Prior to liberalization, the only banks in service were owned, managed and operated by the government of Nepal. This banking monopoly had a detrimental impact on the quality of service, efficiency and competency of the bank and its staff. There are horror stories of people who had to queue up for hours and then offer bribes ranging from tea money to full meals to tellers in order to withdraw their own money. This, unsurprisingly, had a detrimental effect on the economy by discouraging people from investing in banks or even opening a bank account. The opening up of the banking sector has shifted the focus to providing premium customer service, with the growing number of banks increasingly having to compete with each other to secure the services of a limited client base.

Increasing competition also led to the introduction of more services like credit and debit cards along with a variety of loan and financing options which dramatically increased access to capital for both businesses and individuals. Further, a growing emphasis on credit ratings and payback viability rather than patronage and connections in the process of giving loans—ensured that capital was being made available for the most promising projects. The development of professionalism and workforce capabilities through banks has been an important driving force in the expansion of the private sector, and has resulted in an increasing trend towards workplace professionalism and service delivery. The real estate boom that Nepal experienced during the first decade of the twenty-first century was largely financed by a dramatic increase in savings and a capital market which was easier to negotiate. Evidence of the genuine transformations wrought by a reformed banking sector can be found in the change in value of Grindlays Bank (now Standard Chartered Bank) shares. Approximately Rs 10,000 (Rs 9960) invested in 1988 to acquire Standard Chartered Bank shares at the Initial Public Offering (IPO) would be worth Rs 305,100 in face value, and Rs 14.37 million in market value at the end of 2008. If we take the peak price of the shares in October 2008, these shares would be worth Rs 18.71 million. Apart from the value appreciation, the shareholder would have already taken Rs 1.7 million as dividends.[2] Unfortunately, as we will see next, this great economic promise was squandered by a weak political set-up.

Politics Trumps Economics: The Bubble Bursts

The bubble of reform that was seen at the advent of the democracy and liberalization burst all too soon and the economic boom that it had inspired lost its steam all too quickly. The beginning of the downfall was signalled by the volatility of Nepali politics, with the toppling of Girija Prasad Koirala's majority government in 1994 due to infighting within the Nepali Congress party. Rampant corruption, bad governance and the ensuing political instability were to be the defining characteristics of Nepal's multiparty democracy and they quickly neutralized the economic spurt and spirit of the early 1990s. The very foundations upon which the economic growth of the early 1990s occurred proved to be enfeebled and weak. Even though the private sector was ready to take the helm in order to ensure economic growth, the politicians were not ready to take on the responsibilities of democracy. A weak and disoriented government quickly invited back the spirit of profiteering, racketeering and patronizing that had plagued the private sector during the Panchayat era.

The lack of staying power of successive governments and the swiftness with which they lost their political convictions prevented any political party from summoning up the will or the time to push any reform process to fruition. Business lobby groups and labour unions defined policies using money or street-side bravado, while politicians seemed stuck in the middle with little option but to make a quick buck before getting replaced. The myopia of government and the protectionist approach of business and trade unions were to have a tremendously negative impact on the national economy. This situation of policy without conviction was exemplified during the nine-month rule of the Communist Party of Nepal (UML) in 1994—with the leaders remaining wedded to the old socialist rhetoric even as they promised to liberalize the economy during meetings with donors or when seeking funds from the business community. On top of all this, the push for liberalization that the multilateral and bilateral agencies demanded from the government, heedless of local context, did not help.

The fall of the communist government in 1995 and the series of coalition governments that were formed from then onwards made a mockery of the political system. The political parties showed a lack of strong ideological conviction or the motivation to really move beyond electoral preparation and feeble attempts at power retention. If anyone on the street during the mid- and late 1990s was questioned on the role of the political parties, his or her response would have been, 'to keep their seats' (stay in power). Sadly for the nation and its people, the political parties proved incapable of getting their act together and maintaining a government structure for longer than two years. The astounding statistic of eleven prime ministers in the ten years between 1990 and 2000 speaks volumes about the political instability that characterized the Nepal government.

With such instability in the government, it is hardly surprising that no government had the time or the will to really follow through on reforms. The moment a party was able to capture power it immediately became embroiled in a fight to maintain that power. Conversely, the moment a party lost power, it engaged in knee-jerk dissent against those in power, with the hope that it might gain power in the near future. In such a cannibalistic environment, there was no time to think about the greater good of Nepal—ethical thinking broke down and the desire for power overcame better instincts. A complete sense of political hedonism ruled; the idea was to get in power, grab what you could as quickly as you could before you got kicked out and someone else got the opportunity to pillage the country.

This political myopia had a major impact on Nepal's image outside. From a country of hope that could pursue an economic agenda using diplomatic channels to woo investors it was relegated to a state where countries were willing to give aid but not trade with it. Dr Singha Bahadur Basnyat, Ambassador to the UK and Scandinavian countries from 1997 to 2003, expressed to this author his frustration at constantly being told, while overseas, about Nepal's three critical problems—the overly politicized bureaucracy, corruption and political infighting. He felt that there was no interest in the government in using diplomatic missions as trade or investment promotion opportunities. Even when events were organized, the ideas remained bound to party politics—beginning and ending with stratagems that would ensure that political parties stayed in power.

Overall, the squandering of the unique opportunities provided by the 1990s was a direct result of the government's lack of commitment to any specific reform policy. This left the nation in the doldrums, going neither here nor there and led ultimately to stagnation. Each successive government lacked the courage to either wholly embrace a capitalist welfare state, or to follow the discredited Nehruvian model. This confused approach was evident in both the promulgation of pro-labour laws and the manner in which state enterprises were privatized. For instance, a Company Act came into force which accepted the concept of public joint-stock companies but required the wide dispersal of shareholding. The act required large and unwieldy quorums for shareholders' meetings, not to mention the obligation to take on public shareholders. The state refused to accept the basic tenet that businesses are a capitalist phenomenon into which it is hard to inject a socialist ideological element. While laws relating to registration of foreign investments and other domestic investments were reformed in 1992, the laws that could help a business close down came only in 2006 when the Bankruptcy Act was enacted. However, the provisions of the Bankruptcy Act required that a commercial bench of the judiciary be created, to deal with such cases of bankruptcy. While such a bench was created, five years after the enactment, it is yet to deliver a judgement on any case. The business owners have no legal options if a business fails and are thus less likely to take the risk of starting a business at all.

Bureaucracy: Feudalism Under a Veneer

A major hurdle to efficient governance was the entrenched and dysfunctional bureaucracy, which continued as it was from the Panchayat system through the 1990 Jana Andolan and beyond. No major overhaul of the bureaucracy has ever been contemplated or attempted in Nepal, which leaves us with the same antiquated system of governance that characterized the Panchayat years. Bureaucracy still has a working culture moulded out of the system of nepotism and *chakari*, which causes seekers of power and favour to spend most of their time displaying themselves regularly before authority to demonstrate their loyalty. Additionally, the decrease in the quality of education during the Panchayat era led to a direct loss in the quality of service being provided by the bureaucracy. Simultaneously, the preferential propagation of the Nepali language inevitably led to the dominance of the hill culture of the Bahun/Chhettri/Newar ethnic groups within the bureaucracy. Finally, the bureaucracy became a playground for a party affiliated reward system, a transposition of the traditional *jagir* system of the Shah kings via the political parties, where grants of land were replaced with posts in the bureaucracy.

The government also failed to decentralize and delegate responsibility properly to the local and regional levels. This created an evident disparity between Kathmandu and other regions of Nepal. This Kathmandu-centric governance model impacted business as well, with most businesses also remaining Kathmandu-centric. As an example of the dominance of Kathmandu over the entire Nepali economic landscape, it is worth noting that even in early 2008, although the valley had just 7 per cent of Nepal's population, 40 per cent to 60 per cent of the sales of the majority of consumer goods took place there. The region even today consumes around 45 per cent of total electricity generation, uses 75 per cent of all fixed telephone lines and 90 per cent of all mobile phone connections, and is home to 90 per cent of all cars and 80 per cent of all motorcycles.[3] This Kathmandu-centric approach has had a negative impact on the prospects of developing other urban areas and has detrimentally affected the environment and quality of life in the Kathmandu Valley as well.

Labour Woes

If the government followed a capitalistic bent in encouraging enterprise, capital formation and investment, its lack of will to go fully with the liberal capitalistic model was exemplified by its inability and unwillingness to address labour law issues. Of primary concern was the government's unwillingness to release the domain of labour-enterprise relations from its control and allow labour and enterprise to negotiate disagreements independently, without involving the government. Its weakness in addressing labour issues is perhaps best highlighted by the *jagir* system that is prevalent in the bureaucracy and state-owned enterprises, where jobs take the place of the old system of land grants, as payments for favours. The *jagir* mentality spills over into the private enterprises also where workers consider their jobs to be for life, regardless of performance and efficiency. This assurance of the job or *jagir* makes it unnecessary to put one's full effort into the job, adding yet another layer of inefficiency to an already deeply ineffective system. The provisions of the labour laws make it impossible for workers in both private and public sectors to be fired on grounds of inefficiency and non-productivity. The workers, in order to shield themselves from being fired or taken to task, even now choose the route of unionization. Rajendra Khetan, chairman of Khetan Group, shared with this author his view that that this labour culture fits well with the intent of political parties looking for numbers, strength and money. Trade unions affiliated to political parties have members in huge numbers, increasing the total amount coming in as membership fees and in return, the large union cadres turn up for a show of strength whenever the party requires it.

The labour laws and policies that were put into place since the 1990s have been unsuccessful in either creating a secure business environment or in securing the rights of workers, given that the unions were politically affiliated and followed party dictates. From the point of view of enterprise, the preamble of the Labour Act of 1992 only provides for the protection of the interests of the labour community and not those of the enterprise itself. Successive legislative interventions like the Labour Laws 1993, Trade Union

Act 1992 and Labour Court Laws 1995 were no better—each of them made labour and its unions more powerful while compromising the rights of the enterprise. With the strong advocacy of a few bilateral agencies like Swiss Development Corporation (SDC) and the support of a pro-socialist media owned by private businesses and empowered by their political clout, labour groups successfully took advantage of their necessity to enterprise and have essentially held it to ransom. Labour unions and their leaders also started making investments in casinos and other ventures such as real estate. Therefore, they emerged not only as a formidable source of cadres but also as a source of finance for the political parties.

Although Nepal's legal framework provided for the protection of labour, over and above the fundamental rights of workers guaranteed by ILO conventions, the worker still suffered. The worker still did not have access to the rights that government had secured for it. A large part of the problem was that all labour unions in Nepal were politically affiliated and labour rights were often just a pretext for achieving a strong vote bank amongst the labouring class. The rights of the worker were never the fundamental impetus behind labour movements and strikes in Nepal. The misuse of labour unions as means to gaining political clout and voicing disagreements continues to inflict a tremendous cost on the Nepali economy. The militancy of labour that such a culture has fostered has been a severe deterrent to both foreign and domestic investment with labour issues remaining a primary source of concern for those wanting to do business in Nepal.

The reason why labour issues were not reformed is apparent. The politicians and political parties simply had too much to lose by challenging the labour unions they themselves had helped create and strengthen. The unions formed the core of their political voter base and simultaneously provided the strongest muscle power in their political arsenal.

However, in the bargain, labour has lost the most, as the people who really wanted to work for a living chose to leave Nepal, owing to their uncertainty about Nepal's economic future and their inability to handle situations where they were called in to protest rather than work. Many factories shut down, with owners being forced to sell their properties. Businesses closing down meant not only the loss of overtime pay opportunities, of employee housing and profit-linked bonuses, but also the relocation of families in search of work to different parts of the country and abroad, to India. Rajendra Khetan of the Khetan Group blames a handful of labour leaders for inculcating a culture that has kept millions of people out of the employment market in Nepal.

Bandhs Galore: The Business of Closure

The successful use of *chakka jam*s and Nepal *bandh*s* during the Jana Andolan had highlighted the importance and strength of street-level agitation to the politicians. The strategy of closing down the nation or obstructing traffic to make a political statement is perhaps a remnant of the power of the Indian embargo in Nepal. Whatever the cause, the *chakka jam* and Nepal *bandh* soon became an integral part of Nepali society. Political parties, labourers, businesses, social workers and even grief-stricken family members took to the streets in some form of *chakka jam* or Nepal bandh the moment their rights were threatened or demands remained unmet. Websites like www.nepalbandh.com started providing advance information on such events, helping people to plan their days of travel and decide whether to keep offices open or shut. The popular currency of such digital representations of the *bandh* cycle in a nation that was not overwhelmingly tech savvy, is an indication of how deep a hold the *bandh* phenomenon had on the Nepali psyche.

Agitating cable operators cutting off transmission of their channels, taxis expressing grievances by parking along the Ring Road to obstruct traffic in and out of the airport, garbage piling up on the street when someone in the garbage chain is unhappy— these are all routine occurrences. Ironically, businesses and hotels which lamented the impact of *bandh*s on business and tourism,

---

Chakka jam literally means the jamming of wheels, prohibiting vehicles from plying the roads. *Banda/bandh*s are temporary shutdowns in all commerce, that are enforced by the organizers of street-level agitation.

when upset, resorted to calling for *bandh*s themselves. It was as if Nepal and the *bandh* were a match made in heaven—once in the country, everyone seemed to welcome *bandh*s and revel in them. For the by now fatalist and escapist Nepali populace, the *bandh* was just another holiday. It was an excuse to drink excessively the night before and play cards all day long, so most Nepalis relished the many surprise vacations that the nation's political turmoil threw at them. Simultaneously, for the business minded, it presented the ideal opportunity for racketeering and profiteering by providing more arbitrage opportunities to make that extra rupee. The vegetable vendors in Kalimati, Kathmandu as well as the adulterated fuel gas stations prayed for that landslide in Krishnabhir or a strike by any organization—as long as life came to a standstill. Businesses that thrive by capitalizing on such windows of opportunity have served to further the culture of *bandh*s. The business atmosphere in Kathmandu runs on the same wavelength as Kolkata, which even after all its moves towards liberalization, has yet to get rid of the image it impressed upon the world during the 1970s—as a city with more non-working days than working days. In the tourist or economic map of the world, Nepal, with its addiction to *bandh*s and *chakka jam*s, has firmly established itself as Kolkata's younger sibling.

It is very difficult to estimate how much the economy lost on account of *bandh*s, when the Maoists paralysed Kathmandu Valley for five days in May 2010. It was estimated that Rs 15 billion was lost every day.[4] The World Bank Investment Climate Report 2010 pointed out that in addition to the fifty-two annual holidays and fifty holidays because of national occasions, enterprises lost yet another forty-four days on account of such *bandh*s.

A Waste of Youth

At the heart of the *bandh* and *chakka jam* cycle are event coordinators such as student and trade unions. In yet another perversion of economic potential, the politicization of university campuses and trade unions created the need for a large number of young cadres to take to the streets to enforce *bandh*s and *chakka* *jam*s as a real representation of political power. The use of the youth as means of political leveraging is, in effect, the squandering of the promise that the youth hold. Unlike the youth in China, Thailand, and Vietnam, who are driving the economic growth of their countries, young people in Kathmandu are either busy touting party propaganda or spending their nights partying. The youth who were not party material (in either sense of the word 'party') sought out opportunities to leave the country and work abroad. Unfortunately, having been raised in an educational system which lacked the standards that would allow its products to compete in the international market, most of these youth found their skills severely lacking and their degrees ephemeral comforts in a world that was more concerned about quality and brand than heart and intention. For parents, it became more important to provide Rs 6000 for a pair of Doc Martens shoes than buy books for just a tenth of the amount, since Nepali society generally seemed to judge external looks only. For every ten beauty pageants held there was one quiz contest and while ever more places were available to go drink and smoke, there was no place to go and listen to a good lecture. While clubs and dance bars mushroomed, no museums or art centres got built. A business atmosphere that deterred investment for fear of militant labour, energy shortages and constant security concerns, all stifled the growth of employment opportunities in the private sector. The rise in unemployment, dissatisfaction and militancy in such a scenario is thus, hardly surprising.

Opportunity Squandered: The Khetan Experience

The evolution of the Khetan Group as a formidable business group after 1990 and its dilemma about its future plans in 2008 illustrates the trajectory of emergence and squandering that characterized the 1990s. A predominantly trading house, it changed gear in 1988 after Nepal got observer status in the General Agreement on Trade and Tariffs (GATT), a development which enabled it to get into industry. The group invested in three industries along with the government. After the reforms began in 1990, it entered into manufacturing, starting a brewery producing Tuborg beer and into the financial service industry with banks and insurance companies. It even partnered with another local promoter to start an airline. Over the years, it got involved with many more businesses and took a call in the mid-1990s to restructure businesses to focus on food and beverage, financial services and an agency role in representation of international companies. After growing for nearly two decades, they are, in 2012, sceptical about continuing operations in Nepal. Rajendra Khetan, the chairman of the group and also a constituent assembly member, makes statements in public and also to this author, about how they are now being forced into becoming non-resident Nepalis (NRNs) as they have started investing outside Nepal due to the poor business environment in Nepal. He states the reasons for this decision: the deteriorating security situation, the continuous closures on account of *chakka jams* and *bandh*s and a militant labour force. In March 2011, the Khetan Group sold 40 per cent share in Gorkha Brewery to Carlsberg Singapore reducing their holding to 10 per cent[5] and 22 per cent share in Bottlers Nepal, the bottling franchise for Coca Cola, to Gorkha Brewery.[6]

The Tourism Jinx

Nepal's fate as a tourist destination was also afflicted during these years, due to various local and international events. By 1996, the gold rush in the tourism industry had created a situation of oversupply of hotel rooms, while the poor infrastructure (aside from the boom in hotel rooms) could not cater to the rising number of tourists. There was no innovation in the tourism products that were being sold and the golden triangle of Pokhara, Chitwan and Kathmandu became a stale product. The Visit Nepal Year of 1998, that was supposed to provide the impetus for tourist influx paradoxically coincided with the decline of tourist arrival in Nepal. The hijacking of an Indian Airlines flight on Christmas Eve of 1999 dealt the first big blow, with flights from India to Nepal suspended for six months. Thereafter, a riot broke out in February 2001, sparked by rumours that an Indian film star had made derogatory remarks about Nepal. Then, there was the closure of hotels over a service charge row between hotel owners and hotel workers. The already ailing industry was dealt another blow with the Royal Massacre in June 2001. Thereafter, the 9/11 attack on the Twin Towers in New York and the subsequent impact on global tourism carried on the slump till 2002. The escalation of the Maoist conflict in 2002 prompted negative travel advisories and tourist arrivals fell that year to as low as 1990 levels. The Nepal Tourism Year 2011 campaign funded by the government and led by private sector honchos made a lot of noise within Nepal, but failed to create any significant commotion outside Nepal. In 2012, tourist arrival finally crossed the 800,000 mark, which essentially meant Nepal had taken a long and chequered two decades to treble its tourist arrival figures. Malaysia, during the same period, also increased tourism arrivals threefold but from an already substantial 7.4 million to 25 million tourists.[7]

Power Snaps

In retrospect, the twenty-odd years from 1990 to 2012 have been a roller coaster ride for the Nepal economy. The restoration of democracy and the subsequent opening up of the economy sparked much hope, but the squandering of opportunity that began in 1994, was further aggravated by ten years of conflict between the state and the Maoists. By the time the first prime minister of the Democratic People's Republic of Nepal took the oath of office in September 2008, the economy was worse off than in 1990.

The example of the energy crisis perhaps best explains this tremendous decline. The biggest impact of the Indian embargo of 1989 was on the supply of fuel from India, which abruptly stopped. At that time, major power cuts were anticipated and the government, in response, wanted to develop hydropower for energy security as well as rapid economic growth. A Hydropower Policy was instituted in 1992, which encouraged private investment in hydropower, including Foreign Direct Investment. By 1997, Nepal had launched two of what were to be the only ten successful privately financed hydropower enterprises in that decade—Bhote Koshi and Khimti. Both had secured foreign investment.

Shortly thereafter, with the devaluation of the Nepali Rupee and revenues pegged to the US Dollar, these two projects drew a lot of flak and became everyone's favourite punching bags. In 1998, the then deputy prime minister and minister in charge of hydropower, Shailja Acharya of the Nepali Congress categorically stated to a business delegation that included this author, that Nepal did not want the private sector, indigenous or otherwise, to develop power projects with a power generation capacity of more than 10 MW. With private investors out of the picture, foreign donors got into action to fund the Kaligandaki and Middle Marsyangdi power projects, which were to be built and owned by the state-owned utility, the Nepal Electricity Authority (NEA). While the government waited for more donors to line up to build projects, all investors waited for the government to grant licences. All this while, a sizable number of hydropower experts made millions by presenting critiques on the sector. By the end of 2012, more than sixty Power Purchase Agreements* between the NEA and power providers, for the purchase of power by the NEA, were pending negotiation and private developers were sitting on more than 200 survey licences. A historic Power Trade Agreement signed between India and Nepal in 1996 to facilitate power trading between the two countries, was approved by the Indian cabinet but till date, successive Nepali governments have never managed to get the treaty approved at their end. Perhaps this was because of the speculation and hypothesis that Indian interest in commercial hydropower only began after the Bhote Koshi and Khimti projects were well under way in 1996.

Hydropower also generated big activists who stalled many projects. They opposed Arun III, a World Bank–initiated project and a number of foreign investments in hydropower, especially Indian. They opposed and then supported a power project at Melamchi and lobbied hard for Chinese investment in West Seti. Keeping their offices running on expensive diesel generators, these lobby groups did not mind Nepal staying starved of electricity.

As on this date, Nepal is reeling under sixteen hours of daily power cuts, forcing people to resort to inefficient forms of

---

*A Power Purchase Agreement (PPA) is an agreement by which a buyer of power (in this case, the state monopoly, NEA), agrees to purchase power from a power producer.

substitution like battery-operated inverters. The government is left mulling over the possibility of operating a diesel plant producing electricity at four times the cost of the most expensive purchase price of hydropower from private producers. With oil prices having peaked close to USD 200 as of September 2008 and government still controlling the petroleum products market, the situation is as bleak as it was during the embargo. This is a burden Nepal bears for the collective myopia of a government that could not provide a consistent policy framework, a private sector that just sat on licences to trade when it could have built projects, a donor community that kept on funding a financially weak state utility and the silent Nepali consumer who did not complain.

Dr Ram Sharan Mahat, former finance minister and one of the key architects of the 1990s economic reforms says, 'The greatest failure [in these two decades] has been not being able to exploit our hydropower potential, as we could not get political consensus for big or small projects, be it for Arun III or Mahakali.'* On the flip side, he credits the reforms for providing the foundation that has kept the economy from spiralling out of control, since, with the exception of some sectors like banking, these years did see the success of private media, broadcasting communication and information technology. Further, Kathmandu was no longer synonymous with Nepal. Dr Mahat continues on a positive note, 'The greatest gains of [these] years have been the increased role of the community and rural empowerment. Social service delivery, physical and social infrastructure reached rural Nepal.' Yet it is worth noting that during these two decades, Nepal only managed to grow its GDP from USD 3.6 billion to USD 18 billion,[8] while during the same period Malaysia's GDP increased from USD 44 billion to USD 280 billion.[9]

---

*Arun III was a project in East Nepal pursued by the World Bank and later aborted due to pressures from environmentalist lobbies and Mahakali is a multipurpose hydropower project to be built by India.

Communism Is Not Indigenous

The way Nepalis have embraced communism as an antithesis to globalization or westernization is very peculiar. Karl Marx, Lenin or Stalin were never Asian thinkers. Even Mao borrowed the communist ideology from Marx. Whenever a discourse on communism takes place, especially in Nepali, communism is always pitted against western influences. In August 2012, the CPN (Maoist) cadres started a campaign to change the name of educational institutions that had English names. However, the same party cadres are fine with their party offices filled with images of Marx, Lenin and Stalin, and their party leaders continuing to use English initials in their names.

The year 1990 and the few years that immediately followed were times when the Nepali citizenry saw hope and believed in the ability of the democratic process to lead the nation towards economic prosperity. However, by the mid-1990s, this hope was replaced with scepticism and doubt, which, by the turn of the century had turned into despair and apathy. The blame for the failures of the Nepali state and economy can be attributed to many different sections of society and a host of different reasons can be given for each one individually and all of them collectively. The best service to the nation would be to learn from these mistakes so that the hopes and aspirations of the Nepali citizenry after the second Jana Andolan of April 2006, do not meet the same fate as they did in the 1990s. The following three chapters will therefore focus on the private sector, the development sector, the governance structure and social service delivery systems to outline faults and failures as well as successes, so that they may be improved and updated to match the needs of the present age. If politicians and the bureaucracy had their great role in this squandering, the private sector played an equal part, which will be discussed in the next chapter.

4

DISAPPOINTING PRIVATE SECTOR

The private sector runs on the principle of maximizing the return on equity of its owners. The private sector can only exist within an economic model that prescribes to some form of capitalism, with private wealth being free to take part in wealth creation. This is only possible within a state structure that assures and protects the rights of ownership through the rule of law. In a purely communist or socialist economy, the private sector does not theoretically exist, even though the idea of ownership may persevere. In such a society, the state retains ownership rights to all property. Nepal traditionally possessed a feudalistic system that limited the rights of ownership to elites—the granting of property to the aristocratic elite was prevalent. It was only after the fall of the Rana regime and the establishment of the interim constitution in 1951 that a legal and constitutional structure was created for a formal private sector in Nepal.

In 2008, Nepal's private sector was valued at around USD 8 billion.[1] It is by far the most active sector of the economy and its biggest employment provider. The bulk of the private sector, up to 90 per cent by some estimates, is composed of enterprises which can only be classified as small or micro-enterprises. Although these enterprises are Nepal's largest employers, generating more than 90 per cent of the entire country's employment opportunities, they account for a mere 4 per cent of national GDP.[2] For the creation of an employment intensive economy, these small and medium enterprises must be fostered and encouraged. Compared to large industrial enterprises which, on average, create one job for every USD 5000 invested, these small enterprises create a job on no more than USD 150.[3] However, a major reason for stagnation in the Nepali private sector is the inability of these small enterprises to scale up, expand and grow. For instance, a successful restaurant or a store selling handicrafts does not open a second branch or spread over different cities in the country, thereby not leveraging the competencies it has successfully created. While some of this is due to a surprising lack of hunger among enterprise owners, the bulk of the problem remains an inefficient and unregulated market that is unable to deliver easy access to finance, markets, technology and skills.

Barriers to Business: A Look Back at History

Historically, Nepal's private sector remained closely tied to its aristocracy and social structure via the caste system. Ownership, especially of land, was a right reserved for a select group of privileged people. Although Nepal's first company act was coded in 1936, the act only allowed for the formation of public companies on a joint stock model. It was only through the Companies Act of 1951 that individuals were authorized to register private limited companies. The Panchayat government also introduced the Industrial Enterprises Act of 1962, encouraging foreign and direct investment and providing a number of cushions, including a ten-year tax holiday. However, Nepal's land-owning elite, since the time of the Ranas, had found it safer to invest in India than in Nepal. This was a purely market-driven rationale as industries in Nepal, lacking energy and resources, were poorly equipped to compete with the established industries of India. For the Ranas in particular, investing in India remained a hedge against potential political turmoil in Nepal.

As John Welpton correctly points out in his book *A History of Nepal*,[4] the 1936 Nepal Companies Act was largely created to facilitate Rana interests in establishing industries in Nepal. These industries were primarily set up in partnership with Marwari businessmen from Calcutta (now Kolkata), who provided the bulk of the capital for investment while their Rana partners ensured smooth operations in Nepal. However, the Rana regime's unwillingness to invest in infrastructure, transportation and communication along with a strong opposition to market and social liberalization acted as significant barriers to industrial growth. These initial ventures met with limited success partly due to the business environment which was entirely dependent on knowing, befriending and working with the Ranas. Success was hampered primarily due to a shortage in materials caused by the outbreak of World War II. Yet, even after the fall of the Rana regime, the Marwari community's acumen for business allowed it to continue thriving in Nepal. Among the few entrepreneurial communities in Nepal, the Marwari community has by far been the most successful in establishing and expanding Nepal's private sector.

Besides the Marwari community, which made a relatively late entry into the Nepali economy, the commercial landscape of the kingdom had been dominated by the Newars. However, the Newar family and community structures proved to be a significant challenge in adapting to the new business environment that was created in Nepal after the fall of the Rana regime and the liberalization of markets both in the 1950s and 1990s. A fatal flaw in traditional Newar and most Nepali business models was the intimate link between business activity on the one hand and caste, ethnicity and gender on the other. Historically, the caste system had designated particular ethnic and caste communities as the administrators and managers of trade and business. Additionally, these businesses were family run and were passed down through the eldest male descendant of the family. The eldest male then took on the responsibility of heading the business with other family members acting to support him. With the corporatization of businesses in Nepal, few Newar and Nepali businesses were able to switch from this traditional family based operational modality.

Although a few other communities including the Thakalis, Sherpas, and Tibetans were involved in entrepreneurial activities, there are precious few examples of truly great successes. Nepal's fatalistic and deterministic social structures are perhaps major factors in discouraging and suppressing the entrepreneurial instincts of other community groups. Equally at fault is a striking deficit of vision, a lack of interest in dreaming big and capitalizing on opportunities to promote big business in Nepal. For instance, when mobile phones were first introduced in Nepal in 1997, Nepal imported mobile phone sets from Singapore and other East Asian countries. Nepali mobile phone traders quickly realized that due to import duties, the same phones they had in Nepal cost significantly more in India. This encouraged traders to set up informal channels to ship phones from Nepal to India while making a cut through the price difference. However, as was typical of the Nepali trading mentality, arbitrage was seen as a more viable business option than the idea of establishing an actual mobile phone manufacturing plant in Nepal. The comparative advantage in price was also short-lived, for when Nokia and others entered the Indian market by setting up their own manufacturing plants in India, phones started to flow from India to Nepal.

During much of the Panchayat era, that lasted from 1960 to 1990, the growth of the private sector remained sluggish. Although starting a business in Nepal during this time was a lot easier than during the early half of the twentieth century under the Rana regime, significant barriers to entry remained. For instance, if you were from an upper caste family with a good social network and had a connection with a member of the royal family, doing business in Nepal was all fun and games. As Kamal Mani Dixit, former chairman of the Salt Trading Corporation, explained to this author, 'it was difficult to do business without any partnership with *durbariya** members.' Without these royal connections, starting and growing a business remained a challenge.

The deep trade links between India and Nepal were also a problem. The Panchayat government, aware of the dangers of this

---

*People close to the durbar (palace), including royal family members.

situation, sought to build up its trade networks with other countries as well. This proved a challenging task, since all trade with any other country had to pass through India as the only allowed port as per Nepal's transit agreement with India was Kolkata. Given India's protectionist policies targeted at import substitution, New Delhi did not look upon the import of third country goods into Nepal with much pleasure—since these goods were often sold back to Indian consumers at prices that compared too favourably with Indian products. Nepal's position as the provider of top-end luxury goods and electronics for the Indian market was demonstrated by the establishment of Bishal Bazaar, a massive mall in the heart of Kathmandu city, in 1976. Aside from drawing an increasing number of Indian shoppers, Nepali businesses were also able to re-export* goods into India through unofficial routes. However, the problem of re-exporting to India has remained a major bone of contention for Nepal–India trade relations ever since. A significant number of industries, such as steel utensils and yarn-producing factories have flourished in Nepal, taking advantage of export duty differences between the two countries, only to be shut down in a few years once India reacted.

Nepal's traditional trade with Tibet also started to wane. For the greater part of the 1950s and 1960s, Nepali traders in Tibet were being displaced by Chinese business people as they consolidated power in Tibet. The 1962 war between India and China led to virtually all Nepali business people shutting down their operations in Tibet. Nepal could not link up to the various trade points in Tibet with roads, as India continuously expressed concern about the land link between Nepal and Tibet. The strained political relationship between China and India after the 1962 Sino-Indian war meant that all issues related to Nepal were examined by India from a geopolitical perspective. The absence of a good road link with China meant that Nepali imports from China had to come all the way through the ports of Kolkata and consequently both cost more and were subject to constant Indian interference.

---

*Re-export—a popular word used in Nepal to denote the act of exporting an import that was originally imported via India.

The Rise of the Bahun Business Barons

The Newar merchants, who are seen as pioneers in business and entrepreneurship, slowly lost out as the newer generation Newar business people did not change with the times, be it in corporatizing, hiring of professional management, or tying up with international firms to further their business. Internal family feuds that were not resolved due to the lack of openness in adapting to newer ideas kept them away from business. On the other hand, we saw more and more people from the Bahun community do business post-1990, where earlier they had largely held control over bureaucratic jobs. In the world of business they put to use the same networks and their signature style of operating as they did in politics and the bureaucracy. They started engaging not only in trading but also in industry, media and financial institutions. They were also instrumental in providing an 'alternative' to capitalism and starting the 'cooperative' movement. If a survey were conducted to find out which ethnic group was promoting the cooperatives, it would be very clear where the leadership lay. The Bahuns basically followed the same models as the Chettris and Newars, that is, hiring their kith and kin in the business they got engaged in, especially as promoters. However, the Bahuns were a shade more hard-working; and this, combined with heavy networking, led to their acquiring a number of key positions in publicly listed companies as well as business associations.

Give Us Protection

With the liberalization of the markets after the 1990 Jana Andolan, the government put all its emphasis on the private sector as the primary vehicle for economic growth. With this intention, waves of market-oriented reforms were carried out. The financial sector was deregulated along with the tourism, aviation, insurance, and power development sectors and industrial licensing was scrapped. As a result, during the early 1990s, foreign direct investment started flowing into Nepal, and Unilever, Dabur, Asian Paints, Coke, Pepsi as well as foreign banks and insurance companies entered the Nepali market. However, the Nepali private sector which was initially excited at the opening up of the economy, slowly realized that liberalization was the first step to globalization, and that soon they would have to compete in global markets. Despite government efforts to open up the economy, the nexus of the small business elite continued to utilize their political and governmental patrons to frustrate reforms.

Without a vibrant industrial component and lacking any major comparative or competitive advantage, business within Nepal has historically been confined to trade. Trading makes arbitrage a core business strategy whether in the form of working around duties, taxes or the demand–supply gap. As with mobile phones, arbitrage grew into a major industry in its own right with the objective of working the system and making it play to one's favour. This made it essential for businessmen to hobnob with government officials and politicians. Duties and taxes were negotiated over glasses of whisky and loans were handed out for a commission. This form of myopic lobbying, carried out by the private sector with the objective of securing immediate profitability rather than long-term economic prosperity, created a business environment that thrived on corruption. The reach of these lobby groups was such that at times it created distortions in the government's annual budget to the extent of being completely contrary to its long-term five-year plans. The budget started to reflect private interests and accommodate provisions at the behest of private sector individuals or groups. Therefore, customs duties were reduced or increased based on the 'briefcases' that were traded rather than on economic fundamentals.

This shift from market growth to protectionist ploys was the direct result of an increasing realization among local small businesses of the threat international players posed. As a result, the nexus of small business elites used their political and governmental patrons to leverage their position and frustrate reforms. For instance, when J. Walter Thompson, a multinational advertising agency, sought to enter the Nepali market and establish a subsidiary in Nepal, it took them over one and a half years of haggling and bargaining with the government, due to a strong local lobby group that tried to block and discourage their entry into Nepal. Similarly, Maersk, an international shipping, freight and logistics company took a long time to register the company as the government was under immense pressure from smaller local businesses and stalled the registration for more than a year and a half. They saw the entry of Maersk as the biggest challenge to their way of doing business. It was the same case when DHL, an international cargo company, tried to establish a fully owned subsidiary in Nepal. Local courier companies ganged up in an attempt to stop the registration process even though legally, there were no issues for contention. Similarly, not allowing international travel companies to operate in Nepal at the behest of the strong local lobby has made tourist development a fraction of what it could potentially be.

Globalization and Professional Competencies

In the long run, the entry of multinationals into Nepal has been a huge boost to the national economy. They have brought with them a new way of doing business—in their operating procedures, professionalism and service-oriented delivery. Small businesses in Nepal were well aware of the lack of professionalism in their organizations—they knew that their service delivery was mediocre at best and they also knew that they faced serious gaps in management ability. However, instead of seeking solutions to create a more dynamic and efficient organization, most companies took the easier way out by simply blocking all competition. Their lack of ambition has had a significantly detrimental impact on the Nepali economy by discouraging the entry of international companies and foreign investment. It has also prevented most industries in Nepal from developing themselves into world-calibre organizations.

The building of competencies can be explained well by contrasting Nepal's hotel industry, in which international hotel companies are allowed to operate, with Nepal's travel industry, in which international travel companies are not allowed to operate. Thus, we have competent hotel staff, systems and processes but due to the absence of international competencies in travel agencies, there is a lack of ability in scaling up the tourism business. In areas where foreign firms have been allowed, be it consumer product companies, marketing, banking, courier, advertising or market research, Nepali competencies developed to international quality and standards, while in areas where foreign firms were restricted, accounting services and legal firms for instance, the service is way below international standards.

Succession planning and execution is one of the hallmarks of success in business, but, like in politics, the older generation did not want to handover the enterprise to the new generation as family business scions wanted to operate till the very last stage of their lives. In a company, it was not unusual for the family patriarch to be seen coming to office with oxygen cylinders and attendants in tow to sign cheques. The 'younger generation' only got the opportunity to take over the mantle when they were way beyond their productive phase and again, like the previous generation, held on and did not transfer the leadership to the next generation.

The best example of the advantages of the entry of an international player into the local market is exemplified by the entry of Grindlays Bank (now Standard Chartered Bank) into Nepal in 1988 and its impact on the banking sector. While most banks remained identified with the owners of the banks (either the state or private business houses), Standard Chartered focused on building a management team that was distinct from ownership. They brought in international standard operating procedures, checks and balances system, a logistical framework and a sharp focus on service delivery. They not only compelled other banks to develop their own business structures in order to be able to compete with them, but also taught other banks what they had to do. For instance, a major problem banks faced was their inability to retain skilled professional staff, who hopped banks as and when better offers for their services came from other banks. Sujit Mundul, former CEO of Standard Chartered, says that the Standard Chartered training programme along with its management and operational structure (an import from its multinational corporate structure), allowed it to function just as efficiently with a new crop of employees as with a group of experienced ones. He emphasizes the role of international banks in countries like Bangladesh, where new technology, product base and product development competencies changed the face of banking.

In contrast to Standard Chartered, most international brands that were established in Nepal's indigenously developed business sectors have packed their bags and left, or have been asked to leave. The hospitality industry from 1990 to 2000 is a good example of this. The Taj Group of hotels which had entered Nepal in partnership with Annapurna moved out in a relatively short time span; similarly, the Sheraton moved out of Everest, WelcomGroup moved out of Hotel Kathmandu, and Dusit moved out of Fulbari, while Le Meridian was asked to leave from Gokarna. One of the biggest hindrances to the acceptance of corporate culture in Nepal has been the resistance to independent management of companies by their owners. Owners just could not keep from interfering with management, which posed real problems for professional management companies. This lack of corporate culture and professionalism has deterred foreign companies as it poses a significant hurdle to competent management, accountability and transparency. It has also restricted foreign brands from ensuring the quality of service that is associated with their brands.

Since the financial market reforms of the 1990s, there has been a boom in the banking sector, with the establishment of over thirty-one banks, eighty-seven development banks and seventy-nine finance companies up until December 2008. Apart from these institutions there are seventy-five licensed financial institutions that work directly under the Nepal Rastra Bank's directives. There are 26,000 cooperative finance institutions that are not regulated by the Rastra Bank. By the end of 2008, the thirty-one banks had a combined total lending portfolio of USD 4 billion compared to the USD 2 billion portfolio of cooperatives. Although banking penetration outside the Kathmandu Valley remains weak, there has been a gradual expansion of banks into small towns throughout Nepal. The massive volume of remittances that flows into rural Nepal has partly encouraged banks to expand into rural regions. Further, the popularity and success of Grameen Bank in Bangladesh has fostered the expansion of the micro-finance model in rural Nepal. For the first time in Nepali history, people from all sectors, class, castes and walks of life are saving and have access to capital.

Cooperative Movement

There were two types of cooperatives that started to gain popularity. One, a savings cooperative, the other a multipurpose cooperative. These, backed by constant encouragement from political powers, continued to mushroom as they did not have any regulation to adhere to or any stringent guidelines to follow. Families and friends got together to set up organizations that could take public money to be spent at the will of the board of the cooperative. People, especially traditional business people, found a new way of depositing money for higher returns, which was never under the scanner of the tax man or government regulator. The promoters of these cooperatives would form a board of their choice and start investing money at their own discretion and also pay themselves fat perks and benefits. A large set of investments were made in real estate, where, like in a monarchy, the principle was that the gain would be personal, while the losses would be borne by the cooperative. By 2012, 26,620 cooperatives had been registered with an outlay of USD 2 billion that provided access to finance to over 2 million people, or 10 per cent of the population, many of whom could not access the services of financial institutions. However, increased investment in real estate made many of them go bankrupt. With the courts staying away from the recovery process, many Nepalis who believed they did not have enough money or were scared of the processes of the banking system lost their hard-earned savings. The desire among Nepalis for high returns coupled with the lack of innovation within the banking system to reach to the bottom of the pyramid was also responsible for this.

However, the banking sector's success has facilitated the expansion of business in multiple sectors simply by increasing access to capital and decreasing the hassle of obtaining the capital. Bhatbhateni Supermarket is a classic example of a successfully leveraged growth model. Starting as a small mom and pop cold store in a 300-square-foot shutter with Rs 100,000, Min Bahadur

Gurung reinvested in and expanded the business gradually. Leveraging his position along the way, he has expanded the small cold store into the biggest retail outlet in the nation. Mr Gurung, who is founder–chairman of the company, believes in hard work and positive thinking. He quotes a Nepali proverb on how if one works hard, consistently, one can extract oil out of stone. He reports proudly that today Bhatbhateni has 2 million square feet of commercial area in six locations with 2200 people working directly for it and a turnover of Rs 15 billion.

Missing the IT Bus

For all the opportunities a young market like Nepal holds, success stories like Bhatbhateni are very rare. Most Nepali businesses suffer from a chronic inability to scale up, expand and grow. For instance, the IT industry in Nepal opened up shop well before the IT revolution in India. However, as with mobile phones, Nepali hardware vendors were content with making a cut from importing equipment into Nepal and then shipping it over to India. No Nepali IT firm made any attempt to expand its horizons, hardware companies showed an appalling lack of interest in setting up large scale plants to supply to India and software companies showed no interest in taking their products outside of Nepal. As a case for comparison, Mercantile started its computer software division in 1983, two years after the establishment of Infosys in India. By 1987, Mercantile had developed Pumori, an indigenous Nepali banking software which is still in use today. At a time when Indian banks were still on their way into a computerized system, the lack of penetration into the Indian market by Pumori can be seen as a sign of the conservative nature of business in Nepal.

India's successful economic boom driven by the outsourcing industry is another bus that Nepal has so far missed. Although several global software companies have explored the potential of Business Process Outsourcing in Nepal, their two major points of concern in entering the Nepali market remain: labour and labour. First, labour in the form of militant labour unions who propagate direct employment by firms and not through outsourcing agencies and the other in the form of a labour force that cannot match the quality of India's digital clerks, due to weak English and a sub-standard quality of education. With labour unions demanding direct employment by firms, labour was essentially saying that outsourcing would only be a possibility in Nepal if Citibank or Microsoft directly employed the workers here on their payroll. Which in turn would mean guaranteeing them minimum pay for not working, scheduled time to bask in the sun, and time off every time that they would like to celebrate Mao's birthday. The few outsourcing firms that have established themselves in Nepal are all facing this problem and given the strikes that these demands are inevitably preceded by, they have acted as a significant deterrent to the entry of international software companies.

However, the outsourcing landscape is far from a bleak desert and there are a number of success stories that provide a whiff of what Nepal could truly achieve. For instance, one of the success stories of Nepali entrepreneurs venturing out is that of Rudra Pandey, co-founder of D2Hawkeye, which is a medical data-mining company that started with just five people and grew to become a company that was bought out by an international firm, Verisk. It now operates with more than 400 people.

The Politics of Business Associations

Fearing international competition, many Nepali enterprise owners preferred to adopt protectionist policies, fighting for positions in their respective trade associations, rather than making an effort to take their business to a regional or global level. Unlike in India where business associations took on the onus of transforming policy and furthering the reform agenda, private sector associations in Nepal have had very little role in making their members ready for the global marketplace. Like the worker stuck in a union where upward mobility was becoming a union leader rather than increasing productivity or moving up the organizational hierarchy, the businessman was stuck in the quagmire of politics in business associations. Starting trade associations and reaching coveted positions in the associations, chambers or federations, along with wide presence in the media, had overtaken the hunger for building competencies and expanding. In one of the bilateral chambers of commerce, the agenda always remained the gaining of duty concessions on certain products produced by members who were in the executive committee.

The biggest deficiency in Nepal's political and business community has been leadership. Although there have been plenty who would take on the mantle of leadership, most have sadly been lacking in charisma, integrity and drive. The inadequacy of leadership is apparent when the President of Federation of Nepalese Chambers of Commerce & Industry (FNCCI) does not step down despite his name being widely published as a defaulter of bank loans and his firms booked under tax evasion. There is a vacuum of role models for young entrepreneurs. The lack of success stories of people who made it big without taking advantage of political linkages or unscrupulous business practices, speaks for itself. The selection of leadership in the association has always been political in nature and has isolated the few successful businesses and business people who are not keen to join the political bandwagon. There is a distinct lack of co-relation between the size of business and the quality of leadership in these associations. If we were to take the top twenty-five companies of Nepal in terms of turnover, profits, number of employees or taxes paid, then it would be surprising that only a few of the companies are actually involved in the leadership of various business associations. The fact that the leadership of such organizations excludes formidable business enterprises has also limited the efforts of multilateral and bilateral agencies working with such associations, as these agencies see little credibility in the existing leadership.

Myopia in the Face of Opportunity

Even when Nepali business enterprises have banded together and worked positively towards market reforms, certain sections of the business community have always been successful in abusing reforms for their short-term benefit. For instance, when the Indo-Nepal Trade and Transit Treaty came up for renewal in 1996, a group of businessmen from Nepal's FNCCI and India's Confederation of Indian Industries (CII) came together before the official government talks were held and came up with a list of recommendations for their respective governments. The treaty remains one of the few times private sector groups got together and worked out the terms and conditions they would like to see in a treaty that would govern the trade between their two countries. The governments were very receptive to the ideas they proposed and adopted the recommendations of the private sector. With the ink just drying on the treaty, opportunistic businessmen in Nepal started to export vegetable ghee, acrylic yarn, zinc oxide and copper products from Nepal to India. However, all these products were essentially taking advantage of the reduced customs duty between Nepal and India. It harkened back to the trade problem India and Nepal have had from the time of the Panchayat regime—where differences in customs duty unduly dictate the nature of not just trade but even enterprise in Nepal, but only for a short while, until India, realizing its loss, puts a stop to it. For instance, the vegetable ghee industry suddenly boomed by taking advantage of a difference in prices caused by duties. India does not levy an import duty on Nepali imports and Nepali import duties on palm oils from Southeast Asia happen to be considerably cheaper than those levied in India. Simultaneously, the 1996 treaty had imposed a relatively low duty on import and export costs between Nepal and India. This made it possible for opportunistic businessmen in Nepal to import truckloads of palm oil from Southeast Asia, repackage it into smaller packs, and re-export it to India as vegetable ghee at a price that was still cheaper than what was available in the Indian market. This arbitrage, conducted by Nepali businessmen, did not last long and ended with an amendment to the treaty with specific clauses on the certification of origin and value addition in 2002. In another example, rather than establishing a large plant to manufacture vitamins used in animal feed, businesses focused on re-packaging imported finished products into smaller packages and exporting it as product made in Nepal. Time and again, Nepal has been unsuccessful in utilizing a treaty that benefited exporting to India in the long run appropriately and had instead taken advantage of it to capture immediate gains.

The myopia of Nepali enterprise towards the fundamentals of doing business may be understood as a product of the complicated political and cultural history described so far. Yet, it is the customers and end-users of any good or service who ultimately pay the price for the myopia of business. For instance, the private sector is yet to implement a comprehensive consumer protection law that would set a standard for goods and services. Most businesses in Nepal see more benefit in ripping the customer off and making the extra buck than in being concerned about say, customer relations and ethical practices. A striking example of the lack of concern for the customer combined with the increasing pressure business faces from labour is the implementation of the service charge in most labour-dominated service industries. In most countries, the service charge is for the quality that is guaranteed by the business and if this quality is not met, service charges are waived. Without a regulatory framework to ensure levels of quality, services charges are essentially taxes on the consumer. Service charges not only increase the cost to the customer, but also fail to result in improvements to the service rendered. For a country that is heavily dependent on tourism from budget travellers, a 10 per cent service charge can define a better experience in Nepal relative to other countries. The myopia of the businesses agreeing to a service charge, a portion of which comes to them, has impacted the tourism service industry wherein the owners and labour are living off that additional 10 per cent from the consumer, without providing the added edge in service.

However, it is important to realize that the lack of quality services in Nepal is as much a fault of the consumer as it is of business and labour. A good example is the over 300 brands of bottled water that are available in Nepal. The consumer clearly does not care about the brand or quality of the water that is being provided as long as he/she is of the belief that any water poured from a sealed bottle is good, clean and natural. The lack of value the consumer associates with the brand is a telling sign of an economy that has not fully matured and is not aware of the choices it makes. This could partly be the fault of manufacturers and service providers in failing to promote a quality brand, but also at fault is the end-user's lack of interest or awareness in the quality of the good or service he or she buys.

The service providers don't train their staff for effective service and the staff takes their job as a mere *jagir* or lifetime grant—they don't believe that they have to service the customer, even though the customers are actually the ones who, in the end, are paying for their salaries. For instance, at a food court, the staff is keen to close operations before the scheduled time, just like the staff at government offices. The treating of customer-oriented work as mere *jagirs* is part of a culture of work that crosses over into the private sector, making it difficult to distinguish the attitude of a worker at a government utility and the staff at the private sector–owned Internet company or a cable operator.

Another example of the lack of ethical standards and awareness of Nepali businesses is the close proximity of alcohol shops to schools, and sleazy dance bars in residential areas. The former is a clear-cut example of business that does not extend its ethical practices to beyond its immediate interests while the latter is an example of business that is completely out of tune with socio-cultural norms that many still practice. Any event that involves the youth is sponsored by alcohol and tobacco companies and their advertisements as sponsors make one wonder if Nepal has no other business that needs advertisement or can afford advertisements. Indeed, the fact that many a business has thrived on selling alcohol and cigarettes to minors is a clear indication of a business community that simply does not care for anything other than the immediate acquisition of profits. It also is a telling sign of the lack of concern among big business houses on how or to whom their products are being sold and how it is affecting society. But most importantly, it gives a clear indication of a government that does not know its responsibilities and cannot institute basic rules and regulations that any parent would be instituting among their children.

The Continuing Energy Muddle

If the government post 1990 did not adequately regulate the way business was conducted, it practically failed in providing the basic need for any business to function properly—energy. The short-term tenure of every elected government stalled long-term legislative and institutional transformations. In the hydropower sector, in particular, the delay in deciding on survey licences has made Nepal, a country with great hydropower potential, reel under sixteen-hour power cuts every day during the dry months.

One of the greatest failures of private sector and government-led reform policies remains their inability to harness the promise of hydropower. The favourite statement from politicians and businessmen when flaunting their country's riches is about Nepal's potential to generate 84,000 MW of hydropower, out of which up to 44,000 MW is claimed to be exploitable. The reliability of these figures is questionable as these estimates were based on academic work carried out over two decades ago with no other survey being carried out to verify this potential. The Nepal Electricity Authority (NEA), the state-owned monolith that generates, transmits and distributes power, retains an image of incompetency, inefficiency and inability. It is a deeply politically driven institution which has been the subject of several studies, assistance and consultative packages, but has so far failed to deliver its full potential. Currently, with peak demand at around 700 MW, supply fluctuates between 400 MW in dry months to about 600 MW during the wet months, making power cuts a normal feature of life in Nepal. Since 1996, not a single foreign investor has made any investment in this sector.

However, like all sectors in Nepal, there are a few diamonds in the rough, despite the fact that the environment is hostile and corrupt for the successful implementation of a hydropower project. Bhote Koshi Power Company* began as a joint venture in the early nineties, between Soaltee Hotel Limited, Nepal; Harza Engineering, USA and Panda Energy, USA. The project was to develop the 36 MW Upper Bhote Koshi Hydroelectric Project. The Power Purchase Agreement was signed with Nepal Electricity Authority (NEA) in 1996 and financially closed in 1997. The project was financed

---

*The author was involved in this company in various capacities including as the CEO from 2006 to 2008.

under commercial terms through an international consortium led by International Finance Corporation (IFC) and DEG (The German Investment and Development Company). Construction began in 1997 and production began in 2001. The local promoters, Himal International, bought Panda Energy in 2006, at which point of time the entire staff was Nepali. This was one of the best examples of successful foreign investment in Nepal, where technology and funds came from outside Nepal and helped build a facility to be later owned and operated by Nepalis. Prabhakar Rana, the initiator of the Bhote Koshi project, recalls that during that time it was the government that invited him to explore the potential of doing a private project, and with the help of the US Embassy and US Trade Development Agency (USTDA) grant it was possible to do a feasibility study. Large power companies were interested and in the end Harza clicked. It was difficult to raise funds for the project in the international markets despite the government providing a sovereign guarantee and IFC leading the financing. He emphasizes that the success of the project was due to political will, since the project passed through the Deuba-led Congress, UML coalition and the RPP, with the bureaucracy providing support.

The hydropower issue aside, the energy woes in the country have aggregated with each passing year. The losses to the economy due to load-shedding, a product of government ineptitude throughout the 1990s, have been staggering. With such a strong emphasis on hydropower, each successive government has acted as if there are no other sources of energy in Nepal. Alternative energy sources like wind, solar, biomass and biogas energy have all been relegated to the back-burner. These sources have received little to no attention from either the government or the private sector. Aside from the success story of biogas plants in the south and decentralized rural solar lighting, precious little has been invested in alternative energy sources. To compound matters, the government and the private sector have both turned a blind eye to the heavily subsidized oil imports upon which the transportation networks of the country are completely dependent. The recent rise in oil prices and the inability of another state-owned monolith, the Nepal Oil Corporation (NOC), to change prices without turning it into a political issue, demonstrates the extent to which business and politics remain intertwined in Nepal. The former Deputy Managing Director of the NOC, Hariom Dhoj Joshi, who was one of the few to rise up from the ranks, says, 'The appointment by the government of a chairman as well as a managing director in Nepal Oil Corporation, defeated the business purpose of NOC. Most of the time, the organization had to fulfil the interests of the political parties and political masters, therefore sacrificing the interest of the consumer and doing what would have been best for Nepal.' Nepali consumers equally seemed quite content to stand in line for days on end to get a few litres of fuel; if anything, the long queues and lack of fuel provided the perfect excuse for Nepali people to slack off and play a few games of cards.

Nepal's oil supply is controlled and owned by the state through the Nepal Oil Corporation, a state-owned enterprise that has a monopoly on the supply and distribution of oil. However, the end product is sold through distributors, most of whom have thoroughly greased palms for their dealerships. They adulterate the fuel with cheaper oils to plump up profits. In the past twenty years or so, new models and makes of cars have entered the Nepali market. But even if a car owner were willing to pay a premium price for good fuel, there is none available today in Nepal. The only thing we can admire is Nepali ingenuity in using kerosene as a complete substitute for diesel. Nepal's kerosene consumption increased two-fold in the past three years while other oil imports remain stagnant. Kerosene was subsidized for the poor till the fuel adulteration barons figured it could work just as well in the automobile industry. The fact that after kerosene prices were brought on a par with diesel, the consumption of kerosene reduced by 62 per cent[5] clearly indicates what the utility of kerosene was.

The effort of getting Kathmandu to be pollution-free began with the replacement of smoke belching three-wheeler diesel vehicles with clean electric vehicles—popularly known as SAFA tempos—in 1999, six years after electric vehicles first started being assembled in Nepal. However, as Mrigendra Shrestha, one of the producers of the electric vehicles laments, inconsistent government policies on import duties for electric vehicle components, coupled with bureaucratic hassles which required registration through a tardy process of every vehicle produced, left no incentive for entrepreneurs. It was rare that vehicles were registered by the respective government agencies without some greasing of palms. Had the government created a consistently congenial environment for electric vehicles and electricity-powered buses, ropeways and cable cars, the demand would have encouraged some developers to actually develop their own captive power plant.

Each successive government in Nepal has avoided the subject of deregulation of the power sector. It's a political hot potato that could create difficulties for their campaigns. The lack of sufficient energy has cost the Nepali economy an incredible amount of time and money. It has hampered production, distribution and consumption. We should learn from India—Indian consumers today have access to better petroleum products with differentiated utility, thanks to deregulation. Nepali oil dealers, like many other indigenous business players, understand that the government indirectly protects their interests. They also realize that the regional and international players, who will jump into the game if the sector is opened, are not into the adulteration business. Surely, the answer is deregulation of the energy sector. Allow private sector entry into these businesses in a regulated manner and soon we'll have better oil and better air. The entire supply chain in Nepal is well aware of this and is highly unwilling to allow the government to budge from its present stance and allow for privatization. Thus, it is important that consumer forums find a stronger voice, identify better ways to deal with these issues and really pressure the government into ending the monopoly of a state player and a nationalized business cartel.

The Lord of the Lands

The control over land, its distribution and trading continues to be an integral part of Nepali economy. Before the property markets underwent a correction in 2009, everybody started speculating in property and using high-debt leverages for short-term gains. Overnight, small-time entrepreneurs and professionals became big-time real estate dealers. With the money the UCPN (Maoist) had made through extortion and later by channelizing government expenditure as well as investments in business, they had a lot to invest in real estate. In order for the real estate prices not to crash, they continued to informally fund real estate dealers, albeit at high interest rates and strict repayment conditions. Land is still seen as a prime tool for making easy money as well as something that people feel they or their immediate peers and relatives have knowledge of. With increased corruption at all levels, the small parcels of money chasing real estate investments have not stopped, thereby providing a market of small land holdings on a continuous basis. The fact that almost all the apartment developments around Kathmandu Valley are running on a schedule that is delayed by more than two years, without causing an uproar among the buyers, shows that people accept the speculative nature of real estate investment.

The post-1990 period did bring about many business success stories but the story of Kantipur Publication, a private media house, stands out. A media house that had a humble beginning in 1993 with a broadsheet newspaper, it expanded into magazines, radio, television and an online portal by the year 2000. It took advantage of the free media policies and filled in a vacuum created by an inefficient *Gorkhapatra Sansthan*, the state-owned media publication house. By the time the two partners who founded Kantipur Publication decided to part ways in 2008, media reports indicated the company was already valued at Rs 1.5 billion.[6]

While much blame is placed on the government for squandering economic opportunities, the private sector takes an equal share of the blame in not being able to take advantage of the opportunities presented to them. They failed in advocacy after the great experience with the Trade and Transit Treaty with India in 1996, in manufacturing mobile phones, in creating a niche in the IT business, and they never got rid of the myopic habit of arbitrage. After the second Jana Andolan in 2006, an open moment was created for the private sector to take the lead during a political vacuum and build a private sector-led economy that would achieve rapid economic growth. History will always question the private sector leadership for not rising to the occasion to deliver growth for itself as well as for Nepal during those crucial years.

5

THE BUSINESS OF DEVELOPMENT

When talking about development in Nepal, it is important to understand the significance of Nepal's history as a nation that never came under direct colonial rule. However, it would be naïve to assume that relations between Nepal and the British empire were on equal terms. The Rana regime was aware that any direct conflict with the British would mean compromising its most productive lands in the Terai while the British saw sense in using Nepal as a buffer state whose foreign and trade policies were entirely under its control. Thus, although not a colony, Nepal found itself in a position of dependency in relation to the British empire. Following the Second World War and the demise of colonialism, Nepal entered into a new world order in which the former colonial powers of western Europe and the United States became collectively known as the 'First World'. On the other hand, Nepal, along with the least developed of the former colonies— those lacking in industrialization, capitalist institutions, and democratic governance—became eligible for foreign aid as members of the 'Third World'.

The 1950s: Aid Arrives

The first aid package Nepal received was part of the United States-led Marshall Plan. The Marshall Plan was the first international development plan, which combined humanitarian aims with political stability and economic growth in western Europe after World War II. It was also an attempt to directly challenge and restrict the expansion of communism into western Europe. In this sense, foreign aid has a longer history in Nepal than does democracy. The aid package from the United States arrived in Nepal in January 1951, a month before the Rana regime was toppled. Given the strategic importance of Nepal due to its geopolitical location, sandwiched as it was between an expansionist Maoist China and socialist India, the Americans were keen to maintain some influence in the region. Nepal was also an important buffer zone for India against an expanding China. Nepal had traditionally been under the sphere of influence of its southern neighbour and so it came as no surprise when in 1952, India reasserted this influence by starting to provide aid and assistance to Nepal, even though India was itself an aid recipient.

The fall of the autocratic Rana regime was an explicit and historic statement on the part of the Nepali nation of its desire to commence the project of modernization. Within the global framework, Nepal made its entry on the world stage at a time when the notion of development was being propagated by the United States and the 'First World'. Perhaps nothing puts this notion into better perspective than US president Harry S. Truman's statement during his inaugural statement in January 1949:

> We must embark on a bold new program for making the benefits of our scientific advances and industrial progress available for the improvement and growth of underdeveloped areas. The old imperialism—exploitation for foreign profit—has no place in our plans. What we envisage is a program of development based on the concept of democratic fair dealing.[1]

Importantly, this was a statement of purpose for the United States as it made its entry on the world stage at a time when the power of the older European nations was waning and its own rising. This heralded the beginning of the development era, with development being propagated not only as the expansion of capitalism, but as the moral, just and indeed, necessary exercise of liberating nations from poverty and deprivation. Nepal entered this world as an underdeveloped country, as a third world country defined as being between the two battling superpowers of that time, as a country that because of its underdevelopment would be an aid recipient. The nature and identity with which Nepal entered the international arena and the way development was talked about and understood at the international level has defined how Nepal has understood and experienced development.

In Nepal, development has always been understood as its attempts to reach a standard of living prevalent in the United States and Europe. Development meant the building of schools, hospitals, and infrastructure along with nationalization, land reforms, mass mobilization, improving manpower, and creating administrative organizations. In this understanding, the justification for development was the primitive state of the Nepali economy in comparison to the global capitalist economies of the west. The goal was always exterior to Nepal and often the task of development suffered from an amnesia about the past. Nepal was unable to reconcile its feudal past with its westward aims and often completely ignored the ground realities of its historical, cultural and traditional legacy. The lack of any relation between the Nepali people and the project of development perhaps most strikingly reflects the state's failure to garner local support and ownership in this initiative.

Acute Immune Dependency Syndrome

Ever since its first aid grant, perhaps even before that, the Nepali psyche has adopted a mode of dependency. It has made itself believe that Nepal is entirely dependent upon the goodwill of foreigners and without foreign aid, Nepal will face major problems. It is here that the omnipresent and omniscient nature of the Nepali understanding of foreign aid is revealed. Foreign aid in Nepal is understood to mean technical grants, loans, scholarships, endowments and all forms of assistance in cash and kind provided by multilateral organizations, bilateral organizations, NGOs, private foundations and even foreign individuals. This rather nebulous understanding of foreign aid makes it seem as if it encompasses everything, while in essence it remains ambiguous and confusing. However, what remains consistent is the perception that foreign aid is a gift or favour bestowed upon Nepal. Ironically, this view echoes the view of the Panchayat government, which saw its works in national welfare as a gift or favour from the crown bequeathed upon the loyal subjects of the nation. In both cases, there is the creation of a hierarchy of supplicant and provider in the relationship, which precipitates an enduring dependency.

The initial aid grants that came into Nepal were almost entirely composed of bilateral grants—grants that were funded by the tax payers of specific donor countries. As the total volume of aid increased throughout the 1970s and 1980s, the proportion of bilateral grants in that total decreased. Even so, bilateral donors remain the largest contributors to Nepal's aid portfolio, accounting for around 70 per cent of the total aid received since the 1960s. The decrease in bilateral aid corresponded to a decrease in the percentage of aid that is provided in the form of grants and an increase in the percentage of aid provided as loans. Given Nepal's limited revenue generating capacity, during the early years of modernization, loans would have been impossible to manage. This would explain why until the 1960s, almost all aid provided to the country was in the form of grants; this proportion of grants has since then dropped to an average of 76 per cent. The decline in bilateral aid is also attributed to the calming down of geopolitical rivalries that marked the start of the cold war and the tensions between India and China during the 1950s and 1960s. The opening of the World Bank's doors in Nepal during the 1970s played a significant role in the increase of loans from the Bank and from other bilateral donors at a subsidized interest rate below global interest rates.

Ever since Nepal received its first shot of foreign aid, it has become an aid junkie. Nepal was entirely dependent on foreign aid to carry out development work for the first couple of decades after the Rana regime fell. Thus, the belief that Nepal has always been aid dependent is to some extent valid and justified. For instance, the First Five-Year Plan (1956–60) was completely reliant on foreign aid and almost all infrastructure projects since then have been financed through foreign aid. To its credit, Nepal has successfully tapped into aid money from a variety of sources and diversified its aid portfolio of countries and organizations representing the first world. By 1980, Nepal was receiving aid from over thirty-five countries, eleven UN agencies, seven multilateral institutions, and eight private foundations. Validating the growing dependency, Nepal's reliance on foreign aid increased from 2 per cent of its GDP in 1960 to just over 10 per cent of its GDP by 1990. In dollar terms, Nepal saw an increase in aid from around USD 14 million during the entire decade of the 1960s to around USD 382 million between 2001 and 2002. This has made Nepal the most aid-dependent country in South Asia with the highest foreign aid to GDP ratio in the region. If Nepal's heavy reliance on foreign aid needs any further proof then a look at government expenditures will reveal that around 40 per cent of all expenditures are financed through foreign aid. This is startling, as it essentially means that the sovereign government of the nation is financed by third parties, each with their own set of agendas and goals. The haphazard and ambiguous way the government has carried out development can in part be explained by this crosscutting of agendas. It was strange that even post-liberalization economies like the UK tried to provide aid rather than trade. As Dr Singha Bahadur Basnyat, former ambassador to the UK remarks, 'It is strange that a 200-year relationship with Nepal has not seen a single UK prime minister on an official visit to Nepal and no large investments or trade relations with the country.'

Exhibiting an attitude of dependence—Nepal did not bother to have a comprehensive foreign aid policy until 2002. The lack of a national body directing and coordinating aid was a considerable drawback for the country. Not only did it compromise the sovereignty of the nation, it often directly challenged the will and intentions of the government. Without any regulatory framework, donors and aid agencies were at liberty to work out their own strategies based on their own priorities. Predictably, the priority of donors and aid agencies sometimes even came into direct conflict with the Nepali government's own priorities, directions and policies. To put things mildly, there was a significant lack of coordination and cooperation between the two parties. This led to some priority areas getting an excess of aid at the cost of other areas getting little to no attention. To compound things, an appalling lack of communication and coordination between different ministries and departments within the Nepali government itself, caused significant confusion. As a result, there was considerable leakage and wastage of aid money combined with an increasingly complicated bureaucratic structure to be negotiated for the disbursement of funds. For instance, when a very successful livelihood project Livelihoods for Forestry (LFP), under the Department for International Development (DFID), UK, became politicized, its impact was affected when the project moved to a three-donor modality with Swiss and Finnish companies and DFID tendering the work. The bid that Rupantaran,[2] a not-for-profit organization, won was subsequently cancelled at the behest of strong political lobbying and re-allocated in the name of equity. A successful project lost much of its impact as more than three years were wasted.

No Coordination

In 1976, in an attempt to coordinate aid from western Europe, the United States, Japan and the United Nations, the World Bank established the Nepal Aid Group. However, during the early years of donor assistance, the Nepali government's strategy was to get donors to compete with each other rather than establishing an integrated framework for aid that would best meet both Nepal's development needs and the donors' criteria. The government was of the view that getting donors to compete with one another was the best way for the government to get the best deal. In the long run, the entrenchment of this attitude in the bureaucratic environment has made coordination with the Nepal government a difficult task for anyone. As a result of the geopolitical situation that Nepal found itself in, India, China and the USSR chose to remain outside the Nepal Aid Group while still providing aid to Nepal, which further reduced the coordination capabilities of the group. During the 1950s and 1960s, the United States remained the most significant donor and following upon the success of the

Marshall Plan in Europe, adopted a similar model in Nepal. Its development work, carried out on the basis of the modernization theory, a theory propounded by Walter Rostow which outlines the stages a 'traditional' economy goes through to become 'modern', failed for a number of reasons. One was that Nepal did not possess an educated population that was accustomed to industrialized society, while Europe did. Second, there was a lack of willingness to implement major land and agricultural reforms, as the Americans had advised. The Americans had emphasized documentation of land holdings, stronger security for smaller farmers and a ceiling on individual landholdings. Of the reforms that were implemented, there was limited success due to problems in the implementation model itself. The primary reason was that there were too many loopholes in the act allowing large landholders to maintain their control of the land and thus, hardly any success in land redistribution. Also, the Americans faced considerable problems in transferring knowledge to the local level when carrying out projects. For instance, a 1958–63 programme for constructing suspension bridges was meant to be carried out by an all-Nepali team with American equipment under American supervision, but the training turned out to be a complete failure. Of the targeted seventy bridges in two years, only one bridge was constructed in five years.[3] The reason for this failure has been pinpointed as the American inability to transfer technology and technical skills. Further, rivalry between the United States, the USSR and India in securing a strong foothold in Nepal, often impacted which way aid flowed. For instance, funds from the above-mentioned suspension bridge programme were temporarily diverted to fund the purchase of three DC3 aircrafts for Royal Nepal Airlines. This was to prevent the entry of the Soviets, who were interested in setting up Nepal's aviation industry. Finally, political turmoil and instability in Nepal also caused problems for donors in the effective implementation of programmes.

From the mid-1960s, following a decline in the regional importance placed on Nepal by the United States, India stepped up to become Nepal's largest aid provider until the early 1980s. While the Americans were drawn into Vietnam, a more cautious India sought to maintain its power balance against China. Unlike the American aid policy, Indian aid was mostly tied to its own strategic interests of promoting trade flow. With this intention, it initially focused most of its aid money on financing infrastructure developments and the construction of roads. It also diversified its aid portfolio into sectors like education, health, agriculture and power. However, there were considerable disagreements between the two countries over a number of infrastructure and power development projects with India, many in Nepal having identified India as taking an excessive share of the resources. This was particularly the case with Nepal's river sources; for instance, there was heavy opposition to the 1959 Nepali Congress negotiated Gandaki Scheme which allowed India to construct irrigation canals to irrigate five million acres in India, while Nepal would get enough water to irrigate a mere 343,000 acres and a 10 MW power plant. Disagreements on the sharing of resources have since then resulted in limitations on the use and development of Nepal's significant water resources.

Who Is to Blame?

By the 1980s, the obvious inability of foreign aid to kickstart the Nepali economy and put it on track towards development, increasingly challenged the very notion of development. Ironically, the population boom that accompanied the success of foreign aid projects targeting infant mortality and health care limited the impact of the economic growth of the country. Neither the government nor foreign aid projects were able to provide adequate economic opportunities to a growing population. In reflecting this stagnation, a United Nations Report in 1974 states, 'Nepal is poor and is daily becoming poorer.'[4] The reason it gives is that Nepal had on average a 2 per cent annual GDP growth factor while the population growth rate stood at 2.5 per cent per annum. This suggests that during the entire decade of the 1960s, Nepal at best had a zero, if not a negative rate of economic growth. This is a clear indication of a lack of planning and coordination on the part of the government, which was successful in fostering a dramatic rise in population but unable to ensure a future for this growing populace. The growing need to address a dysfunctional system and an increasing disillusionment with the idea of development and the development sector encouraged the Panchayat government to establish the Social Service National Coordination Committee (SSNCC), headed by the then Queen, in 1975. The SSNCC was created as the national clearing house and authority that would approve organizations to receive foreign assistance in Nepal. It would also oversee the establishment of International and National Non Governmental Organizations. While SSNCC wanted to create its own conditionality for donor and recipient institutions, there was, at about the same time, a global shift towards conditional lending adopted by the multilaterals.

In the 1980s, largely due to World Bank and IMF policy changes, the Nepal Aid Group had to adopt a conditional approach to releasing foreign aid and loans. These conditions included neo-liberal policy reforms and structural adjustments within a time-bound frame to ensure the release of funds. These measures were taken to ensure better accountability but also to enforce what the IMF and World Bank saw as necessary economic reforms. However, both the approach and its effectiveness came under increasing criticism and directly challenged the sovereignty of any nation that was coerced into enacting reforms. Critics argued that such reforms and impositions never took into account the actual capabilities of the bureaucracy and institutional capacity in being able to successfully implement such measures. As these reforms were not home-grown out of a need identified by the government and country, but instead imposed by the aid groups, there was a lack of a sense of ownership in Nepal, with regard to them. Since the reforms were imposed upon the government, the lack of interest in ensuring implementation meant that most of these reforms were doomed to fail in practice. Madhukar Rana, economist and former finance minister, argues that the failure was because local data was fitted into an existing model, when for real success, a local model should have been created from scratch. For instance, planning processes began with templates taken from other countries rather than trying to look at whether the information was relevant to Nepal.

The World Bank poured in money during the late 1990s to revive the Nepal Bank and Rastriya Banijya Bank that had half of the deposits of commercial banks, but were technically insolvent. Despite this infusion of funds, the management teams could not deliver the desired results in terms of recovering loans. What was imposed at that time were guidelines in loan recovery practised elsewhere in the world, while in Nepal, in practice, no bank officer would have the guts to take on an existing business head, as there were definitely linkages with political powers to reckon with. Ken Ohasi, then Country Director for the World Bank, said during an interaction that 'recovery of loans is more of an issue of political governance and cannot be resolved technically'. He also asked the government, political and business leaders to use their influence in helping new management to recover the loans.[5] If the banks were sold to international banks rather than getting into management contracting, perhaps, the results would have been better.

It took the post-1990 democratic governments over a decade to establish the Foreign Aid Policy through the Ministry of Finance in 2002. The policy acknowledged to some extent the haphazard and uncoordinated use of foreign aid in the country. It largely accepted the significant role foreign aid had played in assisting in the development of Nepal and unequivocally stated that the nation had benefited from foreign aid. It also underlined the fact that many infrastructure development projects would never have taken place without foreign assistance. However, it also stated, 'Notwithstanding these achievements, foreign aid in Nepal has had its shortcomings. Progress in economic growth and poverty reduction has not been commensurate with the inflow of aid into the country. Foreign aid has thus become very effective in some areas but less effective in others.'[6] This perception of mixed results is strongly shared by the donor community as well as the Nepalese recipients.

Solutions to the Aid Conundrum

Both the donors and the government are aware that development in Nepal has been significantly hampered due to a lack of collaboration and coordination. The first step in resolving this problem is for the government to know what it needs and to identify a long-term vision, which successive governments can pursue irrespective of their political and ideological standpoint. The Foreign Aid Policy in 2002 was the first step taken by the government towards creating a framework for the direction of foreign aid based on the needs and priorities of the nation, rather than that of individual donors.

Fundamentally, all foreign aid that comes into Nepal is for the people of Nepal. This makes foreign aid a public good. Further, with each Nepali citizen under USD 166 of foreign debt (roughly half its per capita GDP), transparency and accountability on all foreign aid is not only justified but required. Irrespective of where the aid comes from or how it is used, disclosure of its source and an account of its spending is essential. Whether it is money donated by individuals for orphans in Nepal or big money grants for hydropower projects, both have to be transparent and accountable. As a public good, the lack of transparency is a violation of the right to information and raises questions of public accountability, fraud and corruption. The Nepali government at present does not have accurate information on all the aid that is flowing into the country. Although the bulk of it is recorded in the Red Book, the government's revenue record, there is a considerable portion of aid that remains undisclosed. For instance, a number of schools are directly funded by the Indian Embassy without having to go through the government. Dr Bhekh B. Thapa, Ambassador to India during Prime Minister Sher Bahadur Deuba's visit in 1996, shares his frustration over Nepal signing an agreement with India as it had with other donor countries like Japan, which ended up allowing all donor countries to provide grants outside the framework of budgetary support. He laments that the 1990s began a 'culture of misguided, unwarranted flood of foreign money totally unregulated outside the budgetary framework'. Without any regulatory framework or requirement to control and record such funding, the donors and aid agencies are at liberty to intervene in Nepali society based on their own priorities, without consulting the government.

Madhukar Rana, an economist and former finance minister, argues that aid has a built-in incentive for corruption—constantly spending on the same thing provides for more incentives for corruption and when this happens over successive short-term governments, the incentives only grow. He cites the example of the Middle Marsyangdi hydropower project built with aid, that is being completed at many times the original cost and time, benefiting all the people who were making money from the project, be it in the form of salaries for those months of delay or hiring charges paid for vehicles and equipment. The golden rule being: the more the delay, the more the opportunity for self-enrichment. The lack of regulations, transparency and accountability placed on foreign aid is directly a result of a weak government. A growing awareness of this weakness forced the then government headed by King Gyanendra to acknowledge the difficulties it has faced in coordinating and effectively using aid via the Foreign Aid Policy. The national needs identified by the government have often not matched donor priorities. To address this shortfall, King Gyanendra's government also established a department within the Ministry of Finance for channelling foreign aid in a more effective manner.

Influencing Culture

The cultural challenges that resulted from the entrenchment of the development sector are perhaps best exemplified by the changes that government bureaucracy underwent from the 1980s onwards. Prior to 1990, the government of Nepal had a strict code of conduct and guidelines for hosting official parties and dinners. One such code was that no government agency would be allowed to serve alcohol during government sponsored dinners, nor were government officials allowed to drink during official functions. However, this changed with the dinners and luncheons that the aid agencies started hosting since 1990. As Toyanath Bhattarai, a senior government secretary, recalls, the codes of conduct for official parties were violated constantly and are, to this day, under the influence of aid agency culture. Another kind of change was occasioned by the fact that aid agencies started to 'compensate and encourage' people for attending their workshops and seminars, which, from the Nepali perspective, was the equivalent of getting paid to attend a seminar. To attend a seminar, a government official would be paid transportation costs equivalent to that of travelling in a cab and also get paid for his participation in the seminar. Travelling by bus instead of a cab, the official could then make some additional money and if required to spend the night, could make some money on a per diem. Meetings started to be held after office hours, to be able to apply for compensation in the form of meeting fees and transportation allowances. Given the stark difference in salary between the development worker and the government official, in some cases this was a necessity rather than voracity. This tradition of giving out allowances for attendance, popularly called the *bhatta pratha*, was initiated by aid agencies in the villages to compensate daily wage workers but became even more popular in the cities. The donors started a tradition of compromising with transparency. For instance, in a governance project, a consultant was told to reduce the rate but increase the number of days of involvement just to adhere to the rules. Thus Nepalis learnt to tweak many rules because they thought that was the way of life.

Most aid agencies work closely with the Nepali government through the establishment of projects targeting specific issues. Although the aid agency's project functions under its own administrative and logistical structure, it will often have government officials assigned to it. These officials work in close collaboration with the agency's staff. This structure seems admirable until one calculates the levels of distortion the project creates. For instance, a project driver could earn a salary that could put him on a par with a senior government official while a junior-level bureaucrat would find the driver's meal to be well above his own budget. Further, if the same junior-level bureaucrat were assigned to the project, he would be making his way to office in a new four-wheel-drive SUV while his former supervisor would be taking the bus or driving a two wheeler. In such a work environment it is easy to see why government officials are easily disheartened and exasperated with their work. Sadly, it also gives a clue as to why corruption is an accepted way of life. It was made necessary as a means to maintain some *dignity* while working for the government. Although some scholars have argued that foreign aid and the development sector have supported the traditional social hierarchy, the truth is, within the government, it has directly challenged the hierarchy of the bureaucracy. Foreign aid has also had a significant impact on the real estate market in Kathmandu Valley. Houses are often rented from people who are close to the renting agency's staff, while vehicles are rented from influential individuals at rates higher than the going market rate. These provided nice commissioning counters for development agency staff workers and a secondary source of income for well-placed and high-ranking officials. For instance, a politician or government official could request a particular aid agency to rent a vehicle or house for office or residence premises from his or her relative. With no definitive procurement policies, these contracts were made at higher than market prices, thus allowing an indirect source of income for the concerned politician or government official.

The donor communities imported development workers who have found life in Nepal to be quite a charm. From a two-room apartment on the outskirts of New York City, the development worker finds himself transported to a three-storey independent house in Nepal with a large compound, where his tax-free income places him at the upper elite levels of the pay scale and gives him or her the freedom to eat out at expensive restaurants citing work, throw massive parties and own expensive cars paid by his or her country's tax payers. Further, being a foreigner, he enjoys preferential treatment from both Nepali people and foreigners, and can muscle his way through the Nepali masses as their saviour. Passing guidelines such as requiring the foreigners to furnish homes and offices with furniture from their own country has made a mere mockery of the policies. The differential in cost between high-quality locally made furniture and imported furniture can in fact provide education to hundreds of girl children. It would be interesting to know how tax payers in the host country would react if they came to know of the expenses and lifestyle of an aid worker.

From being a sector that people joined out of sheer passion to serve humanity, the business of development work became a great investment for people's careers. Young parents started to take up positions that gave them multidimensional support in having and rearing children amidst a social life that they could never dream of. They enjoyed privileges they would not be able to afford to in their own countries, while at the same time talking about how there were real hardships in these positions for which they received allowances.

Thankfully, there are exceptions. There are many development workers who have contributed towards the development of competencies and capacities in Nepal that have been of invaluable assistance in creating a technically skilled workforce in Nepal.

A good example of the advantages of an effective assistance programme is the Nick Simmons Institute (NSI) which was established as a philanthropic project of James and Marilyn Simmons from the United States, in memory of their son Nick who had worked in Nepal as a volunteer and was concerned about the standard of health in rural areas. The Institute's mission is to train and support skilled and compassionate rural health care workers. Dr Bhekh Bahadur Thapa, chairperson of NSI, says that it is an institute that runs under Nepali leadership and Nepali management, receiving only temporary input from abroad for the sole purpose of enhancing local capabilities and capacities. Such institutes that work on becoming genuinely Nepali institutions while receiving only endowments from foundations, can pave the way for new aid architectures for Nepal.

Best Talents Wasted in the Development World

Given the large distortion in salaries that the development sector creates, it is inevitable that some of the best and brightest in Nepal enter the development field. Indeed, for many young Nepali people recently graduated from a college with a bachelor's degree in business administration, the development sector holds the most attractive career prospects. Pulling a few strings through familial ties, she will be able to secure a junior-level position at an NGO and after two or three years of hard work, will be able to move up the organization ladder. She will now easily be earning more than she would at any job in the government or private sector. At this point, having garnered sufficient experience and established a good network, she will be able to secure a job at an INGO. Starting from a junior-level position, she will be able to successfully move up in the organization while attending a host of capacity development trainings and workshops. She will now easily be earning more than any of her friends who joined the private sector. Within two or three years, she will have embraced a specific issue and can then apply for a master's degree through one of the scholarship programmes. She could apply for a master's in a hot potato subject like conflict management, gender, development studies, or peace studies which would give her the qualifications necessary to take on more responsibility and move up the grade scale. Returning with a master's degree, she will bide her time working on lucrative, short-term, high-flying consultancy work for INGOs and multilaterals by tapping her old network. Assessing the field, she can then enter an INGO at a senior level or join a bilateral or multilateral agency at a managerial level. By the time she hits her mid-forties, she could head up a major INGO department or become a senior project manager in the United Nations. By sixty, she could retire and work as a consultant, charging fees upwards of USD 500 a day while travelling the world for a series of conferences that her own small NGO sponsors or multilaterals pay her to attend. Yet there is actually nothing to differentiate these fifty Nepalis in terms of their contributions to the country, from the thousands who have made a substantial difference to Nepal's development—and not necessarily by authoring volumes of reports and making zillions of presentations. The biggest irony for Nepal is that people have been made to believe that the highest money that a Nepali could dream to earn was the USD 700–800 per day fees or honorarium that they could charge an INGO, bilateral or multilateral agency. The same jobs performed by non-Nepali consultants are paid at international rates that, excluding travel, food and board are a minimum of two to three times more than what domestic 'Nepali' consultants make. Nepalis have lived with such differential treatment, their ambitions in the development world limited to earning a 'magic' figure that is steeply lower than what aid workers of other nationalities make in Nepal.

The development industry in Nepal is estimated to account for 10 per cent of the national GDP, compared to the 3 per cent contribution of tourism and 7 per cent contribution of manufacturing. With the ability to pay two to four times more than the wage rates of the private sector for any qualified candidate, the development sector is clearly the better employment option. Aside from the wage structure, the benefits and on the job training that come along with the job set a standard that very few private firms have been able to match. Further, with the decline of the government and bureaucracy in the 1990s, the development sector has become the most prestigious industry to work in. The glamour of the industry is further highlighted by new social elites of Nepal— foreign consultants and development workers. Just as diplomats and ambassadors used to love hobnobbing with the royals during the Panchayat era, this new elite loves to mingle with the socialites of Kathmandu. The business of development became an easy choice for complacent Nepalis who could get a fancy designation like specialist, advisor or a programme manager just by being in the job. Unlike in engineering, accounting, law or other professions, development workers need not go through any examination or invest in any skill-upgrading programmes. People who toil for many years to become a department head in a corporation encounter a country director or country manager of a programme with just a fraction of their qualifications or experience. The fact that people can get fancy designations in a designation-conscious society, along with excellent perks and benefits, has made the development world attractive.

With degrees from good universities and the influential networks of their families, these people have embarked on discussing poverty during the day and partying during the night. This new class of socialites find themselves on page 3 and in the glamour magazines while penning op-ed pieces and political analyses. Jet-setting, high flying, high-end living, and fancy car driving—what is elsewhere perceived as the investment banker lifestyle, unfortunately, in Nepal, is the ultimate allure of the development world.

The development sector has perhaps impacted the private sector the most through the loss of some of the best people to the development organizations. It remains an unfortunate feature of work in Nepal that people, during their most productive years, spend most of their time churning out reports, sitting through seminars and moving from one project to another. At the end of over fifteen to twenty years of work in the development field, many people are beginning to question their work, its actual significance and impact. Having worked for over twenty years in a development organization, a senior development worker reflects that perhaps it was a waste of time. He finds himself frustrated and the victim of a false dream. Perhaps most telling about his predicament is his feeling that he is stuck in a system that, at his level, becomes a tangible representation of imperialism. For one thing, as a Nepali citizen working in his own country for its own development, he is precluded from holding the top-most positions in the organization he works for. These positions are reserved for the foreign born, most likely from the country of the organization's origin or funding. Further, in spite of being more qualified in his area of work than most of the foreign consultants hired to work for the organization, he knows that because he is Nepali he cannot demand the same allowance and pay as his international counterpart. This clear and categorical hierarchy not only reinforces the psyche of dependency but is hypocritical and reflects a colonial mentality at best and racism at worst. Madhukar Rana, a former finance minister, refers to it to as the colonization of human capital and intelligence.

N(O)GOs

The psyche of dependency and the hypocrisy of the proclaimed inclusiveness of the development sector are made even more apparent when one explores the hierarchy of organizations within the development structure. At the lowest rungs of the development ladder are the home-grown NGOs who primarily sustain themselves through their ability to write proposals, identify problems and provide solutions. Once established, these organizations can also be recruited by those higher up on the ladder, to carry out specific projects. Proposals are forwarded to organizations with the money and with an interest in the problem. This higher rung of the ladder is predominately made up of a Western class of donors, including INGOs, bilateral and multilateral agencies. Acceptance of a proposal depends on what the donor's priority areas are, as also on the recipient's credentials, history and network. Once selected, a detailed documentation exercise begins, which is aimed at recording proof of the project's execution. If the project ends in failure, there is much to learn, but if there is success, expansion possibilities are on the cards. The report or document produced is the holy grail; it forms the basis upon which senior management can sleep with a good conscience about having successfully put their tax payers' money to good use and more importantly, created documented proof of having done so.

By end 2012, there were over 36,000 NGOs registered in Nepal through the Social Welfare Council; most of them at the bottom of the development sector food chain and carrying out most of the work. In 2011–12, their total reported expenditure was NPR 8 billion (USD 100 million). With budgetary restrictions, these NGOs do not have the financial muscle to hire or retain their best staff. Yet, the reporting demands placed on them are grossly overbearing. The success of their work in most cases depends on the quality of the report written about them, rather than on their work. For instance, a water and sanitation project in the northern hills close to Manang was considered successful in building the targeted number of toilets. However, six months down the line, none of the toilets was usable, as they were full of stones. The project implementers had failed to understand local customs and to realize that stones were a substitute for water or toilet paper in the region. A success story on paper, the work remains of poor quality. The heavy emphasis on reports makes it necessary for small NGOs to divert an excessive amount of funding towards report writing by hiring expensive consultants with a good command of English. With what some claim to be the highest per capita number of reports, Nepal suffers from the 'project mentality'. This syndrome makes the report more the actual work, than the reported work itself. This mentality is prevalent not just in the development sector but is also well entrenched in state-owned enterprises and government bureaucracy. Those infected with this mentality in government will often propagate a problem, so that the necessary reports justifying the continuation of a programme to solve it, can be created. This helps them secure their seats. The logic being that more problems identified, a longer time to a solution and more reports needed would all correlate to a minimization of work while maximizing income through salary. Passive until absolutely necessary, they act only when projects need to be displayed or inspected and when the possibility of funding increases.

The entire development sector is not self-sufficient and self-sustaining. It is entirely dependent on and caters to the direction in which aid flows. At the top, INGOs, despite having their own sources of funds, play the role of effective managers for a large chunk of the money released by bilateral and multilateral organizations. Some scholars have accused the development sector of being too top heavy, with a large chunk of the money that enters the country being used up along the way, as it trickles down to its intended targets. Beyond consultation and overhead fees, there remains a fundamental Catch-22 with all development work. All development organizations are, as *development* organizations, working, on paper, towards their own redundancy and unemployment. To forestall such an outcome, mediocrity is built into the system—too much success threatens employment, too little threatens loss of funds. The donors themselves seem to emphasize this through the relatively quick rate at which they keep changing their leadership. Every three years or so, a new director enters the organization with his or her own set of agendas, working styles and preferences. Nepali staff have to accommodate the whims of every new leader. A good example of this was the running of a national visioning exercise that was started under the impetus of one leader but was quick to go out of favour and funding once the leadership changed.

The insurgency allowed the development sector to hide all its inefficiencies and failures. The conflict became the golden ticket to not only excuse past failures but also to shift gears from the largely unsuccessful campaigns of poverty alleviation to that of conflict resolution and human rights. It also provided an excuse to hold lavish workshops and seminars in high-end hotels (rather than out in the field), to discuss the problem of poverty and the means to contain the insurgency. With participants from the districts being flown in to attend these conferences, the high-handed, centralized and patronizing nature of the development sector created a peculiar understanding of development at the local level, which will be described below.

Imported *Bikas* and Original *Bikas*

The people who were supposed to benefit from development, to this day associate and identify it with the government and foreigners. Development to the average Nepali is something they lack, something that is not present at the local level—a well-honed and nurtured development industry over the past half century has successfully hammered in this notion. The onus of development lies with the state, for it is something conducted by the state and by others who are not local. Development is an external factor; something imported into the country and distributed by the government. Thus, the concept of development as introduced to the Nepali people was not something they ever identified with. It has never been internalized by the Nepali people and they never saw it as something that involved them personally. This understanding is clearly demonstrated by the use of the word *bikas* to describe things ranging from imported apple varieties (*bikase shyau*) to character, education, infrastructure development and employment. The Nepali dictionary understanding of *bikas* is very close to that of the English word development, but it can be used in colloquial speech in reference to anything foreign or imported. This has created further stratification in Nepali society, with an almost racial distinction between those who were 'developed' and those who received the 'development'.

Of Course There Are Success Stories

Although this chapter focuses on the largely negative impact of the development sector, the success stories also warrant a critical analysis. The USD 5.2 billion in foreign aid from the 1950s till the end of the twentieth century has had a limited impact on poverty, education, health, gender and the environment—all part of the United Nations defined Millennium Development Goals (MDGs).[7] However, there have been a few success stories that highlight the potential of foreign aid when applied to the local context, within the existing social structures, through the community, with the intention of divesting ownership and rights to the local population. Within such a framework it promotes sustainable living, entrepreneurship and ultimately, the growth of a strong private sector.

In 2000 The Forestry Sector Policy, an updated version of the Forestry Master Plan Policy and subsequent amendments to that document, was released. The policy statement of 2000 for the forests of the Terai, the Churia hills and the Inner Terai provided explicit management options for the forests in the hills and mountains of these regions. This gave rise to increasing local management of community forests, which significantly benefits the livelihood of people. For instance, a community forest is established amongst families using the forests and they become members of forest user groups. They elect executive committee members for the management of the forests, who initiate many income-generating programmes like handicraft making, sawing, making agricultural tools, etc. The executive committee also decides on whether or not to provide loans, with the loan money mostly coming from taxes and fees levied upon the users of community forests in return for proper management of these programmes.

Nepal's community forest success story is premised on participation and consensus, transparency, local decision making, management and ownership. That is why there are provisions for the marginalized to also benefit from the local governance of community forests. The Forestry Master Plan of 1990 laid out these principles and they are being followed till date.

Another good example was the success of the Biogas Support Programme (BSP), an NGO that works to promote biogas plants as a key renewable energy source in rural areas for household cooking use. Villagers pay for these units and the programme supports them through subsidies as well as by providing technology and training. Saroj Rai, executive director of the programme informed this author, 'A biogas plant is a wonderful product with multiple socio-economic and environmental benefits to the user, the community and the whole world. Nepal's success in developing the biogas technology and disseminating it, benefits around 17,000 additional rural households annually through a public–private partnership model, has been exemplary. The modality is being replicated in Nepal and elsewhere for promotion of biogas and similar technologies. Five teams of visitors from Asian and African countries have come to Nepal in the last three months to learn from us and replicate the success in their countries. Nepal, with around 200,000 biogas plants, comes second to China only, in terms of per capita biogas plants in the world.'

The Greenhouse Project for Medicinal Plants of Dabur Nepal, also explains the potential of private sector-led partnerships with communities. Most of its herbal raw material grows naturally in the Himalayas and even those that are found in the wild can be cultivated. Just stripping herbs from the forest would be unsustainable, so the greenhouse tries to cultivate them to create a sustainable source of medicinal and aromatic herbs. A nursery in Banepa since 1998 and another one in Marpha, have been involved in conservation and research into twenty-five species of endangered Himalayan Ayurvedic plants. Banepa alone produces six million saplings of medicinal plants per year, and these are distributed to forty-six farmers' cooperatives in nineteen districts across Nepal, giving direct employment to 5000 people and indirectly benefiting 25,000 others. The Banepa nursery employs eighty-five workers, all women from surrounding villages. However, there are few such examples of development achieved through partnerships between the private sector and the development sector.

ॐ

By and large, the business of development, a term imported specifically for Nepal, has remained controlled by the producers of the concept, with Nepalis falling prey to it, as they do to other imported cultures, without questioning the rationale or the sustainability of development aid in the future. The development industry has created a large pool of development workers that keep churning out reams of reports, keep the hotel and catering industry busy with seminars and conferences and ensure that the business class seats in international airlines always have a waiting list, despite the economy class seats being empty.

6

GOVERNANCE WOES

In a democratic system, the role and responsibilities of the government are formally defined in the constitution, which not only sets limits to its government's powers but also seeks to establish a checks and balances system that ensures that no one party can exercise absolute power. However the government is defined in the constitution, it is the way it governs that defines its success. Governance, as defined by the World Bank, is the exercise of political authority and the use of institutional resources to manage society's problems and affairs. Yet governance is only the act of governing; to be successful at it a government must not just govern but also ensure good governance. Good governance, as I've written elsewhere, is made up of four key features: accountability, transparency, predictability and participation.[1] Accountability holds officials responsible for their actions. Transparency allows everyone the access to relevant and comprehensible information. Predictability allows for laws and regulations to be clear, logical, systematic and uniform. Participation gives an individual the right to act and challenge the government through legal means to ensure good governance. In most liberal democratic countries, the government is responsible for meeting basic needs and providing basic services for the entire population of the country. For a capitalist welfare state, the kind of state which in my opinion is best for Nepal, the government has to guarantee the welfare of its citizens by ensuring efficient social service delivery.

For a nation formed from the institutions of governance present in the small hill kingdom of Gorkha, it is tragic that even 200 years after its unification, Nepal's governmental structure remains ineffective and inefficient. The Shah and Rana rulers of Nepal ruled with absolute authority but expressed little interest in reforming governance structures that had been in use since before unification. With an economy based primarily on agriculture, the land ownership system remained the primary means of governance. Although the size of the kingdom had dramatically increased and the rulers were aware of limitations in the existing governance structure, they were either unwilling to change it or unaware of any alternatives. By the early 1900s, it was clear that the Rana rulers were strongly opposed to any changes in governance which could challenge their stranglehold on power. It was only with the fall of the Rana regime in 1950 that substantial changes in the governance structures of Nepal occurred.

The manner in which the Rana rulers understood governance and the role of government, precluded them from taking part in the process of modernization. The Rana government viewed the state and its populace as something that effectively belonged to them. Given this view, it was no wonder that the entire state apparatus was designed to fulfil the needs of the rulers. All state revenue in excess of administrative costs, without any transparency or accountability, went directly to the Rana rulers. This was strongly reinforced by a popular culture which, even during the devastating 1934 earthquake, meant that the public was unwilling to accept aid from the government, because it was seen as money that belonged to the king. Given that anything spent on administration ate into their source of income, the Ranas were miserly in their administrative spending and sought to maintain the smallest administrative units possible. Indeed, the bulk of administrative spending was on the maintenance of an army. This modality of governance created a further disincentive, aside from the fear of popular dissent, for the Ranas to invest in progressive measures like health care and education. Thus, when Nepal initiated its modernization project after the end of the regime in the early 1950s, it had a non-existent public service sector, only about fifty doctors and just 200 primary schools. Needless to say, with all institutions of governance and public service having to be built from scratch, modernizing Nepal was no easy task.

The following sections will discuss the various roles the government undertook in administration, education and health. It will become apparent that in the fields of health and education it has been quite unsuccessful in comparison to the private sector. Even in administration and regulation it has met limited success due to its insistence on being involved with both service delivery as well as regulation.

The Panchayat Era: Improved Governance in Nepal

With the introduction of the 1951 Government of Nepal Act, Nepal took its first steps towards developing a formal constitution. The 1950s were formative years for most of Nepal's bureaucracy and democratic institutions. The Nepal Civil Service Act was passed in 1956 in an attempt to streamline and define the authority of all civil servants working for the government. Attempts were also made to construct administrative units based on the modern Indian model of ministries and departments. With a small pool of educated Nepali citizens to choose from, the initial government bureaucracies were populated by former elites and rich landowners. In a nation without a private sector, educated Nepalis saw the expanding government, which by the 1960s was employing around 31,000 civil servants, as the best employment option. The Nepali government during the 1950s was progressive and discarded many of the old regime's hierarchical and exploitative structures. It focused on development and sought to bridge the social divide by attempting to create a more inclusive government, towards establishing a democratic and modern society.

By the time of King Mahendra's coup in 1960 and the establishment of the Panchayat government, considerable progress had been made in terms of civil services. Along with a growing administration geared towards development, the government had focused considerable resources on expanding its educational system to ensure that qualified people entered the modern economy. As a result, over 4000 primary, 500 secondary and thirty-two tertiary-level schools had been established, along with Tribhuvan University. The Panchayat system however, adopted a different form of administration, which it claimed to be grass-roots democracy. It instituted a four-tiered system consisting of panchayats at the local, district, zonal and national levels. The lowest tier of the system, called the *gau sabah** or panchayat, was the only democratically elected council in the entire system. The country was divided into seventy-five districts and fourteen zones of which each district was composed of fifty to seventy *gau* or village and *nagar*, or town panchayats.† Each district and regional panchayat was vested with the responsibility of carrying out directives from the central level while maintaining law and order and executing and coordinating development work. Despite the institutionalization of the Panchayat system in Nepal, the focus on economic development and a semblance of democracy remained. Although the Panchayat system was in essence an authoritarian regime, it actively sought to distinguish itself from the Rana regime by identifying itself as the agent of democracy and economic development.

Panchayat rule explicitly tried to institutionalize the equality of all citizens and took over governance in the education, health care, financial, business and development sectors of the economy. It prevented the formation of unions, other than the six class organizations—of peasants, labourers, students, women, former military personnel and college graduates, that were sanctioned by the government. It also shifted its tax system from one based on a direct tax on land to one based on indirect taxes, with a large portion of the revenue coming from imports. It instituted some major land reforms in 1964 which included the seizing of some large Rana estates. The land reforms were largely a failure but the people of Nepal saw the king as the harbinger of democracy and

---

*Village assembly

†Town panchayats had more than 10,000 people living in the area.

change, allowing the Panchayat government to consolidate its position for the next three decades.

Multiparty Democracy, Graft for All

Even after the Jana Andolan, the democratic movement of 1990, the Panchayat administrative system was not changed, other than being rechristened and put under the directives of the Ministry of Local Development. Thus the gau, nagar and zilla panchayats became *gau bikas samitis** *nagar palikas*† and *zilla bikas samitis*‡. The bureaucracy by this time had expanded to over 100,000 civil servants and required considerable restructuring and streamlining. With this objective in mind, the democratic government took a number of initiatives including the passing of a new Civil Service Act in 1993 which sought to strengthen the bureaucracy, increase accountability and decrease the ability of ministries to tamper with the bureaucracy. Unfortunately, these well-meaning attempts ran up against entrenched obstacles to efficiency, as will be outlined below.

With multiparty democracy, the art of graft that had formerly been limited to people in close circuits of power was also democratized. Corruption became rampant and started becoming accepted as a way of life. This can also be attributed to the socio-cultural phenomenon where one does not ever hesitate to offer sweets, money or promises to gods. Dubbed as the 'two-laddoo' syndrome, it encompasses the tendency to corrupt even the gods people worship, with offerings of sweets in return for favours. Such a mentality could only have led to the formation of a society where corruption was not taken as a social evil and people flaunted the wealth they acquired by graft or even talked about it openly. Phrases like '*kar ma basyo bhane ghar banincha, bhansar ma basyo bhane sansar banincha*', meaning, 'if you work at the tax department you can build a house and if you work at customs you will make

---

*Village Development Committees

†Municipalities

‡District Development Committees

your world', became common proverbial phrases of wisdom. The need for political parties to fund their elections and to take care of their cadres and all their aspirations for better lifestyles, also fuelled this culture of graft. Government positions started getting auctioned to the highest bidders behind closed doors and the business–bureaucracy–politician nexus manufactured plenty of fodder for the vernacular tabloids.

The inability of the government to ensure accountability and transparency was attributable to a judiciary that remained weak and has never been independent. Although the stated aim of all political forces, since the fall of the Rana regime, has been to promote an independent judiciary, constant intervention by political figures and government officials has meant that practice is different from intention. In the 1950s, major improvements in establishing a coherent set of laws and developing substantive procedural mechanisms had been made, in comparison to the arbitrary and punitive laws of the Ranas. However, the lack of a clear demarcation in the Panchayat system thereafter, of the limits of the judiciary versus the executive and the legislature, weakened the authority and independence of the judiciary. The heavy involvement of the government in the judiciary even during multiparty democracy and republicanism posed significant challenges to the integrity of the judicial system.

Education Mishaps: Politics over Governance

The Rana regime had been strongly opposed to the idea of educating the population of Nepal. This was not simply a matter of inefficiency, there were real political reasons behind it. Take the example of one Rana prime minister, Chandra Shamsher. He had studied in Calcutta University in the early years of the twentieth century, witnessing the first waves of the Indian independence movement. He established the first college in Nepal, Tri-Chandra College, in 1918. Given that education would ultimately encourage the Nepali people to revolt against the regime, this may seem like a surprising move, except that his intention in establishing the college was not so much to provide quality education as to ensure that Nepali students studied in Nepal. He saw the college as a means to prevent Nepali students from being exposed to the radicalism developing in India. Tri-Chandra College had limited success, with the majority of Nepali families who had the means and the awareness, continuing to send their children to study in India. This long-standing preference for studying in India highlights two major issues, the indifferent quality of education on offer in Nepal and the prestige placed upon an English language education. Ironically, this prestige was partly due to the fact that Jung Bahadur, the founder of the Rana Regime, had insisted on an English education for his children, in preference to a traditional Sanskrit education. Although Jung Bahadur's children were educated by private tutors in their stucco palaces, the royal preference for an English education eventually led to the establishment of Nepal's first modern school, Durbar School, in 1892.

Dev Shumsher, the Rana prime minister in 1902, brought about some radical reforms in a then exclusive and elite educational system. He promoted primary education in the Nepali language and even opened up Durbar School to commoners; this was perhaps why his stint in power lasted a mere four months. However, his brief four-month stint as prime minister ensured the establishment of a few Nepali language schools in and around the urban centres of Nepal. This was on a very limited scale and by the end of the Rana regime in 1950, merely 310 primary schools, eleven high schools and two colleges were present in a country of around five million people. Consequently, the elite Bahun, Chhettri and Newar families in the 1940s and 1950s had no hesitation in sending their sons to Banaras and Calcutta (now Kolkata) to complete their formal education. Even though it placed a burden on them, it was a great source of pride and prestige to send a son to study in the English-medium schools of India.

Nepali Only—A Grave Misstep

While the sons of the well-off were heading to Banaras and Calcutta, the new Nepali government founded the National Education Planning Commission (NEPC) in 1954. This was its first step in attempting to establish a modern public education system in Nepal and ensuring educational access to the general population of the country. This initial educational plan was drawn up with substantial American assistance and the programme met with considerable success in increasing access to primary education through an expanding network of schools. However, meeting the increasing demand for qualified teachers and creating a comprehensive and well-structured curriculum, proved to be a stiffer challenge. The shortfall of teachers was addressed to some extent when the Americans assisted in the establishment of a teacher training centre in 1954 and also in the subsequent opening of a college of education two years later. Although the Americans and the NEPC had strongly advocated a decentralized system that involved the community in the management of schools, the educational system remained centralized under the Ministry of Education in an attempt to establish uniformity throughout the system.

The Banaras and Calcutta-educated sons of the elite came back to a changing Nepal and entered the bureaucracy. Their strong English-based education became a considerable asset to a government heavily reliant on foreign aid, as major donors, including the UK, USA and India along with the World Bank and IMF, used or preferred the use of English. Even though the democratic exercise ended all too quickly once Panchayat rule was established in 1960, for most civil servants, little changed and they continued their work. By 1959, the nation's first university, Tribhuvan University, had been established and a network of schools was in place. The Panchayat system continued with the centralized approach to education and found it a more convenient means to propagate the system's ideology and support for the crown. From programmes and policies to textbooks, all were prepared centrally and then distributed throughout the nation. The primary objective of the education system was to create a population that would remain loyal to the crown and produce crops of graduates who would be best suited for clerical work. The heavy emphasis on the use of Sanskritized Nepali with a very limited English language curriculum, was meant to ensure these goals. The teaching of Sanskritized Nepali helped promulgate the 'one nation, one language, one dress' philosophy of the Panchayat regime, while the insularity of the Nepali language ensured a limitation of content and ideas from the broader chain of Western intellectual thought. The influence of nationalist education and the practices they had imbibed at Banaras induced in them a sense of social supremacy. They combined the best of religion and politics and used nationalism to keep from integrating into a world they did not want to learn about and could not take control of.

There are over ninety-two local languages and dialects in Nepal and over a hundred different social groups based on caste, ethnicity, religion and language. The Panchayat regime's promotion of Nepali, even though it was not the mother tongue of a considerable portion of the Nepali citizenry, created an unfair advantage for those who spoke Nepali. Nepali speakers mostly comprised Bahuns and Chhettri, the top two tiers of the traditional Nepali caste system and the state-imposed Nepali language thus became a symbol of oppression, especially among ethnic and linguistic groups who did not speak Nepali. Although this system effectively instilled Nepali language as the primary means of public communication, even by 2001, only 28 per cent of the entire population spoke Nepali. Equally worrisome is the fact that a number of languages unique to particular ethnic groups in Nepal are in danger of dying today.

It is important to note that most tertiary-level education relied on books written in English which were impractical or posed significant challenges to translation. Given the lack of a formal English education in Nepali schools, the level of English of most students was simply not adequate to the task of lecturing in English or comprehensibly reading from the book. This essentially forced teachers to teach in Nepali even though the books were in English and any research or collaboration internationally required a strong command of English. The New Education System Plan (NESP) introduced in 1972 attempted to make the teaching of Nepali mandatory below the tertiary level, only worsening the plight of Nepali education and further encouraging parents to send their children to India. Although NESP was shut down a decade later with a broad consensus that it had largely failed, the damage done has been considerable. It has produced a whole generation of Nepalis with a very low standard of education, who, upon entering the bureaucracy have had a significantly detrimental impact on it.

Part of the reason that the Nepali language was enforced by NESP was a growing and increasingly worrying stratification of society between English-teaching private schools and government-run public schools. The establishment of St. Xavier's School in 1951 provided the first instance of an English boarding school under foreign management and was soon followed by the all-girls' school, St. Mary's School, in 1955. In 1972, Budhanilkantha School was established under British management, with the intention of making it the Eton of Nepal. The quality of education these schools provided and the command of English that their graduates had, distinguished them from the government-run public schools of Nepal. Anyone in Nepal who understood the value of education and realized the prestige that a good command of English could buy them, wanted their children in these schools. They simply were the best option for most families who could not afford to send their children to India or who wanted to keep them close to home. All of them knew that graduating from one of these institutions was a sure ticket to success. Aware of the value of an English education, it was mostly the first-generation intellectual Bahuns, business-minded Newars and aristocratic Chhettri families that formed the bulk of the student population in these institutes, even though a certain number of seats were reserved for students from rural and poor backgrounds.

For the rest, especially the small land holder and rural elite, things were getting tougher. Of those born in rural Nepal, few would have made it to school; those who did were mostly from the higher rungs of the social ladder. Language was an issue for some families, while most could not afford to lose their labour force. Someone born in rural Nepal in the mid-1960s would have gone to school under the new Nepali language education act during the 1970s. A Bahun from the village elite, he would have a good orientation to Sanskrit and excel at the memorization-based Nepali education. He would then join the urbanization trend of the 1970s—which saw the urban population grow annually by

8.4 per cent—and move to Kathmandu. Living in a one-room apartment shared with four other people or with relatives, he could graduate in the 1980s with Sanskrit as a core subject and appear for the public service examinations. Passing due to his knowledge of Nepali he would then enter the government services. Receiving job training in the staff colleges while still stuck in a box of a room, he would get back in touch with his relatives and people from his hometown. By the 1990s, having worked his way through the bureaucracy from the low-income level, he would buy a small plot of land and build a small box house around Koteshwor or Sinamangal. Still living in a box he would send his children to an English boarding school and then try to send them abroad. Working hard for junkets, he would go visit his children and see the bigger world, but would come back to his box and retire from government, unknown to anyone six months before retirement. But then he would resurface as a consultant, working all those connections in the donor community that he had established during his years of government service. He could now travel abroad to see his children once a year, while his wife raised his grandchildren abroad.

Private Schools and a Foreign Education

By the early 1990s, Nepal had made dramatic improvements to its educational system with over 17,000 primary schools established by 1990 including an equal rise in the number of secondary and tertiary-level institutes. However, the literacy rate had only increased to around 40 per cent by 1991 and the quality of this education was questionable. Most tertiary-level education occurred in the field of the arts with very few opting to study technical subjects like engineering and medicine. This was largely due to a weak primary education in English and the limited seats available for students to enter technical fields. The low quality of government education had fostered the growth of the private English boarding school industry from the 1980s onwards. After the liberalization of the 1990s, the private school industry experienced an economic boom. This had a very salutary effect on Nepal's educational sector and its economy overall. Charging higher fees, these schools could pay less to teachers than government schools did, but were able to teach English to their students from the primary school level on. Although many schools acted only as money-making ventures, it is without a doubt that private schools in general immediately set a new benchmark for education in Nepal and challenged the hegemony of a government school education among the Nepali middle class.

Suddenly in the early 1990s, three things shook up the educational sector: passport access was decentralized, an English-speaking generation was produced, and the educational consultancy industry was established. With limitations on both the capacity and quality of higher educational opportunities in Nepal, going abroad to study was an alluring prospect. The precedent of going abroad to study had already been established by the older elite English boarding schools and foreign degrees carried an undeniable prestige. Attached to the prospect of going abroad was the eventual opportunity to work and live on in the foreign country. It was an attractive prospect for many, to shed the Nepali image and acquire a lifestyle that fitted with their perception of the West.

Peer pressure forced rent-earning parents to sell their property or to mortgage it, in order to finance their children's overseas education. This was the only way for them raise enough money to send their children abroad as they did not see a future for their children in Nepal. It is not surprising that children, adopting their parents' world view, also saw a brighter future abroad, one much better than anything imaginable in Nepal. The educational consultancy industry literally opened up a world of opportunity. An educational market that had thus far been cornered by students of the elite schools in Nepal was suddenly made accessible to the rising masses from newly established private English boarding schools. This is perhaps a story best told in terms of numbers; in 1994–95 only about 1000 Nepali students were present in the United States, by 2012 this number had risen to 10,312 Nepali students per year.[2] The return rate among these students remains extremely low with most choosing to stay on legally or illegally.

Given the establishment and rapid expansion of private English boarding schools throughout the nation and the subsequent rise of educational consultancies, it can be argued that education in Nepal has been an intrinsically market-driven phenomenon. With the limited scope and quality of government education in Nepal, there was an increasing demand for better educational standards and practices, especially with a growing number of educated middle class parents who were increasingly aware of the opportunities a good education could provide their children. These children, educated in the private school system, were even more aware of the opportunities they could grasp and set their aspirations much higher than their parents did. Thus, the educational consultancy industry was born out of this demand for quicker and easier access to universities abroad. The 'secrets' of the application process, that only students at elite schools had been privy to in the past, were made available to all—for the right price.

Private Institutions of Higher Learning

The impact of privatization was felt throughout the educational sector. Aside from the private school boom, perhaps the biggest revolution to shake the foundations of the Nepali educational system was the establishment of Kathmandu University. Established in 1991 through an Act (Kathmandu University Act 1991), it is the first private institute of higher learning established in Nepal and posed the first direct challenge to the educational monopoly of Tribhuvan University. In 1992 Kathmandu University started its first class with intermediate-level courses only; since then the university has quickly expanded into undergraduate and post-graduate studies. It currently operates six schools based on the disciplines of arts, education, engineering, management, medical science, and science. It has enrolled, including in affiliated colleges, a total of around 3300 students. Setting an educational benchmark that places it in a different league than the government-mismanaged Tribhuvan University; there is an increasing trend among private secondary and tertiary institutions to seek affiliations with Kathmandu University. Constant strikes, delays in examinations, delays in publishing results, and disillusionment with the entire quality of education at offer in Tribhuvan University means that any student with ambition shuns it.

Although privatization went a long way in improving the standard of education in Nepal, the lack of governmental regulation on private schools meant that a considerable amount of profiteering occurred. Although some private schools gave you all you paid for, in terms of education, facilities and access, some, if not most of them, took the easier way out. By charging increasingly higher fees while doing nothing to improve the quality of education or the facilities of the school in return, it is safe to say that private schools often became a cash crop. By selling sub-standard uniforms through designated contractors, books through cartels of booksellers and book publishers associations and charging parents for foundations, events, fairs or excursion trips, education became the best unregulated private sector. Some private schools justified these expenses by attempting to provide an international standard of education. For instance, the Kathmandu University affiliated Kathmandu College of Management started charging around Rs 100,000 for a year for undergraduate studies but armed students with laptops and hired the best professors available, with the objective of creating world-class business managers. Its ability to deliver, albeit by charging such high fees, has encouraged some Nepali students to study in Nepal.

The costs of all levels of private education remained relatively high with the cheapest private schools in Nepal charging rates that were easily higher than those being charged in private schools of the same standard in neighbouring India. With school fees up to Rs 1000 a month, private education was not a luxury that low income people, with their low minimum pay, they could afford to provide their children. These high fees have been a bone of contention between private schools and the government, add to it increasing pressures from the government to have control over such private schools and soon private schools grouped together to form big cartels with strong negotiation powers. With 5 million children in school, this provided the largest base of customers that the service providers could profit from.

Preference for Paper Degrees

A fundamental flaw in the traditional Nepali attitude to education was a yearning for degrees rather than education. A desire to have the accolade rather than the knowledge, to have a title rather than expertise, is a trait shared by most Nepali students. This is perhaps best exemplified by the fact that an estimated 15,000 teachers[3] of the total 150,000 qualified teachers in Nepal possess fake certificates bought in the bazaars of Patna where one could buy degrees for around USD 150 to USD 500 depending on the appearance of authenticity and the demand for the degree. Although this story has been in the popular media for a while, little to no action has been taken against those holding fake degrees. Considering that this is a presentation of statistics only in the education sector, the number of fake degree holders touting professional expertise in the economy must be considerable. For instance, a sharp decrease was noticed in admissions to an MBA programme in India when admission tests were introduced. Before the admission tests were introduced, more than half of the class size consisted of Nepalis, which dropped to less than 5 per cent as soon as the system of admission tests was put into place. Such a love of degrees combined with a disregard for actual knowledge and learning are dangerous signs of an economy that neither has regulations, nor values expertise.

The Nepali people are resilient and are looking for the best deal as much as anyone else in the world. It is no surprise that a number of major Indian educational institutes have shown a keen interest in investing in the educational sector in Nepal. One such example is the establishment in 1994 of the Manipal College of Medical Sciences in Pokhara, in collaboration between India's Manipal Group and the government of Nepal. The hospital is also a medical school and is one of the finest examples of a successful public–private partnership and of the potential that exists in Nepal, not just for education but for educational tourism and medical tourism. Manipal, registered as a for-profit company, pays a significant amount of taxes in Nepal, apart from providing employment opportunities for locals. Spread over thirty-eight acres with a 700-bed teaching hospital, clinical teaching departments, and hostels for medical students, it is truly an impressive institute. In the first decade since its establishment, Manipal has been able to churn out more than 1000 doctors, most of whom are non-Nepali. The hospital has been able to provide top-class medical services to the surrounding region at an affordable price while significantly contributing to the Nepali economy and producing some outstanding doctors.

Manipal and other private medical colleges that have been established have, to some extent, addressed the great need for health professionals in Nepal. However, one recently graduated doctor had this to say about being a doctor in Nepal: 'Any doctor with moral or ethical integrity about how a patient needs to be treated will either not work here at all, or will try his or her best to leave. The standards here of especially the larger public hospitals are pitiful; there are neither enough beds nor equipment nor most importantly, time to do very much. And then the militancy! We give our hearts but since there are no proper malpractice laws or security for doctors, failure is as dangerous for the doctor as for the patient.' Thus, the lack of a proper health care system in Nepal follows a similar trend to that of education; both have a failed government system and an unregulated private service sector. Given the relatively similar situation under which both the government and private sectors entered into the project of modernization in 1950, and the limitations on producing qualified professionals in both fields, the failures of government in both sectors have many similarities, which will be examined below.

Health Care Woes

By the end of the Rana regime in the 1950s, Nepal's modern health care was represented by 649 hospital beds and fifty doctors. With the complete absence of modern medicine from interior regions, the Nepali health care system in these areas was composed of *jhankari*s and *vaidya*s. *Jhankari*s belonged to a superstitious and astrological tradition of popular folk medicine while the *vaidyas* were the masters of a system of medicine developed in South Asia by the Hindus over 2000 years ago. Ayurvedic medicine utilizes an extensive knowledge of medical plants, roots, herbs and fungus in treating medical ailments. The Nepali government has made some attempts in ensuring the preservation of the knowledge of Ayurveda through the establishment of a national college of Ayurvedic medicine in Kathmandu. However, in the promotion and expansion of the modern health care system, the government has met with considerable obstacles.

One of the primary problems the government has faced since the 1950s in expanding the health care system, as with the educational system, has been the unavailability of qualified professionals. The Nepali educational system has not prepared and indeed, has actively discouraged students from pursuing a tertiary-level education, especially in the technical fields of medicine and engineering. Lacking educational facilities in Nepal, most Nepali students who wish to study medicine have to study abroad with funding from one or the other of Nepal's donor countries. In this regard, the United States, India, USSR and Britain are the primary education destinations and sponsors. Aside from the USSR, all other countries require a command of English that Nepali education is unable to provide, which biases such opportunities towards the Nepali elite who send their children to English boarding schools in India. The first medical college in Nepal, the Institute of Medicine, was established in 1972 but only started recruiting students in 1978 and operated under Tribhuvan University. This meant that the five-year course in medicine normally took six years to complete, due to a variety of strikes and delays at the University.

By the end of the Panchayat era in 1990, the modern health care system in Nepal had only expanded to around 1200 doctors and 3000 nurses serving a population of around nineteen million, of which most doctors were all situated in the urban centres of Nepal. The government had established 123 hospitals, eighteen health centres and 816 health posts throughout the country, largely with the help of donor money which had to be spent, but did not value long run operations. With only one doctor for over 20,000 people, the lack of qualified professionals meant that those health posts left operating were run by the janitors rather than by any qualified professional. The improvements in infant mortality and the death rate from the early 1950s to 2007 were of some consolation—

infant mortality rates improved from 210 per thousand to 43 per thousand and death rate from 27 per thousand to 6.5 per thousand.[4] But these achievements could be attributed to the success of various vaccination and disease eradication campaigns along with an increasing awareness of sanitation, basic health care and childbirth procedures.

As with the education sector, the inability of the government to deliver quality health services meant that with the liberalization of the economy after 1990, private hospitals began to appear to meet health care demands that were not being met by the government. Without adequate government regulation and rules on medical practice and standards, a host of private nursing homes, hospitals and pathology labs sprouted all over town. The sector remains unregulated and lacks proper malpractice or liability laws, which essentially creates an environment of complete laissez faire anarchism. Public sector doctors refer patients to the private sector so that they can charge more money, pharmaceutical companies cut a commission with doctors to sell their medicines, and customers vandalize hospitals if a patient dies. There are no regulations on medical professionals that ensure that they remain updated and capable of performing their duties, nor are there adequate checks with the issuance of drugs. The Nepal Medical Council, which remains the central source of authority in terms of issuing regulations for doctors, has been much politicized along the lines of the Federation of Nepal Chambers of Commerce and Industries (FNCCI). With the council playing regulator, those elected by the general doctors' assembly wield considerable power in accrediting and guaranteeing the quality of various medical institutions in the country. Accreditation and quality guarantees have proven to be a lucrative business. Charged with the responsibility of working with the government to institute best practice standards, malpractice laws, liability laws and addressing issues of continuing education, the Council has instead largely ensured that the quality of doctors is neither maintained nor regulated.

As in education, although there are still considerable challenges to ensuring an effective and efficient health care system that is accessible to all, it is without a doubt that the expansion of the private health care services has expanded the reach of modern medicine much further than the government had been able to. Further, the establishment of some world-class health centres in Nepal has set the benchmark for what people expect in terms of health care services in Nepal. Some of these private ventures have been resounding successes and have made a massive difference to Nepali society at large. Hospitals like Dhulikhel Hospital, Tilganga Eye Hospital and doctors like Dr Sanduk Ruit, a Magsaysay Award winner who made corneal transplantation affordable and accessible and Dr Ram Shrestha, a surgeon who returned to Nepal after working for fifteen years in Europe to start a world-class affordable hospital for the masses in Dhulikhel, have shown what can happen when efforts are undertaken thoroughly with a worthwhile intention. The need for the development of proper health care services in Nepal is undeniable.

Dhulikhel Hospital that began operations in 1996 with small facilities has today grown into a full-fledged hospital complex with a medical school. The sheer determination of one man, Dr Ram Shrestha, enabled the provision of health care to people at just Rs 25 for a check-up and Rs 250 per day for a bed including meals. In 2011 the hospital treated 121,070 outpatients and 15,417 inpatients. The same year, the hospital conducted 15,246 surgeries compared to 3000 general surgeries in the largest government-owned-and-operated Bir Hospital in Kathmandu. With an annual turnover of Rs 4 billion, Dabur Nepal, a private sector company in the wellness business, is one of the success stories of the new economic policy of the early 1990s and one that demonstrates that foreign investment in Nepal is still a viable proposition. Dabur exports 70 per cent of its production and the rest is sold within Nepal, proving that the Nepali market now has a critical mass of consumers who could make a manufacturing industry very profitable. Dabur's range of products include juices, honey and a spectrum of health products that use herbal ayurvedic raw materials cultivated in greenhouses and by farmers across Nepal. In contrast to the Dabur example, medicinal Yarchagumba plants, which are a natural resource base for Nepal, are being collected and sold as a raw material. Although the government requires collectors to pay a Rs 10,000 royalty per kilo of the plant, in most scenarios collection remains free from government control. When purchased from collectors it is bought at a mere Rs 2500 to Rs 3500 a kilo, and by the time the same kilo of Yarchagumba reaches Nepalgunj or Kathmandu, it is trading at a staggering Rs 12 lakh a kilo. It then makes its way to China and Hong Kong where it is processed to extract medicines and tonics.

The inability of Nepal to capitalize on the natural supply of Yarchagumba and establish processing plants to add value to the resource harkens back to the Nepali mentality of arbitrage. It follows along the same path as mobile phones in which Nepali businesses were content with just being middlemen and did not seek to establish manufacturing plants. Nepali businesses should learn from the Dabur success and realize that its natural resources are much more valuable processed and packaged rather than in the raw form. The government must realize that with the institutionalization of companies like Dabur, it can reap benefits in taxing the suppliers as well as the processors. It must also seek to protect its natural resource base from over cultivation and excessive use which leads to depletion and possible extinction. Here the donor community, wildlife conservation agencies and the government can play a critical role in setting up a system that allows for the local community to maximize its share of returns while keeping its natural resource base intact and ensuring maximum profitability for both the private sector and government.

In conclusion, the major problem with governance has been a lack of vision in terms of the role of the government itself. It is clear that the government has been unsuccessful in acting as a discounted service provider in the education and health care sectors. It would be much better off focusing its energies on trying to establish a capitalist welfare state that derives its welfare system from the prosperity of the national economy. If the government were to focus on being a regulatory body with the intention of acting in the best interest of business, the consumer and the worker, it would best be able to address the needs of the national economy.

7

CONFLICTONOMICS

In 1972 when King Birendra ascended the throne of Nepal, he made a call to the international community asking for the recognition of Nepal as a Zone of Peace. This proposal was a political manoeuvre in keeping with the non-aligned philosophy Nepal had adopted to manage its neighbours India and China. Birendra may or may not have seen the dark irony of calling Nepal a Zone of Peace, given the nation's violent history. Nepal was forged through conquest and held together by sheer brute force. Little to nothing of Nepal's early history suggests that the Nepali nation and identity predated late 1700s Shah conquest or that the conquerors, the Hindu Chhettris of Gorkha, and the conquered of various ethnicities, indigenous cultures and religions, had a common identity. The Nepali unification under Prithvi Narayan Shah was not a Gandhian non-violent nationalist movement but a product of a monarch's vision, ambition and leadership.

Long History of Violence

Court intrigue, murder and duels were a regular occurrence in early nineteenth-century Nepali royal courts. Seats of power were to be grabbed and seized, not attained through merit or wit. In congruence with this tradition of violence, the Rana regime was established in Nepal through the massacre of almost the entire aristocracy in 1846. The fall of Jung Bahadur's clan in 1885 to that of his brothers, the Shumsher Ranas, was equally a case of violently seizing power through a coup. It is important to acknowledge the role of Nepal's southern neighbour India, especially during the Shumsher Rana coup in 1880s and the Nepali Congress-led insurgency of the 1960s. Jung Bahadur's descendents, who were in exile in India, were effectively held back from carrying out an insurgency against the Shumsher Rana usurpers by the British, who saw a greater benefit in supporting the usurpers. In the following century, the Shumsher Ranas found the newly independent Indian democratic government unsupportive of autocracy and eager to see democratic reforms in Nepal. The close relations the Nepali Congress party had established with the Indian Congress party were a factor here, along with the democratic ethos of the Indian leaders.

Following the royal coup by King Mahendra in 1960, the Nepali Congress had started an armed revolt based out of India, against the monarchy. The Nepali Congress, with the backing of an Indian government, which had placed an unofficial embargo on Nepal, pushed the royal regime into a precarious position. However, the monarchy was saved by the sudden outbreak of war between India and China in 1962, which forced India to cosy up to the royal regime rather than risk losing Nepal to the Chinese. The Nepali Congress-led insurgency continued intermittently until the 1990s on a much reduced scale, most prominently through the hijacking of a Royal Nepal Airlines flight in 1973 by the Nepali Congress. That the belief in insurgency as a means to legitimate power permeates the Nepali political landscape is perhaps best attested to by the fact that the mastermind behind the hijacking was Girija Prasad Koirala, who went on to become the prime minister of Nepal four times. The hijacking of the national flagship carrier was carried out partly for media coverage, but also for the Rs 30 lakh it was carrying from the Rastra Bank to Biratnagar. The hijacking was physically carried out by Birendra Dahal, Koirala's former political advisor, and Durga Subedi, a senior leader of the Nepali Congress. The hijacking was a success, as both hijackers escaped without being caught and thus considerably tarnished the government's security record. Koirala has also admitted that during the 1970s, the Nepali Congress was involved in printing counterfeit currency as a means to raise funds for their political activity. Aside from political insurgencies, there were a number of smaller ethnic insurgencies that occurred in Nepal during Panchayat rule, but these were successfully resolved by the government.

The royal massacre of June 2001 continues to haunt Nepalis and raises many questions about the seemingly enduring place of violence in Nepal's political culture thus far.

The People's War

Given the reasonably good success rate of armed insurgency in seizing political power in Nepal, the People's War started by the Communist Party of Nepal (CPN-M)—also known as the Maoists— in February of 1996, was a calculated and understandable strategy. The stated objectives of the People's War were to: 'remove the bureaucratic-capitalistic class and the state system, uproot semi-feudalism and drive out imperialism, in order to establish a New Democratic Republic with the view to establish a new socialist society'.[1] While the state system in this case was the monarchy, they attacked semi-feudalism as a system under the rule of kings and other feudal lords, that exploited people as a means to their own prosperity, leaving them poor.

Dr Baburam Bhattarai, senior Maoist leader, explained to this author that Nepal has been bestowed with many resources but the feudal lords were parasitic, extractive and rent-seeking and used these resources only for their own benefit. They were never interested in development but only in leisure and the living of luxurious lives. The Maoist struggle was needed to ensure that this class could be removed, thereby allowing a model of people's participation in Nepal's future economic development.

Unlike past insurgencies, the Maoists were unique in that they wanted to capture and control land in Nepal, apart from challenging the state structure. This was a strategy that they took from Mao's books and it proved powerful enough to win the support of the vast number of Nepalis who had long suffered under the burden of poverty and oppression. Starting out in the districts of Rolpa, Rukum and Jajarkot in the mid-1990s, the Maoists started with the removal of select local 'tyrants' who formed the local elites and police. The Maoists were very successful in these early phases, partly because of a government that did not care to act and partly because their strategy was immensely popular with the impoverished and exploited locals. This also allowed them to set up their own local government structures in these regions, totally supplanting the government's administrative and judicial structures. After just three years of building, expanding, recruiting, extorting and raiding, the Maoists were able to formally announce the formation of the People's Army in February 1999. Although raids, sabotages, ambushes and kidnappings had formed the core areas of competency for the Maoist guerrillas, the establishment of the People's Army marked a new phase in the war. On the 25th of September 2000, the People's Army successfully launched their first full-scale assault on Dunai, the headquarters of Dolpa district in the western part of Nepal. The victory was a big boost to the Maoist war efforts and subsequently led to the escalation of the war.

The People's Liberation Army during the course of the decade-long insurgency from 1996 to 2006 is estimated to have had anywhere from 4000 to 8000 core combatants with a support structure of 20,000 to 25,000 armed militia.[2] The Maoists had to have significant political and administrative capacities to operate such an army, as well as run a parallel government structure in roughly one-third of the entire nation. Part of the success of the Maoists has been their ability to not only manage and coordinate but also to ensure loyalty and respect for command hierarchy within their organization. This partly stems from the fact that they were a militia, conducting extensive guerrilla training and compelling discipline. The Maoists were also successful in recruiting former British and Indian Gurkhas and ex-Nepal army personnel to lead their training exercises. This has allowed them to develop a level of professionalism and create a soldier's culture within the ranks of PLA, which would not have been possible without specialist military trainers.

Child Soldiers

It is the nature of children to follow the examples set for them; when trained from a young age they can be indoctrinated into anything. The extensive use of child soldiers by the Maoists allowed them to have a highly dedicated and ruthless army at its disposal. The brainwashing and induction of child soldiers within the ranks of the PLA has been a common occurrence. Estimates of the total number of child soldiers used range from 3500 to 4500.[3] The Asian Human Rights Commission and the Coalition to Stop the Use of Child Soldiers have estimated that as much as 30 per cent of the Maoist force is aged fourteen to eighteen, with children as young as ten being conscripted into the militia.[4] The use of children in particular was part of a Maoist strategic offensive launched in 2004, to meet the increasing need for armed militia to carry out attacks. To this end, the Maoists demanded a child from each family in areas under their control. During this period, they were also involved in the abduction of students from schools, either for ideological indoctrination or for basic combat training and recruitment.[5] In addition to child soldiers, the Maoists were very successful in tapping into support from women and minority and oppressed caste groups, due to their heavy emphasis on gender equality and strong anti-casteism propaganda.

The forced recruitment of children into the Maoist army compelled many families to move out of Maoist-controlled regions and into the city. Increasingly unbearable extortion rates and constant harassment by both security forces and Maoists have together internally displaced several hundred thousand people in Nepal. A large majority of the displaced are youths who ran away out of fear of being conscripted into the Maoist army. The abduction of students from schools and the persistent persecution of teachers have significantly retarded any progress made in education during the past forty years. Teachers were a particular focus for Maoists as they were the most influential people in the village, with progressive and liberal leanings. The Maoists often took them to be representatives of the state structure they were fighting. Abductions have discouraged parents from sending their children to school and encouraged teachers to flee from schools. Considerable damage has been done to school infrastructure. Illiteracy among this lost generation of youth in Nepal will be a significant price to pay for the conflict, on top of the psychological trauma that many abducted and orphaned children now suffer from.

War Economics: 'Business Opportunities'

The Maoists' major revenue was obtained through extortion and the levying of donations and taxes on the general populace. The donations and taxes in particular were most severe in Maoist-controlled areas where they targeted teachers, government officials and farmers in addition to local businessmen. The payment of a tax to the Maoists ensured protection from Maoist violence, but did nothing to protect the payer from the security forces or from opportunistic hoodlums. It is estimated that by the year 2000, the Maoists' extortion and tax racket had allowed them to accumulate over Rs 5 billion.[6] By 2001, the Second National Conference of the Maoists in February 2001 declared Pushpa Kamal Dahal or Prachanda the party chairman, and the party officially touted a doctrine that was popularly called 'Prachandapath'. The doctrine is an extension of the ideological line expounded by the Communist Party of Peru and is an attempt to localize the doctrines of Marxism, Leninism and Maoism in the Nepali context. It was also around this time that the People's Army was renamed the People's Liberation Army (PLA) and placed under the direct command of Prachanda. It now boasted three divisions, nine brigades and twenty-nine battalions and was far better equipped than before, thanks to the automatic weapons and explosives looted from police posts and army barracks. There are also unofficial rumours that suggest that the Maoists were successful in procuring AK-47 assault rifles from black markets in the Indian states of Bihar and Uttar Pradesh.

Cost estimates of financing the PLA vary from source to source, from around Rs 250 to 800 million.[7] What we do know is that the Maoists spent frugally on the payment and equipping of their forces; however, they did spend extensively on training them and preparing them for battle. At the individual level, it is estimated that each solider received Rs 150 as monthly allowance, was given a non-vegetarian meal every week and in total no more than Rs 17,000 a year was spent on each combatant.[8] Aside from extortion, looting, and kidnapping, the Maoists were successful in raising funds from the trading and taxing of Yarchagumba plants. They also were able to tap poaching and the illegal trade in forest wood for which they followed a similar informal taxation model to that of Yarchagumba, requiring direct payments to the Maoists based on the value or volume of goods. Further, the Maoists were successful in establishing Nepali Maoist trade unions in countries where Nepalis worked, including in the Middle East and East Asia. These sympathizers were then able to channel considerable funds to support the Maoist movement.

The insurgency came with its own unique set of advantages. For one inclined to do business for the sake of profit without the restraints of ethics, these proved particularly bountiful times. Corruption allowed a great deal of trade in Nepal under the cover of the insurgency. From the smuggling of goods to poaching and from printing counterfeit notes to the creation of artificial shortages, Nepal's swindlers and double dealers had a field day. A weak state structure invites all these irregularities and promotes the proliferation of racketeering. The hugely popular use of blockades, *chakka jam*s and strikes was particularly effective in creating artificial shortages that allowed businessmen in Kathmandu to make a few extra bucks on things ranging from kerosene to tomatoes. With no consumer protection laws and few alternatives, the people had to pay up.

These *chakka jam*s, blockades, raids and lootings also meant that newsworthy events were now happening all over the country and suddenly, Nepal was Kathmandu no longer. Nepal grew vast, and suddenly began to represent many places previously unheard of and unknown to the urban mind. Here was a crash course on Nepali geography that most people would have done better without.

State Apathy, Royal Takeover and the End of the Conflict

The government during the late 1990s was involved in a number of inter-party and intra-party squabbles that allowed the Maoists to operate without much state resistance. The lack of popular support behind the Maoists, especially in Kathmandu during their earlier days, made them of only fringe interest to the then government. Indeed, if anything, the political parties were willing to use the Maoists as leverage to play their own power games. This was perhaps best exemplified by the political shuffle within the Congress party when Krishna Prasad Bhattarai's government was displaced by his own party colleague Girija Prasad Koirala in March 2000. The stated reason for this shuffle was that Prime Minister Krishna Prasad Bhattarai's government was unable to initiate dialogue or tackle the Maoist problem. At this point, the Maoist violence had escalated to a considerable degree and was increasingly impacting the national economy. The inability of the government to effectively deal with the insurgency and the weakness of its administrative and security structures was quickly revealed. The police force was poorly trained, poorly equipped and extremely corrupt. The police structure was centralized with all recruitment and placements occurring in the capital, thus dissociating the police from the local community, to whom it appeared as a foreigner representing state repression. In many sections of the police, the insurgency suddenly created business opportunities in directing the placement of police officers around the nation. A nice bottle of Black Label whisky to a senior officer could be the difference between going to the heart of the Maoist insurgency in Rolpa or to the tamer town of Dharan. The police also lacked discipline, were guilty of harassment and prone to lash out randomly when threatened. With such a culture of corruption and unruliness entrenched in the police, it is not surprising that they were disliked and despised by people as a reckless and irresponsible group of hoodlums. Thus, when the Maoists first attacked the police, there was actually considerable public sympathy for their actions.

The government also faced major problems in mobilizing the army. Although the army was, in theory, under the control of the government through the National Defence Council, it retained its allegiance to the king. The king using his army to kill fellow Nepalis always became a moral issue that he had to address publicly to retain legitimacy. Therefore he refrained from using the army despite the level of escalation in violence. The army in turn, chose to abide by its traditional allegiance to the king, instead of following the wishes of the democratic government. Although the army had a good public image in comparison to the police, corruption was endemic in that budgets and spending were neither accountable nor transparent. The army's unwillingness to join the conflict in situations where it could have assisted police forces and its lack of cooperation with the prime minister and parliament, caused considerable consternation to the government. For instance, during the Maoist attack on Dunai in September 2000, local army barracks opted not to intervene in the fight and allowed the Maoists to take off with 50 million rupees from the local bank, which had received this surplus money that very day. The unwillingness of the king to get the army involved and the lack of the army's interest in entering into the conflict forced the government into the formation of the Armed Police Force in 2001. It was primarily established as a paramilitary force to maintain law and order, contain the insurgency and fight terrorism. The general feeling among the Nepali people was also against the use of security forces by the government. This was largely due to a fear that the use of the army would lead to an escalation of the crisis. The constant political turmoil and infighting between political leaders further reduced the faith of the Nepali people in the ability of the democratic government to successfully manage the army and handle the conflict.

If the escalating violence due to the insurgency was not enough reason for worry, the Nepali nation was shocked in June 2001 by the massacre of the entire royal family and the ascension of Gyanendra Shah to the throne as King of Nepal. Shortly thereafter, within two months of the World Trade Centre attacks in New York, the Maoists launched a full-scale attack on an army barrack in Dang in western Nepal, breaking a ceasefire and leading, finally, to the government mobilization and deployment of the Royal Nepal Army. The timing of the Maoist attack seemed to be in line with their shift in propaganda, attacking American imperialism rather than Indian hegemony. In an interview, Prachanda himself states, 'In the process of waging war we managed to snatch a few rifles from the armed police. It is these rifles that are now capturing automatic weapons from the royal army. Thus, weapons sent by George Bush to suppress Nepalese people will soon be reaching the hands of Nepalese people, and will be directed against imperialism.'[9]

Although there were several peace talks between 2002 and 2005 between the government and Maoists, none of them was successful in resolving the crisis. The primary reason for the failure of these peace talks was the government's unwillingness to cede to the Maoists' demands for a constituent assembly for the drafting of a new constitution. There are also claims that the Maoists were only using the peace talks as a means to consolidate and strengthen. The argument goes that the peace talks were used by the Maoists as time to recuperate, gather supplies and plan for their next offensive. There is some justification for this argument as after the breakdown of each talk, the Maoists became stronger and launched more and more daring raids.

By the time of the royal coup in February 2005, when King Gyanendra sacked the prime minister and began direct rule, the conflict had become a stalemate, with the Maoists controlling considerable tracts of the countryside while the government controlled the urban centres. After the royal coup, there was a crackdown on civil liberties, which caused considerable opposition to the royal regime. The Maoists were increasingly aware of their inability to defeat the army in a protracted military struggle and saw a unique opportunity in tying up with dissenting political parties and taking part in a non-violent campaign against the monarchy. This eventually led to the April 2006 popular non-violent uprising called Jana Andolan II, that effectively brought an end to the conflict and the reinstatement of the parliament under a coalition led by the Nepali Congress. The subsequent constituent assembly led to the abolition of the over 200-year-old monarchy.

Prohibitive Cost of War

Ten years of conflict have done immeasurable damage to Nepal's economy, society and culture. A significant amount of infrastructural damage was caused by the Maoists in their quest to remove the old feudal structures. For instance, they targeted many government installations as a way of attacking, destroying and superseding representatives of the state, to demonstrate the state's weakness. Primary Maoist targets were offices of Village Development Committees, school buildings, municipality offices, District Development Offices, and other Government offices. They also targeted communication installations, power relay stations and bridges, as a way of gutting state infrastructure and creating a parallel administration and also because these targets were identified as components of the feudal state. In total, over a ten-year destructive spree the Maoists were successful in vandalizing and destroying infrastructure worth 30.55 billion rupees in 1841 rural VDCs.[10] These structures, which had been built over the course of forty years of development now have to be rebuilt and reinstated.

The nation also had to bear the cost of a dramatic rise in spending on security forces and other necessities for the state's war against the Maoists. The security force used to be a 50,000-strong personnel army and a 50,000-strong police force, but it soon incorporated an entirely new branch—the paramilitary outfit of the Armed Police Force. By 2005, the combined security forces had expanded to over 100,000 strong. This was accompanied by a rise in budgetary spending on security from Rs 5.38 billion in 1996 to Rs 18.33 billion in 2005.[11] During this time, the government security forces and the army in particular, were responsible for purchasing weapons, including 5000 M16 rifles and 5500 M246 Minimi rifles. The total budgetary spending on security forces during the ten years of insurgency totalled a whopping Rs 107.8 billion.[12] If this money had been used to build power plants, then Nepal would have had a 625 MW power plant!

It is estimated that the conflict cost the nation around 2.5 per cent of GDP growth per annum since the escalation of the violence due to the insurgency, starting from the year 2000.[13] The impact on the GDP is the result of a combination of factors including the decline in tourists, losses in business, drying up of foreign direct investment, and loss in human capital. The conflict has impacted the ability of the government to provide basic needs to the people in the form of drinking water, education and health services and has impacted the capacity and extent to which development work on such things as roads and communication has been carried out in rural Nepal. The most significant of the costs that the nation and the people have had to bear is the invaluable cost of the lives of over 15,000 Nepali citizens. This has had an impact on their families, relatives, friends and local communities. The war has led to a mass migration of young men and boys fleeing the war out of fear of both sides. Between 100,000 to 200,000[14] people have been displaced from their homes and have been forced to shift to the urban centres, primarily Kathmandu, in search of safety, security and work.

The Psychological Impact of War

Given the substantial number of people the insurgency has directly and indirectly impacted, a strong undercurrent of resentment can be felt in Nepali society. Feelings of anger, hatred and revenge have established themselves in the minds and hearts of many Nepalis and pose an invisible danger to the social fabric. There is no way of predicting or being prepared for the possibly violent reactions of people who have themselves witnessed and suffered from violence. This invisible danger will be an investment risk for doing business in Nepal for the next two generations. The insurgency has also caused immeasurable damage to the intricate networks of trust and friendliness for which Nepali society was once known throughout the world. Nepali people no longer walk the streets and implicitly trust those they cross paths with; there is an air of mistrust and suspicion that hangs over Nepali society. It is no longer considered safe to talk to people at random or be involved in discussions about politics and society out in the open. There is a fostering of the perception that there are eyes all around and one wrong move in front of the wrong set of eyes could have drastic consequences. For instance, during the conflict, it became difficult for a lodge owner to decide whether to rent a room to a stranger as both the Maoists and the state were keeping an eye on people's movement. If the guest was a Maoist, then the security forces went after the lodge owner and if the guest had any level of allegiance to the state, then the Maoists went after the lodge owner. Spontaneous chatting in tea shops in villages, carrying of parcels for a relative or acquaintance or just travelling in a local bus became more and more difficult for the common citizen.

The Insurgency: A Great Excuse

The insurgency also provided an ideal excuse for the private sector and the development sector to excuse their inefficiencies and failures and blame it all squarely on the insurgency. The insurgency, in this sense, became the tastiest scapegoat to have ever lived beyond two *dasains*.* For the donors, the insurgency was the reason for the failure of many of their development programmes even though many of these programmes had been in business— unsuccessfully—for far longer than the insurgency itself. It also gave the donors the excuse to quietly close down programmes that were not working, without acknowledging their failures. Some donors were romantic about the promise of socialism and bought into it like a dream once lost. These donors continued to operate their programmes in Maoist-held territories, willingly paying the 10–15 per cent tax they had to bear in order to operate within these regions, despite knowing full well that their money was being used to buy weapons and finance extortions. Even so, the donors and international community in Nepal did not want to see a Maoist victory. This would have been dangerous in not only encouraging other such revolutions but also in terms of the instability it would invite into the region.

Of all the nations involved in Nepal, India stood to lose the most from a Maoist win. Not only would a Maoist win significantly boost the morale of Indian Maoist factions in Uttar Pradesh and Bengal, but Nepal would also become an actual base of operation for the Indian insurgents. Further, a Maoist win endangered India's security not just in terms of possibly losing its sphere of influence in Nepal but also in risking the use of Nepal by other terrorists groups based out of Pakistan. Given all this, and India's strong

---

Dasain: a two week-long Hindu festival known for goat sacrifices.

commitment to assist the Nepali government in combating the Maoists, their inaction is surprising. India had declared the Maoists a terrorist outfit much earlier than Nepal itself had and it was well known that most Nepali Maoist leaders and troops were based out of India. Historically, it should be noted that any insurgency in Nepal has not succeeded in Nepal without some form of explicit or silent support from India. The Indian government's inability to tackle the Nepal insurgency is either a sign of limitations in its ability to control its northern frontier or an indication of a much deeper political manoeuvre.

The rapid and rather unexpected conclusion of the insurgency through the non-violent uprising of April 2006 and the eventual peace accord of 2006 also came as a trump card for the donors. It became a means for the donors to immediately get their hands dirty and prove that their involvement in Nepal for the past few years in their newly touted subjects of conflict resolution and peace studies were coming to fruition. This proved an ideal platform for the development community overall to vindicate itself and justify its work. The streets of Kathmandu started being flooded with people of various nationalities, and eating places and watering holes started buzzing with people working for the United Nations Mission for Nepal (UNMIN). Nepali development workers found a new Mecca for high-paying jobs and rhino-horned SUVs* started being seen in parking lots. Media guesstimates of expenses of the UNMIN range from USD 70 million to USD 100 million in the first year of operations.

The Discovery of the Fourth Estate

Perhaps one of the greatest finds of the entire insurgency and the royal takeover was a realization of the power of the media. The literacy rate grew, in spite of the attacks on schools, since parents sent their children away to cities for an education, accompanied by

---

*Rhino-horned SUVs—the communication antennae on the front of big, white and expensive UN vehicles earned them the popular title of white rhinos.

relatives. An increase in newspaper readership along with the expansion of radio and television meant that everyone anywhere in Nepal could follow news from around the nation instantaneously. When the rights of the media and the press were challenged during the insurgency and particularly during the royal regime, not just the journalists and media houses but also their readers, viewers and listeners expressed a strong opposition to any such suppression of the media. This public outcry was perhaps the strongest signal that the fourth pillar of a vibrant democracy was taking shape.

The Terai Story

An offshoot of the Maoist insurgency in Nepal was yet more insurgencies, especially in the Terai, where the Maoist attempt to unite socially marginalized and excluded groups is really taking shape. A major underlying reason for the spread of insurgency was the economic stagnation that most districts in the Terai were experiencing. The old land-based agrarian economy was on the verge of collapse and could no longer accommodate the growing workforce, while labour intensive, employment generating industries were few and concentrated in the southern Terai cities like Birgunj, Biratnagar, Nepalgunj and Janakpur. At the same time, aspirations among the youth had dramatically increased, leaving them but two options, either join an ethnic political party and become a small cog of the larger patronage politics or enter a militant group engaged in crime and extortion. This has dramatically increased political unrest and crime leading to a decrease in investments in the region, which in turn has limited economic growth and employment. This is slowly becoming a vicious cycle.

The eastern Terai is extremely low on socio-economic indicators and landlessness is an acute problem. In a context where land determines your income, social status and political power, not having land means being at the bottom of the hierarchy. The *dalits*, who form the chunk of the landless, face the brunt of both social discrimination and economic deprivation. This provided the ideal base for the Maoist-led political mobilization, but as is now evident, has created a backlash. Prashant Jha, who writes a column called

'Terai Eye' for the *Nepali Times*, a well-regarded English-language weekly, explains to the author, 'It was not only the high caste landed elite which was worried about what the Maoist influence may mean. It was also middle-sized landowners. Someone may have five *bighas* of land, his sole income source, barely providing enough for his large family. This is the asset he mortgages when he sends his child to school or pays for medical treatment. Suddenly, this person started fearing that "revolutionary land reform" would mean his only asset would get snatched away. He did not believe the Maoists when they tried to reassure him that he was not in their line of fire. Instead, this class became the bulwark of the anti-Maoist resistance along with those higher up in the socio-economic ladder. They together formed the nucleus of the Madhes movement and gave it the anti-Maoist tilt that it came to assume in the post 2006 period.'

The Madhes must have an ironical bitter taste for the Maoists who were the ones to first raise the Madhesi issue. A major reason for the split between the Maoists and Madhes is because of a lack of Madhesi representation within the Maoist leadership. Most Maoist leaders in the Madhes happen to be *pahadis*, from the hills, which has created considerable resentment as it is seen as a continuation of the old system of hill dominance. However, some might say the reality is that the *pahadis* have not dominated Madhesi people, but it is the upper-class Madhesi people who have dominated the various subgroups within the Madhes. The Madhes issue is also about a caste struggle between the *yadavs*, who form the bulk of the supporters of the Madhesi parties, and the *dalits* with whom they have a strained relationship on the ground. Finally, the Madhesi issue is not one just of class, but is intrinsically an economic issue as well. It is primarily about the mid-sized landowners who are fearful of losing what little they have, to the landless.

The Madhes identity received a significant boost as Nepal got its first President and vice president both from the Madhes, after which the Madhes continued to be a significant voice in deciding ruling political coalitions in Kathmandu.

The Illusion for Many

By the end of 2012, the Maoists who had fought the 'people's war' continued to race ahead in the struggle for power like any other political party by using nepotism and money. Leaders who had walked in the jungles and found four-wheel vehicles the epitome of imperialism suddenly started to own them; leaders who had gained public sympathy by banning alcohol could now not live without their favourite imported Scotch; leaders who had burnt down private schools were now educating their own children in elite private schools. Maoist leaders started working closely with businesses to further their personal fortunes and used the party as a veil to hide the benefits of capitalism that they had discovered. Suddenly, the people who had lost their youth, relations and livelihoods during the ten-year insurgency started to question the necessity of the revolution.

Legacies of the Conflict

The conflict has relegated Nepal to a situation similar to West Bengal in 1977 where after the Naxalite war, a Left Front government with coalition partners belonging to various left parties came together and won the elections. The only difference is that it was not the Naxalites that led the government in Bengal in 1977. After coming to power in Bengal, the Left Front worked on various ways to consolidate and stay in power and they have done that brilliantly, with more than three decades of continuous rule. They came to power promising vigorous agrarian and political reforms just as the Maoists in Nepal have. They called for a 'reversal of the trend toward industrial stagnation by constraining monopoly capital, encouraging small-scale industry, promoting worker self-management and an expansion of the state sector. Corporate industrialization was to be minimized in favour of industrial cooperatives and the public sector.'[15] This is very similar to the Maoist policy pronouncements in Nepal. What the Left Front in Bengal did was to woo the landless through distribution of land, get youth votes through various voluntary employment programmes and free largesse in the form of loans that did not need to be repaid, get the workers into the fold through strong unionization and patronize some business groups to enable control over business. This way, the Left Front relegated West Bengal to a state of negative growth, lagging far behind the national average, until Chief Minister Buddhadeb Bhattacharya starting reversing failed policies and pursuing market oriented policies.

On the whole, the conflict in Nepal has had a physical, financial and psychological impact on Nepal that will take a while to overcome. The development clock just stopped in 1996 and the urgency of getting it to start ticking again, is being felt. The biggest impact of the conflict can be felt in the fact that the youth are leaving the country. The open borders with India provided the best shock absorber for Nepalis as they could move south in search of jobs and livelihood. A trend of migration to India that began as an escape from both the state and Maoist harassment, has now extended to many other countries including Malaysia, Hong Kong, Saudi Arabia, Qatar and the UAE. In 2012, an average of 1200 Nepali youths left the country every day to work in foreign lands.[16]

8

EMERGENCE OF THE
REMITTANCE ECONOMY

During the first three decades of Nepal's quest for development, after the fall of the Ranas in 1950, there was very little real GDP growth. In the 1960s, GDP growth averaged 2.5 per cent while the 1970s it averaged a mere 2.1 per cent. During this time, the population growth of the nation stood at 2.6 per cent. In layman's terms, it means that the country was at best able to maintain the standard of living it had during the 1950s. During these three decades, what with the expansion of road networks, health and education services and the spread of mass media, the socio-culture experience of the Nepali citizen had dramatically changed. At the same time, rural Nepali subsistence farmers were increasingly finding themselves with too little land for too big families. A tradition to go work in India as seasonal workers in the 1950s and 1960s intensified and an increasing number of Nepali youths made their way south. Part of the reason that these workers chose to go to India rather than Kathmandu was because the big Indian cities remained considerably more accessible, due to road linkages, than Kathmandu and also held more opportunities.

Historically, as we have mentioned in previous chapters, Nepali migrant workers and merchants were selling their labour and plying their trade from Tibet to the fertile Gangetic plains. Aranika, a great architect who migrated to China in the thirteenth century and took many artisans of the valley with him, heralded the era of Nepali migration and remittances. The classical Nepali epic poem, *Muna-Madan*, written by the poet Laxmi Prasad Devkota, is based on the central character of Madan, who leaves for Tibet with the aspiration of working there and making himself rich in Lhasa. Successful in making his riches, Madan nonetheless fails to make it back with his new-found wealth, highlighting another aspect of working abroad—its high risk and danger. Risk and danger have been the name of the game for many Nepali foreign workers. The Nepali tele-series' view of life as a high risk and high return gambling game is an accurate expression of the way Nepalis perceive making money and going abroad. This perception perhaps stems from the enduring benchmark of success for all Nepali workers: mercenaries in the service of the British and Indian armies. Sanctioned by the state in most cases, but equally a choice made by many young Nepali men, the exporting of mercenary soldiers or *lahures* has been a lucrative business in Nepal since the conclusion of the Anglo-Nepali war in 1816.

First World War: Gurkhas Start the Remittance Economy

During the First World War, the then prime minister of Nepal, Chandra Shamsher, had sent over 55,000 recruits to serve in the Gurkha regiments of the Indian army. On top of this, he had also sent around 18,000 Nepali soldiers into India to take over garrison duties. In total, including Nepali soldiers in the British Army and those working for the British-controlled Military Police in Burma, it is estimated that over 100,000 Nepali men were involved in the war. Of this total, over 10,000 were killed in action while another 14,000 were wounded or were missing in action. For his contribution to the war, the British provided Chandra Shamsher an annual subsidy of one million rupees, although the Rana rulers had pushed for a return of some of the territories Nepal had lost to the British in the Sugauli treaty of 1816. The Rana rulers' unquestioning loyalty to the British was again demonstrated in their support for the British during the Second World War, in which over 200,000 Nepali recruits and soldiers are estimated to have played a role in the victory of the allied forces.[1]

In the process of fighting for other countries, for causes that never have been their own, Nepali soldiers have earned a reputation for unparalleled ferociousness, loyalty, and bravery in the face of insurmountable adversity. The Gurkhas have fought on the side of the British in almost every military campaign from 1816 to the present day. Conservative estimates place Gurkha casualty figures at 150,000 wounded and 45,000 killed in action in the two world wars and other conflicts before and since. More than 6500 decorations for bravery, including thirteen Victoria Cross awards and two George Cross medals,[2] have been awarded to British Gurkha soldiers.

The Gurkhas have effectively carved out a name for themselves at home and abroad with their khukris and blood. As Nepal entered the modern era in the 1950s, the legendary success of the Gurkha in foreign armies in foreign lands was already well known, both worldwide and at home. The Nepali economy had defined its comparative advantage and its primary export: its loyal, trustworthy, and brave youth. Simultaneously, the Gurkhas who came back home brought with them tales of technology and progress unheard of and a world richer than their wildest dreams. Most importantly, the Gurkhas who returned were richer than anyone else in the village. Thus was the myth of the money and success of the bideshi (foreign) Nepali workers or *bipalis** nurtured.

Migration as a Way of Life

Despite being in the business of exporting its human resources, Nepal showed little interest in capitalizing on a niche market in labour in the global economy. Other than during the World Wars,

---

Bipali is a neologism coined by this author from the words 'bideshi', or foreign, and 'Nepali'. He first used it under his nom de plume Arthabeed, in his 'Economic Sense' column of 16 October 2003 in *Nepali Times*. He has used it extensively since its first publication.

when the ruling Rana aristocracy made a considerable profit exporting Nepali soldiers to the British army, there has hardly been any government interest in the area. However, the lack of government interest did not stop Nepali workers from dreaming of the riches to be earned in foreign lands. Taking full advantage of the porous and deregulated border it shares with its southern neighbour, India, a steady stream of Nepali workers set out into the world pursuing their dreams of riches and glory. Given the similarities in language, culture and tradition, India was easily the preferred choice for Nepali workers. In the 1952–54 census, around 157,000 Nepali workers were estimated to be working in India out of an estimated population of 8.25 million, accounting for around 2 per cent of the total population.

During the 1960s, it was estimated that at any point in time, around 25 per cent of the entire population was on the move, either going home after working or seeking work elsewhere. Of this, as many as 87 per cent of those travelling were composed of male workers. This trend of overseas migration also encouraged internal migration and resettlement, with the bulk of the migration happening from the hills to the Terai as well as to urban centres. By the 1980s the bulk of the population had shifted from the hills to the Terai, with the hill population decreasing through migration by 20 per cent in 20 years.[3] Migration to the Terai was made more attractive by the availability of land there in the 1960s, through deforestation and the proximity of the Terai to India as a destination for seasonal work. The preferred destination of most Nepali workers before the 1990s, India still accounts for a substantial portion of the migrant workforce, with estimates as high as a couple of million Nepali citizens working in India. Of them around 250,000 are officially recorded as working in the public sector in India. India also provides a considerable market for seasonal migrant workers from Nepal who spend a few months working in India during the non-farming months and then return home during the farming season.

When the Indian prime minister, Indira Gandhi, declared a state of emergency in the 1970s, a large number of young Nepalis who traditionally went to India, started to look further abroad. The oil boom in the Middle East during the 1970s provided the perfect destination for such aspiring youths. By the 1980s, the opening up of the labour markets in Korea, Japan and the Middle East provided the opportunity to work for greater rewards than working for the stagnating state-controlled economy back home would. However, restrictions on passport issuance in Nepal encouraged many Nepali citizens to go through India as Indian citizens or through illegal channels. Even those who could get their hands on passports often found it easier to transit to their destination countries through India rather than directly from Nepal. Additionally, given Nepal's weak financial system, these workers had to take loans either from their immediate family or from moneylenders. All this—the loans, the illegal transit through India, was part of the risk of going abroad. Much like the mercenary *lahure* of old who put his life on the line for his money, this new breed of *lahures* put everything, including their integrity and property, up for sale, for the opportunity to make a living. These workers are the tragic heroes of contemporary Nepal.

Passport to Prosperity

There are four categories of migrants. First, a small number are people who have high-level skills like medical doctors, accountants and nurses who migrate to the UK, Australia or Europe. Second, there are students who go to the US, the UK and Australia for education and never return to Nepal. To put the numbers into perspective, in 2009, 11,233 Nepali students entered the US for education, making Nepal eleventh in the list of countries sending students there. The third category comprises semi-skilled workers—plumbers, carpenters, mechanics, etc.—who migrate to countries in the Middle East, South-East Asia or Korea. Finally, a significant number of unskilled workers leave, mostly for India. In 2009–10, the combined remittances from Nepalis working abroad totalled NPR 231 billion (USD 3 billion). It is estimated that an additional USD 500 million enters Nepal through informal remittance channels. In 2009–10, remittances accounted for 25 per cent of GDP.

The source of inspiration for the *bipalis* is not hard to identify either: impoverishment and the lack of employment. The financial success and social respect earned by returning *bipalis* adds to the allure of working in foreign lands. Without strong economic growth, hardly any examples of entrepreneurial success and the continuation of a feudal system of *chakari* and nepotism, working in Nepal has held no promise or hope. It has also made many ambitious young Nepali look beyond her borders. With the establishment of multi-party democracy in 1990, steps were taken to liberalize the market for foreign labour. The most significant of the democratic government's acts was the decentralization of passport control so that issuing passports was now the responsibility of the district offices. Until then, passports were issued only by the Ministry of Foreign Affairs in Kathmandu. However, with this move to decentralization, anyone could obtain a passport from their local district office within a week of applying for a passport. The availability and ease of access to passports had an immediate and drastic impact on labour migration. Suddenly, every Nepali had the opportunity to become a *bipali*.

The situation for a villager in the far western hills of Nepal is getting increasingly difficult. Villagers with no land of their own would have to work another person's land to make ends meet. Someone born in the 1960s in such a situation would have grown up in a family where his father would not be home for up to eight months each year. His mother, in the meanwhile, would toil away on someone else's land to earn enough to feed herself and the family. He would be acutely aware of ever-present hunger and the limited availability of food. By the time he turned fourteen he would have half a dozen brothers and sisters and would likely even be married himself. Once sixteen and already a father, he would follow in the footsteps of his own father and head down to Mumbai and work as a manual labourer earning his keep and saving as much as he could to take back home. By the time he was twenty-five, he and his wife would have a family bigger than they could afford, and since life in the village would only have become tougher, they and their children would starve. Even so, when his oldest son turned eighteen in the early 1990s, he could send him to the Gulf by taking a loan from the local landlord. Then things would suddenly take a turn for the better, this son sending in enough to pay back the loan and buy enough food. Seeing the money to be made in the Gulf, the father himself or his second son might also go off to the Gulf.

Before the liberalization of passport control, the majority of Nepali workers used to work in India with official estimates placing India as the primary destination for over 93 per cent of all *bipalis*. By 1991, with the liberalization of passports, this had already dropped to 89 per cent,[4] which was also matched by an increase in the amount of money being remitted into Nepal. Since the early 1970s, the amount of money being remitted to Nepal has gradually been increasing, reflecting the increase in the numbers of Nepali workers going abroad, to a variety of destinations. Remittance effectively doubled in five years from Rs 90.7 million in 1974–75 to Rs 216.8 million in 1980–81 and then tripled by the end of the 1980s to Rs 676.8 million. These figures are recorded by the Nepal Rastra Bank and represent the volume of money that was transferred into Nepal through official channels. However, there is a significant informal mechanism for the transfer of money, which would not be factored in or accounted for in the Rastra Bank estimates.

The disparity between actual remittance flows and those that are recorded by the Rastra Bank is best displayed when one takes into account unofficial estimates of USD 150 million of British and India Gurkha remittances during the mid-1980s, at a time when official remittance figures were only around USD 100 million. The primary reason for this disparity lies in the fact that the bulk of remittances coming in from India are from seasonal workers, who do not use formal channels and often carry their meagre earnings back home with them. Given the volume of such workers, these earnings form a significant but unaccounted contribution to the national GDP. There is an extensive informal system, a culture and society of recruitment and money transfer that has developed in Nepal. Migratory patterns suggest that once a person has established himself abroad, he will attempt to draw his relatives and local villagers to the same place. This allows for a semblance of home away from home and provides a social security net in case of sickness or injury. The act of being able to place others into jobs abroad also means an increase in stature for the recruiter.

Along with this support network, the collection of relatives and villagers also allows for an easier and cheaper means of money transfer. Usually when one worker goes home on leave, all other workers within his circle will send money home through him. This avoids the cost of transferring money through informal or formal channels. Workers also tend to use the informal *hundi* and *hawala* systems of money transfer. *Hundi* and *hawala* are informal money transfer systems that rely on an informal business transaction mechanisms and are often part of money laundering rackets. The attractiveness of the *hundi* system is both economic and cultural. Economically, *hundi* is cheaper, faster, more versatile, and more far reaching geographically than banks or money transfer companies. Culturally, the people who run the system are trustworthy members of the community and there is some tie of kinship, ethnicity or personal relation between the users and the operators. The operators generally tend to make money through a minimal service charge or take advantage of the exchange rate spread.

Till the mid-1990s, the government of Nepal, major donor institutions, private businesses and scholars saw rural Nepal as consisting almost entirely of subsistence farms. Although there was some mention in the local media and some donor recommendations of the need for more information on the migratory patterns of Nepali workers, there was hardly any interest in migration until the late 1990s. Unknown to the rulers, ground realities were forcing people to adapt and change according to the needs of the local and global economy. Matters were moving much faster than the policy makers, and often policies were moving even slower than the policy makers. The Nepali government's historical amnesia might play a part in its inability to capitalize on a remittance economy and labour industry that was established along with the modern nation of Nepal. The major cultural factors for this relative blindness should also not be discounted, for going abroad anywhere beyond India was considered equivalent to losing one's caste and culture. Going to work in another country, although a means to get rich quickly was, among the elites, frowned upon as being 'unpatriotic'.

Most importantly, the lack of government interest and involvement in this entire industry reveals a stark lack of understanding of the national economy amongst the ruling elite and consequently, an inability to shape the economy.

Conflict Pushes, Remittance Surges

The escalation of the Maoist insurgency and the growing problem of the conflict during the 1990s, added yet another incentive for young men and women to seek employment in foreign lands. The sudden rise in foreign workers was a boon in disguise for the Nepali economy. With hardly any economic growth in the country, the growing volume of remittance money flowing into the country was able to prop up the national economy, enabling it to avoid a complete collapse. The surge in remittance flow also helped bring into public debate the previously little talked-about economy of foreign labour migration. A growing realization of the volume of money involved in the business of labour migration, quickly got the private sector interested. However, the government was to take almost another decade for the establishment of a body to address the needs of these Nepali workers. The lack of government regulation and worker rights protection has possibly ruined the lives of countless poor Nepali workers who were cheated by swindlers and shady manpower agencies. The lack of any regulations allowed for massive amounts of profiteering and large-scale fraudulent activities. Nonetheless, deteriorating economic conditions at home meant that the number of Nepali workers going abroad in search of work kept on increasing.

With such a booming labour supply industry, the private sector quickly got into the act both in terms of supplying labour and ensuring proper training and in setting up channels for the flow of remittance money. The objective of manpower or human recruitment agencies is to serve as a link between Nepali workers seeking work and companies who need workers in another country. These agencies are responsible for matching the worker with a job and after selection, arranging visas, air travel, and documentation. They are also responsible for conducting medical check-ups, job orientation and training, to make sure the worker has some understanding of his job. However, most of these agencies have acquired a poor reputation and are approached with suspicion. This is largely due to a weak government that cannot ensure that these companies follow standard regulations that ensure the protection of the workers.

Although manpower agencies have established themselves as the primary channels through which to gain access to foreign employment, the lack of trust in them has emphasized the importance of informal channels. Particularly in India and more recently in some regions of the Gulf, entire Nepali villages have captured the niche market of migrant workers. This has led to local migrant labour monopolies; for instance, it is estimated that almost all Nepali migrant workers in and around the city of Bangalore are from Bajhang district in Nepal. Such trends have been established in the Gulf as well.

The volume of the migrants and their importance in the national economy is by now fully appreciated and valued. Part of the reason the importance of overseas remittances remained unrealized for so long was because the money came in through informal, undocumented channels. The private sector and Rastra Bank, since the late 1990s, finally got into the game, realizing the great volumes of remittance that were flowing into the country. Before the Rastra Bank loosened its monetary policy in the 1990s, it had placed a tight control on the circulation of foreign currencies in Nepal. With restrictions on the amount of foreign currency a person could withdraw or obtain, a rampant black market for these currencies existed. Due to the high demand for foreign currencies, both the remitter and recipient/operator stood to gain by carrying out transactions at a rate higher than the official exchange rate. In an attempt to divert more of the remittance flow through official channels, the Rastra Bank loosened its monetary policy in the 1990s by granting manpower agencies the right to open foreign currency accounts in Nepali commercial banks. It has also slackened its grip on foreign currency supplies for Nepali citizens leaving the country. This has reduced the importance of the foreign currency black market and has had a positive effect in bringing more remittances in through formal channels. With the private sector getting its act together and starting to reach out across the country, offering cheap money transfer services, a significant amount of remittance has been diverted through formal channels.

The Educational Pull

For many Nepali youths, migration is alluring given the limitations of the local economy in allowing them lifestyles that accord with the youth consumer trends marketed by Hollywood and Bollywood. For many this means getting into a university anywhere outside Nepal and not looking back. The growth of the educational consultancy industry facilitated this trend among the youth. The private sector benefited from a class of society that actively pursued the focussed quest of moving out of Nepal. While the youth wanted to escape the suffocating confines of the Nepali economy and society, their parents too were ambitious, wanting to see their children move into the developed world as successful individuals.

Many Nepali students, in following this dream of foreign education, went abroad to mediocre universities and worked full time to pay for both their part-time education and the loans that they had amassed in making their way overseas. Many may have worked at a menial job like dishwashing, but nevertheless enjoyed the freedom of Western society and the priceless feeling of independence. This was all it took to convince them that staying abroad was the way to go. Back home, all that awaited them was a socially backward family and an economy where they could not get a job. They could not work menial jobs at home for it would be a loss of face to have studied abroad only to work in a menial or clerical position. Thus, they chose to stay on and toil and enjoy the fruits of their labour and as they worked, they truly did progress, for having known the absence of wealth, they were keenly attuned to attaining it.

Those with a steady job then came home and married the girl their parents had picked for them. For the girl this was a ticket to freedom. More so than boys, a girl truly valued the freedom that life outside Nepal offered. She no longer had to remain confined by the socio-cultural norms of Nepali society and could develop her full potential and follow dreams that could never become a reality in Nepal. These parachute weddings* not only allowed for easier migration but also allowed the family back home to ease its concern at the possibility of having to entertain a foreign spouse in the family.

NRN Dreams and Nepal

For many young men born in the villages and sent to school by their parents, working on the farms in the 1990s no longer held much interest. Having passed the School Leaving Certificate (SLC) examinations, considered quite an achievement in the village, the general consensus would be that he was too qualified to be working on the farm. However, the employment market in Nepal remains limited and nepotistic and he finds it impossible to get a good job in the city. Back home, he sees how all the older youth in the village have left for the Gulf and are regularly sending money back home. In exploring the scope of work in the Gulf, he meets a manpower agency's representative who easily sells to him the lure of foreign lands. Seeing this as his opportunity to make it big, he prepares his passport and all the necessary documents. With the support of his father, he mortgages most of his land to raise the Rs 80,000 necessary for him to pay the broker and get all the necessary documents ready. He then goes for a round of medical check-ups and gets a briefing at the manpower agency on the nature and scope of his work. Then he finds himself at the airport wearing a baseball cap with the manpower agency's logo on it, standing with a group of people who will be his unlikely friends and family for this new journey and experience. As he rides the escalators up, he senses himself moving towards a brighter future. The entire airport experience for him is new, frightening and yet marvellous. He is seeing and hearing things that he has never been

---

*A reference to the swift two-week trips made to Nepal by *bipali*s, to pick up wives.

exposed to in his village. After his first ever flight, he lands in Doha, is picked up by the local agent there and whisked away in a van with his friends. They are all enthralled by the skyscrapers and malls and fancy shops. Now for the next two years he will work like there is no tomorrow, but the sound of Nepali in his ears as he works with his Nepali friends keeps him going and deep in his heart, he sees a bright future, a motorcycle, a house in the city, and kids in school learning new languages.

At present, the bulk of remittance inflows from migrant workers are doing little to support economic growth and job creation within the country. Instead, the majority of the money is put into real estate, which has created a considerable boom in the construction and housing market and led to a considerable appreciation of land. Houses have been built as a means to earn income through rent. However, with everyone seeking to build a house, the supply of rentable houses has far outstripped the demand for them. This harkens back to the rent-seeking orientation towards wealth and wealth creation in Nepal. There is a serious lack of effort on part of both the government and the private sector in exploring ways in which to reinvest this cash inflow into long-term growth engines. The country should also be thinking along the lines of maximizing remittance inflows by adding value to the labour it provides. By ensuring its migrant workers are moving up the value chain, it not only secures better pay and work for migrant Nepali workers but also ensures higher volumes of remittance inflows. Incidentally, it is when *bipali*s move up this chain that they turn into NRNs (non-resident Nepali). A *bipali* is a Nepali working in a foreign country and sending money back as remittance to support a family, while an NRN is a Nepali living in a foreign country *with* his immediate family.

The inflow of remittances tells only half the economic story of *bipali*s and NRNs. There are an increasing number of Nepali citizens who not only migrate abroad but make their destinations their new homes. An interesting feature of the Nepali diaspora is how close they still are to their Nepali roots. There is a sense of pride in being from Nepal; the strong cultural and traditional influence of Nepali culture does not dissipate with distance. A community *Mha Puja* or celebration of Nepal *Sambat* (calendar) of the Newars is as important as *dasain* or an exhibition of a Nepali artist's work. People flock to watch Nepali concerts and films. The diaspora is emerging as a remarkable market for the arts. As other South Asian countries have started realizing in the past decade, the biggest market for the arts is often the diaspora.

The sense of a strong cultural identity binds NRNs to Nepal. Their zeal for the Nepali state and politics is but an indication of their interest in Nepal. Many NRNs are searching for a means to invest in Nepal, many are actively contemplating the idea of returning to Nepal and still more would like to try short stints working in Nepal. Although a general atmosphere of gloom shrouds their views on Nepal, the will to do something for the motherland remains strong since having left is almost seen as an NRN's original sin. The myth of 'I shall return back home one day and change it', remains embedded in the NRN mindset from the days that they aspired to seek their fortunes abroad. The Nepali diaspora, although a considerable source of income through remittance and a potential source of investment in Nepal, also needs to be understood as Nepal's loss of some of the best human resources the country is producing. Exporting our human resources cannot be a long-term strategy, but should instead be a means to further develop existing human resources for better and more effective use in the future.

PART III

UNLEASHING NEPAL

The chapters till now have perhaps presented an overly grim picture of the Nepali economy and its future development potential. However, the intention was to provide a critical analysis of the past as well as the present, as a way to chart a more productive future of accelerated and inclusive economic growth.

Nepal's political parties decided to come together to fight against King Gyanendra's direct rule in November 2005. They approached the then-underground Maoists to join their campaign for the reinstatement of the parliament dissolved by the king. In April 2006, after a nineteen-day non-violent popular street-level protest referred to popularly as Jana Andolan II, the king stepped down and reinstated the parliament. The monarchy was abolished on 28 May 2008. An interim government under the leadership of Prime Minister Girija Prasad Koirala then led the nation to its first constituent assembly election which subsequently led to the establishment of a Maoist-majority government in September 2008. The constituent assembly saw four different coalitions in power and four prime ministers, and yet none of them could complete writing the constitution despite two extensions, after which the constituent assembly was dissolved in May 2012. However, the peace and reconciliation agreement between the political parties and the Maoists on the political front eased nerves all around and immediately brought the sagging economy into focus.

In the next four chapters, attempts are made to present solutions to problems analysed in the earlier chapters while also generating ideas for unleashing Nepal's potential. The chapters discuss mechanisms of alleviating poverty and creating wealth, scaling up to take advantage of available opportunities, using youth as an engine of productivity and growth and last but not least, redefining Nepal's economic boundaries. These are discussed with a positive frame of mind, dreaming and visioning for a Nepal that will be a better country in all aspects for every Nepali.

9

ALLEVIATING POVERTY, CREATING WEALTH

The reinstatement of peace has allowed Nepal to focus on development and economic issues with a renewed urgency. The country has emerged from the turbulence of a decade-long insurgency in better shape than most critics might have expected. The situation could have been much worse. Had the king resisted his removal, had the Maoists pushed for a People's Republic (along the lines of Mao's China) or had the Nepali people grown complacent and not resisted the king's undemocratic dissolution of parliament, things could have turned out very differently. The escalation of the People's War in 2001, and the extreme state responses to it, had created the possibility of a dramatic escalation in violence and brutality. The worst case scenario of massive bloodshed in form of a full-scale civil war was avoided, but this itself is not a reason for optimism. Perhaps the most valuable realization from those tumultuous times is that the Nepali people will not accept constant violence as a means to solve any problem and that all political players in Nepal are aware of this and abide by it.

For Nepal to truly progress in measurable and human terms, it has to set into motion economic growth that can include the poorest of the poor. In so doing, it must not compromise on Nepal's hard-earned civil liberties and democratic government or on the entrepreneurial spirit necessary to create a vibrant economy. Unfortunately, post-conflict Nepal has joined the league of South Asian politics and has adopted the Indian states of Uttar Pradesh and Bihar as its role models—politics is about ethnicity, goon power and financial clout. Yet, irrespective of the political climate, there appears to be a clear consensus on the agenda for the future—the economy. The challenge that Nepal now faces is bringing about an economic transformation in order to alleviate poverty and move Nepal up the development ladder from a Least Developed Country (LDC) as defined by the World Bank, to a respectable developing country. The World Bank defines poverty as living with an income level of or less than USD 1.25 per day. By this definition, 24 per cent of all Nepali citizens live below the poverty line.[1]

The Maoists are yet to resolve the internal bag of contradictions and dilemmas that are a product of their own history, power base and the economic intentions for which they fought the decade-long People's War. On the one hand, they have to meet the expectations of their cadres who fought a ten-year war based on Maoist ideals of redistributive economics and far-reaching land reform. On the other hand, they have to meet the expectations of a significant section of the populace, who desire a vibrant and prosperous economy based on entrepreneurship and economic liberalization. To add to these complications, the Maoists are well aware of the failure of a series of centralized governments in Nepal and realize the difficulty of implementing anything close to a Chinese growth model. Further challenging such a model is the level of integration between the Indian and Nepali economies. The similar culture, open borders and a shared interest in television soaps and Bollywood films have already allowed the boom in entrepreneurship in India to create ripples in Nepal.

The Business of Wealth Creation

One of the primary benefits of entrepreneurship and a vibrant economy is that the creation of wealth it stimulates inevitably leads to the alleviation of poverty. Government initiative alone has consistently proven to be of limited success in tackling poverty. Even in cases, like China, where the government set upon the task of poverty reduction, it did so by promoting business and liberalizing its economy. The simplest way of ensuring wealth creation is to create free, fair and competitive markets, which are accessible to all levels of society, class and caste. Although this is an idealistic vision, it retains a level of structural realism that utopian societies, such as those envisioned by the Maoists in their early conflict days, cannot match. The structural resilience and flexibility of democratic and market-oriented governments in comparison to ideological communist regimes attests to the more successful strategy of the former. The primary reason that an open society is more likely to create wealth is that people in such societies are secure in the knowledge that their rights—to do business, create wealth and earn it—are all protected by the law. I assert that wealth cannot be created without the existence of a private sector that has the right to do business. In this, wealth mimics democratic governance, as it is created by the people, for the people and belongs to the people who earn it. While poverty can be understood as a complete lack of wealth, wealth is a luxury beyond subsistence. Wealth is created by first creating job opportunities, investment opportunities, entrepreneurial assistance, a secure business environment and stable political governance.

People who live in poverty do not and cannot create wealth. A subsistence level of existence restricts people in terms of opportunities and capabilities and forces them to focus only on survival. It is also important to distinguish between being wealthy and being rich, wealth is not just being rich, but the ability to become richer through the investment and utilization of one's riches. Wealth is created by people working above the poverty line, individually or through the creation of small enterprises and cooperatives. The first prerequisite for wealth creation is to ensure that people at the bottom of the pyramid are assured of basic necessities. Only then do they have the luxury of exploring opportunities, taking small risks, and engaging in wealth creating activities in the economy. Alternatively, wealth can be created through the creation of employment opportunities in large enterprises. It is true that large enterprises initially require massive capital investments, making wealth a necessary prerequisite for the creation of additional wealth. Poverty can only be reduced when it is possible for those without wealth to take part in the project of wealth creation, either through employment or individual entrepreneurship. Therefore, the twin-pronged approach of creating wealth through creating job opportunities in large enterprises and creating of entrepreneurs in micro and small enterprises, must be pursued.

Neither a government dependent on foreign aid nor a plethora of development agencies can generate wealth as they are not in the business of wealth creation and only disburse money. Poverty can only be addressed when the poor can participate in the private sector through ownership as shareholders or as employees in large enterprises or as self-employed people in micro and small enterprises. The poor can only participate in wealth creation if barriers to their entry into the private sector are reduced. It is in ensuring a level playing field, that the government, donor agencies and civil society can best serve the Nepali people. To make this happen, Nepal must embark on the path of becoming a *capitalist welfare state*, a state that believes in private enterprise as well as in the welfare of its citizens.

The transformation of Nepal into a capitalist welfare state requires a consideration of:

- how Nepal will integrate rapidly into the global economy;
- how the private sector can be reformed;
- how the government can facilitate this process of reform;
- how the multilateral and bi-lateral aid agencies can contribute;
- what role the plethora of community-based organizations can play;
- how partnerships can be forged between these different players.

The remainder of this chapter and the following three chapters will consider precisely the above issues.

Refining and Embracing Globalization

Globalization can be understood as the seamless process of integration between global markets and citizens worldwide. It is important to understand globalization not just from the perspective of the market economy, but also to consider it from a socio-cultural perspective as the simultaneous globalization of attitudes, ideologies and practices. These range from human rights campaigns to animal rights activism, from religion to the horrors of terrorism, and from the spread of culinary delights to the sound of music. For Nepal, the challenge is not just one of market integration but of identifying and capitalizing on its unique brand and identity, so that it can contribute to and benefit from the socio-economic process of globalization.

For Nepal to truly capitalize upon the advantages that globalization has to offer, it needs to fundamentally reorient itself and re-brand itself on the world stage. It can no longer stick to its old aristocratic views of isolationism and protectionism and must embrace the dynamic and horizontal world of the twenty-first century. Nepal has to lock the symbols of its archaic past into world-class museums in Nepal, and start marketing and leveraging the sacred symbols of culture that are housed in such museums. It nonetheless has to preserve history and meaning—not as an impediment to progress but as a tool for marketing. It is critical that Nepal and the Nepali people participate in this new age of consumerism and remain in tune with changing fads and fashion. In participating in the global community, Nepal must also understand the nature of consumerism and learn how best it can capitalize upon its unique location and history. Its rich history and culture provides a unique setting for tourism of all strains while its location has potential for production and industry in both the agricultural and energy sectors.

Nepal also needs to modernize its mindset and lifestyle, it has to change its calendar from an archaic Bikram* calendar and start

---

*The Bikram calendar is a solar calendar which is sixty-two years ahead of the Gregorian calendar. It begins in mid-April and is inconsistent on how many days are in each month of the year. It is also occasionally inconsistent on the number of months in a year.

using the Gregorian calendar used worldwide. It has to get into tune with global financial markets and let the sun shine on a weekly Sunday holiday, instead of on Saturdays. It needs to institute a five-day work week, but operate 24 x 7 otherwise and also ration out public holidays.* It needs a stricter work ethic and a working schedule that does not end at 4 p.m. during winter just because it gets dark earlier. Efficiency will never become the norm when workers come in an hour late, take an extra hour of lunch and two half-hour tea breaks and then leave an hour early. Finally, Nepal needs to smarten up and fully support the English language as the primary national language for all Nepali people so that Nepalis are fluent in the language of globalization. Importantly, this does not mean forgetting other languages and dialects, but understanding that a common language without historical baggage in Nepal, which is globally acceptable as well, could only be an asset to a country that is trying to make its way into the global mainstream.

The reasons for the above recommendations are apparent—globalization cannot occur within the confines of a national system and context. The Nepali economy needs to be integrated into the global economy and Nepal must realize it cannot dictate the rules of engagement. This is a result of the relatively minor role Nepal plays in the global economy. As a country, Nepal is competing with all the other developing countries for limited global economic resources, whether it is foreign aid, foreign investment, tourists or trade. If the Nepali economy is unsuccessful in reorienting itself, it will be relegated to the far fringes of the global economy. Nepal as a nation and the Nepali people as members of a global community must realize that integration into the global economy will be difficult if we use a calendar that occasionally has only eleven months.† Unlike the United States, which is a superpower, Nepal

---

*In 2008, there were fifty-two public holidays and even more after Nepal became a republic.

†There was a strong public debate to keep the Bikram calendar at only eleven months in the year 2066.

cannot ignore the metric system. We cannot integrate into the global economy without adopting mobile commerce technologies like iPhones, iPods and PDAs. We cannot develop standard international practices without adopting newer versions of banking software, GPS systems in cars, online ticketing systems for flights and the like, across industries. If we are to trade Nepali shares on the New York Stock Exchange or have brokers in Hong Kong trading shares on the Nepal Stock Exchange, we need to adhere to and adopt the fundamental structures of the global economy.

The global financial crisis that escalated at the end of 2008 is evidence of a world which has become a smaller place, as a share price fall in one country affected the stock markets of many others. Nepal was not substantially impacted by the crisis due to its limited integration into the global financial system. In fact, the global meltdown could actually provide some unique benefits and opportunities to Nepal. The lack of global trust in the financial markets and a strong unwillingness to invest in financial instruments opens the door to investments in brick and mortar, infrastructure investments. This could be a huge boost to the hydropower, real estate and agro-based industries in Nepal. Another opportunity is the incentive for not-for-profit foundations and conservative investment trusts, to put a portion of their funds into less developed countries which have limited exposure to global financial markets. This allows for a greater diversity in portfolios, a safer investment spread and also directly benefits Least Developed Countries (LDCs) like Nepal. There is a significant opportunity now for Nepali social entrepreneurs to tap into social venture capital funds that focus on investments into social ventures that would like to cover basic interest costs, which means that these ventures gain access to capital at an interest rate that just covers inflation. Commercial firms can tap enterprise funds that are willing to invest in small and medium enterprises in LDCs.

Nepal also needs to learn how to play its LDC card in a globalized world carrying the moral burden of eradicating poverty. It needs to understand and take advantage of the preferential treatment it will receive in the Bay of Bengal Initiative for Multi-sectoral Technical and Economic Cooperation (BIMSTEC) a treaty amongst seven countries on the Bay of Bengal rim and the World Trade Organization (WTO). For instance, exports of pharmaceutical products from Nepal to Europe will still enjoy a duty benefit while exports from other countries to Europe won't. While Nepal, as an LDC, possesses the right to exercise the advantages stretching non-tariff barriers like different levying various cess, fees and taxes in addition to customs tariff and buying enough time to make their own industries and services competitive. It is important that this should not be seen as an opportunity to extend protectionism but instead as an opportunity to catch up. Globalization comes with its own risks and Nepal as a nation must be willing to take on and manage these risks.

Nepal must learn from the experiences of other developing countries as they sought to integrate into the global economy. For instance, the closure of the Thai airports for a week in December 2008 highlights the need for seamless global operations and the risks in failing to achieve that goal. The closure of the airports in Thailand pushed the supply chain of computer suppliers in the United States out of gear and cost the Thai economy as well as the computer companies in the US a considerable amount of money. Taking heed of these developments and learning from its own past failures, Nepal needs to understand that integration into the global economy cannot happen if constant labour disputes, strikes, inconsistent policies and low productivity govern the nation's economic life.

Towards a More Ambitious Private Sector

Although Chapter 4 evokes pictures of a private sector with as many problems as the government of Nepal does, the private sector's freedom from a bureaucratic deadweight gives it the opportunity to quickly and effectively mend its ways. The future of the private sector depends on its ability to realize its own inadequacies and to lead the nation in the goal of wealth creation. The central quality the private sector needs is ambition—it has to be ambitious enough to take on the global economy. For this, it needs to step outside the box of protectionism, believe in itself and develop the necessary capabilities and competencies to compete on the global stage. Selling instant noodles in Sikkim in India can no longer be the ultimate goal of international trade and sending night watchmen to Mumbai, cannot be called competing in the global economy.

The private sector needs to forge alliances with multinationals, seek foreign capital and technology, venture beyond the country and bury protectionist attitudes. Simultaneously, it has to work on developing professionalism and building contemporary administrative structures that follow ethical codes and believe in making adequate disclosures. Although regulating the private sector is the responsibility of the government, it is the private sector that must step up to the plate and dictate the most appropriate regulatory frameworks, to ensure that best practice models are being followed. The private sector can no longer be complacent about a lackadaisical government and must realize that local regulatory frameworks that do not match international standards affect their credibility in the international market. In a global economy, it is safer and easier to do business with firms from nations with regulatory models that match international standards.

The building of strong private sector institutions which assist the government in policy formulation and act as advocacy bodies for industry requires a paradigm shift within the private sector. The private sector has to move away from its dependence on political nexuses, kowtowing and lobbying for individual gains. Instead, it has to work by means of institutions led by business people and managed by professionals. Their lobbies should target policies that support fair competition and expansion opportunities. Business groups like FNCCI and CNI should include businesses based on their contribution to taxes and the number of people they employ instead of cobbling together the motley crew of organizations that currently come under their umbrella. Madhukar Rana, a former finance minister and an economist, suggests the formation of a National Economic Council along the lines of a similar council in India, comprising members of both the private sector and the government. The council would be composed of industry specific sub-committees, each of which would be jointly headed by the concerned secretary from the government and either the head of the concerned private sector association or the CEO of a prominent private enterprise.

The root cause of political corruption lies in the inability of political parties to raise funds legitimately. This forces them to resort to taking political donations illegitimately, in return for favours. The private sector needs to work with the government to formulate policies that enable the funding of political parties legitimately and most importantly, accountably and transparently. Each business should be given the right to contribute a certain percentage of their profits or turnover to a political party, thereby ensuring proper tax disclosures by companies who want to play politics and by politicians who want to collect contributions. These contributions should be tax deductible, but would require political parties to issue financial audits and public disclosures of their collections and expenses.

Privatize the Private Sector

Unfortunately, in Nepal, the private sector has even lagged behind the government in reforming itself. The private sector needs to move away from the rent-seeking, power-and-opportunity-grabbing mindset and needs to develop long-term sustainable practices to ensure they are profitable, growth-oriented and make a larger impact on society. The segregation of ownership and management is a must and there is no other option but to corporatize and inculcate professionalism. Succession planning for family businesses is a must and embracing global benchmarks in strategy, accounting and tax practices needs to be used to gain comparative and competitive advantage.

The private sector must walk its talk on Corporate Social Responsibility (CSR) and pursue corporate social opportunities (CSO). While corporations should focus on their core operations of making profits, they can pursue CSR through creating private not-for-profit foundations. However, the challenge for the corporations would be to go beyond CSR and pursue the corporate social opportunities (CSO) that exist. With one of the highest

Gini-coefficients* in the world, there are tremendous opportunities for people at the bottom of the pyramid in Nepal. These could range from tapping self-help groups to market products, creating procurement centres in rural areas or the distribution of better goods and services at lower costs. For instance, village centres can be created that can only buy local products like agricultural produce and handicrafts but that can also sell through these centres basic commodities that the rural people consume for themselves, such as agricultural inputs and materials required in the process of producing handicrafts.

In the future, the most successful players in the Nepali private sector will be those who are the first movers in grabbing opportunities that the existence of a large low-income population provides. For instance, less than an eighth of Nepal's population is linked to formal banking channels and less than a percentage participates in capital markets. There is therefore tremendous opportunity to serve this latent demand of the population through leveraging technology. The possibility of transferring money through using mobile phones would immediately make services of money transfer available to an additional 10 per cent of the population. Similarly, starting community mutual funds by using just a few thousand of rupees collected by the self-help groups in villages can increase their participation in the capital markets substantially.

The private sector and business people must lead by example. They have to repackage themselves for the public eye as responsible citizens of the nation and shed their image of profiteering and racketeering. Businesses have to present themselves as professional entities with long-term goals that prosper along with the nation and not as rent-seeking arbitrage units. For this, they need to involve themselves in consumer education, inculcate strong corporate governance and revive the culture of the 'giver' who helps social causes. If there were no Bill Gates, there would be no Microsoft and there would be no Gates Foundation, which contributed USD 3.5 billion in 2011 and over USD 25 billion since

---

*The Gini coefficient is a measure of inequality in wealth and income distribution.

inception to the needy sections of the world.[2] Historically, Nepali businesses and business people have been strong believers in philanthropy and have contributed significantly to their local communities by building social service delivery institutions, be it the Rajbhandary business family supporting Dhulikhel Hospital, the Kedias starting eye hospitals or the Khetan group supporting schools and universities, working by means of separately administered trusts called *Guthis*.* Reconnecting with this past, Nepali businesses can build solid foundations in social service delivery for the firms of tomorrow.

A Different Role for the Government

The government in a capitalist welfare state† has two significant roles. One is ensuring that it provides an environment for private enterprise to flourish; the other is ensuring an equitable delivery of welfare to all its citizens. As Dr Ram Saran Mahat, a former finance minister and senior Congress leader puts it, 'Growth will depend on the future model of politics—free flow of ideas, real competitive politics and liberal values.' For this, the government needs a clear understanding of its role as a regulator and as a service provider.

The government must realize, understand and believe in ensuring and protecting economic freedom as a non-negotiable. Economic freedom is directly correlated to economic growth. The collapse of the Soviet Union and Eastern Europe in the late 1980s adequately demonstrates this. On the other hand Sri Lanka, despite grappling with three decades of civil war, has persevered with the provision of economic freedom and thus ensured steady economic growth. It is of paramount importance that any government formed by any political party should never compromise by even suggesting that

---

*Guthis are trusts that are formed in the interest of their beneficiaries and regulated by a separate law.

†A capitalist welfare state is here defined as a country with economic freedom and free enterprise but with the state ensuring the welfare and freedom of its citizens.

economic freedoms might be curtailed. This would have a significantly detrimental effect on investor confidence. Further, it is important to understand economic freedom as not just the freedom to do business but also the freedom to shut, close and exit business. For instance, as discussed in Chapter 4, the lack of bankruptcy laws and the non-implementation of insolvency-related laws in Nepal scare investors, as there are no exit strategies available in case of failure. Nepal also needs the next wave of economic reforms in a 'flattened world'. The government needs to learn its lessons from the first wave of economic reforms in the early 1990s and the positive impact they had. For example, allowing money transfer firms to compete for remittance from abroad has brought remittances under a legitimate framework, thereby increasing tax revenues.

Similarly, by allowing Nepali citizens to invest abroad in an organized way, Nepal can take advantage of globalization. For example, a businessperson in east Nepal understands well the market of nearby Siliguri or Sikkim across the border in India, while a business person in far west Nepal understands well the business opportunities across the border in Uttaranchal. Neither particularly understands the opportunity in Kathmandu, yet they cannot legitimately invest and capitalize upon their understanding of neighbouring countries' markets. Current investments abroad are all illegitimate as they contravene the Foreign Investment Prohibition Act 1964 which stipulates that no Nepali can invest outside Nepal.[3] This needs to be replaced by a Regulation of Investment in Foreign Countries Act, which will benefit the state in the same manner as allowing the establishment of money transfer firms has. Economic and financial prudence would suggest that Nepalis be allowed to invest in the economic growth of China, India and other neighbouring countries. The Nepali national investing in a Nepali fund that invests overseas would have the benefit of getting returns not limited to the Nepali economy. If we take the Grindlays Bank multiplier we discussed in Chapter 3 where a Rs 10,000 investment in 1988 would have grown to Rs 15 million in twenty years despite taking a cash dividend of Rs 1.5 million over the last twenty years, every Rs 1000 invested can become millions over two decades. We should not prevent Nepalis from availing of this world of opportunity outside Nepal. We need to recall that India's growth in the past couple of years has been fuelled by Indian investments abroad wherein Indian investors have been able to increase the value of their portfolios through the growth of assets in the developed world.

The fewer restrictions the government places on the flow of money, the greater the benefit to general investors. In the same way that Nepal became the first south Asian country with a digital telephone exchange in 1985, it could become the first South Asian country to allow 'virtual commercial financial transactions', or electronic and mobile financial transactions (e-commerce and m-commerce), allowing investors to transfer money and transact financial instruments like shares using mobile and online technologies. Reforms are not rocket science—a copy of the *Doing Business Report* published by the World Bank that ranks countries based on the ease of doing business in and with them, provides a list of best practices,[4] emulating some of which will take Nepal a long way on the road to economic success.

Critically, such reforms would mean the state taking on the role and responsibility of a strong regulator. In an age of automation, regulation is best done through automation, be it automating the entire functions of the Company Registrar's Office that regulates the registration and operations of companies, or the Central Bank that regulates the financial and monetary sector. The government has to embrace technology. Additionally, the government has to understand the value of outsourcing and explore the possibility of outsourcing select regulatory functions to credible international companies. It has to accept that outsourcing the customs function at the International Airport to an international company or outsourcing the Auditor General's function to international audit companies, does not compromise the nation's sovereignty.

Six Areas of Reform

There are six areas of reform that the government, with the assistance of a strong private sector, needs to pursue: land reform, tax reform, capital market reform, financial sector reform, labour reform and fiscal reform.

Land reform debates have been limited to putting a ceiling on land ownership and redistributing land seized from owners of large tracts. Often, redistribution involves selective distribution based on the possibility of developing a future vote bank for one political party or the other. A better approach to land reform is through the management of revenues from land rather than land itself. For instance, someone who owns a *ropani** of land valued at Rs 320 million (around Rs 62,000 per square feet) in downtown Kathmandu, currently will not pay land taxes in excess of Rs 28,300 per annum, less than a 0.01 per cent tax on value. Clearly, land ownership taxes should be based on the market value of the land, thereby taxing owners on the basis of higher value rather than larger plots. Land revenue management requires a shift from a land area paradigm to a land value paradigm, allowing the government to determine a revenue system based on land value that maximizes its revenue. This revenue can in turn finance or subsidize housing schemes or provide agricultural land for the poor.

Additionally, an Inheritance Tax can be levied on the transfer of the ownership of land beyond a certain value, thereby not only increasing revenue streams but also helping transform the mentality of the urban Nepali who lives off rents from ancestral properties. To initiate such land reform, it is necessary to reform the process of record keeping from handwritten records to state-of-art-digital records with a nationally networked database so that one can find out the total land holdings of a particular individual all over the country. Land reform would require the categorization and zoning of land based on usage—agricultural, commercial or residential. The land ceiling for cooperative and large-scale commercial farming by institutions also needs to be relaxed. One major reform that will be necessary in order to increase agricultural output will be the consolidation of land holdings to achieve economies of scale.

Ropani is a plot measuring 5174 square feet.

Dr Baburam Bhattarai, current finance minister of the Communist Party of Nepal (Maoist)-led government, emphasizes to the author the need for far-reaching land reforms to ensure that subsistence farming gives way to industrial and commercial farming. He prescribes farming through cooperatives to bring in scale as well as increase productivity and efficiency.

Tax reform requires changing the attitude of tax collectors rather than tinkering with pieces of legislation or the entire institutional framework. Currently, a business in Nepal pays 25 per cent Income Tax apart from 13 per cent Value Added Taxes and 5 per cent taxation on dividends earned. Apart from that, businesses have to set aside 8.33 per cent of salaries as a bonus for *Dasain* (a major festival), 10 per cent of profits as Profit Sharing Bonus, 5 per cent of profits as provisions for employee housing and in case of the hospitality industry, there is a further 10 per cent Service Charge levied on the customer. This plethora of taxes does not really encourage people to do business. Further, the people who are in the tax net are always penalized further, be it through additional taxes or harassment. People who have not paid taxes till date run scot-free and are offered low tax programmes through Voluntary Disclosure of Income Sources popularly known as VDIS, where at 10 per cent of the total income one can bleach black money into white, while people who religiously pay taxes pay a high rate of 25 per cent. The government in 2008 end brought out a provision requiring all salaried employees to deposit a day's worth of earnings into a fund that would finance unemployed youth in starting small enterprises. Successive governments come up with such populist programmes that would create funds that political appointees could manage for political gains. However, this is done at the expense of the regular tax payers, while in tangible terms, the fund has not been able to provide any employment for the unemployed. Those who are already paying taxes, pay such additional taxes, while all those who are evading taxes do not have to contribute towards such funds.

Investors are scared away by the very thought of the complicated income tax and other tax laws as well as by stories of the treatment meted out to tax payers at tax offices. They end up working through informal channels involving the tax authorities personally, which in the end, reduces government revenues. Similarly, the Custom and Excise tax systems require further reform along the lines of automating systems that will reduce the likelihood of human intervention.

Tax revenue is augmented by the easing of tax laws, simplification of processes, automation and proper implementation of laws, because all of these reforms increase business activity. This has been clearly demonstrated in India where the automation and simplification of income tax collection since 2001 has increased tax collections significantly. Tax reforms also need to address the capital formation issue by rewarding tax payers who save and invest. With urban housing becoming expensive, health care costs rising, and retirement costs soaring, there have to be tax breaks for people who invest in their own dwellings and buy health insurance or retirement fund products. The housing boom in India was due in part to the fact that payments of housing loans instalments were made tax deductible up to a certain limit.

Capital market reforms are a priority that the government has either never understood or never leveraged. A cash-strapped government should always be on the lookout for ways to encourage the raising of money. For instance, securing funds from private or public companies for infrastructure development would reduce the burden on the state exchequer. Nepal desperately needs funds to build its infrastructure and accelerate the pace of development. Money that is locked in non-performing assets like jewellery and speculative property investments needs to be released and re-invested in infrastructure and other projects, to fuel economic growth. Bringing about legislation to make commodities trading in gold, metals, etc. legitimate and bringing in legislation to allow establishment of real estate and infrastructure funds, would give people incentive to liquidate non-performing assets and invest in more productive asset-based markets. This would require a series of legislative changes, apart from a change in the mindset that making money is somehow reprehensible. When a common citizen starts investing in stocks and mutual funds to augment his/her wealth and can thus directly feel an investment in the success or failure of enterprises, the business of doing business becomes more acceptable to the public.

The investment of Rs 10,000 in Grindlays Bank (Standard Chartered Bank) building to Rs 15 million in twenty years demonstrates not only sharing of wealth but also the need for capital markets. The success of such examples in creating a public mindset favourable to the free market is apparent in India, where some vegetable vendors and daily-wage earners can relate to the fate of the Indian companies as shareholders and do not therefore think of themselves as the victims of a great class divide. For instance, anyone who has been investing a mere one-time investment of Rs 1000 in a good IPO like that of Grindlays can suddenly see their wealth swell, taking care of their children's education with dividend payments and getting their children married off through the sale of their shares. On the institutional front, the government needs to restrict itself to a regulatory role and leave the demand and supply to the markets. The role of the regulator can be augmented by allowing international credit rating agencies, legal firms, and auditing firms to operate in Nepal, as well as by raising disclosure and accounting standards to international norms by adopting systems like the International Financial Reporting System (IFRS). The critical factor would be to allow for the maturity of the money markets by instituting the necessary regulatory legislation for the establishment and operation of mutual funds, pension funds and other institutional fund management instruments. Tax laws need to recognize these funds differently, thereby making investments through such institutions secure and financially beneficial for the common man. Additionally, capital market reforms need to be augmented by financial sector reforms.

Financial sector reforms comprise a gamut of changes not only in the legislation but also in the structure and functioning of institutions such as the Nepal Rastra Bank, Nepal's central bank. While political will is critical to implement all forms of reforms, the financial sector, having a direct bearing on money, requires that politicians and bureaucrats in power walk that extra mile. The reinstatement of the Governor of the Central Bank by a court in 2001 and the sacking of the Governor of the Central Bank in 2007 are instances of a deep political-business nexus that always hinders reform. The global financial crisis of 2008 has demonstrated that the financial sector is the most difficult one to regulate but then, reforms should not be stalled just because the government wants to play a zero-risk game.

Nepal has more financial institutions than it needs. As of January 2013, there are thirty-one commercial banks, eighty-seven development banks, seventy-nine finance companies, seventy-five financial institutions of other categories licensed by Nepal Rastra Bank and over 26,000 cooperatives that also undertake financial transactions. The entry barrier has to be raised to allow entities with competencies rather than pure financial targets to enter the financial sector. Laws are required to make the financial institutions more transparent and make possible the use of financial instruments like leasing, guarantees, venture capital funds, social enterprises funds, mutual funds, and private equity. Further, mergers, acquisitions, restructuring and distress asset sales need to be facilitated by providing specific legal provisions that are currently absent. The absence of specific legal provisions relating to mergers has restrained financial institutions that intend to merge for operational efficiency or increased market share. This needs to change, as in the banking and financial services sector, more consolidation will be required to gain the economies of scale that would allow the sector to compete with global companies entering the market. Sujit Mundul, CEO Standard Chartered, remarks that in Malaysia, mergers reduced the number of local banks from twenty-four to six, which enhanced the capacities of the local banks and allowed them to compete with multinational global banks.

While reforms are required in the legislative and institutional framework of Nepal Rastra Bank and the Securities Board of Nepal, the establishment of a independent regulatory body in form of a Financial Services Commission that will enact and regulate the operations of the various commodities markets, venture capital funds, private equity funds and similar instruments will go in a long way in making funds available for existing and new business ventures.

Labour reform, at the end of 2012, has become the most critical of the reforms that business people, donors and investors alike have started demanding. Changes in the Labour Act, Trade Union Act and other relevant acts are necessary if we are to address the following four fundamental issues. First, labour wages should be linked to productivity and wages allowed to be set for different individuals doing similar jobs based on output and performance. We need to take into recognition that there are good workers and bad workers, people producing two different levels of output should not be paid the same wages. If an efficient housekeeper cleans more rooms than his or her co-worker or an efficient worker in a garment factory produces more than another co-worker, the efficient worker should have the right to earn more.

Second, negotiations between labour and employer should remain an enterprise-specific issue and should not be conducted at the industry or national level. Every time an issue emerges in a specific business organization, the national-level unions gang up against the enterprise and disrupt business creating a culture where, for instance, all workers in all hotels are involved in the negotiation of an agreement about a particular hotel.

Third, employers should be able to hire employees based on the need and seasonality of the jobs and relieve employees if there is no need for them or if there has been a disciplinary issue. Beyond the basic issues prescribed by the law, every enterprise should have the liberty to negotiate with labour depending on the nature of operations. If a hotel or travel industry negotiates wages with its workers taking into consideration the seasonality in the industry, where the number of people employed vary with tourist seasons, or if tea plantations hire more people during tea leaf-plucking season, they should be left to do so and no national-level unions should be able to interfere and secure guarantees of jobs at all times.

Finally, trade unions have to drop their political affiliations, else the vote banks that the politicians want to preserve may lead to the country's bankruptcy. The political parties that needed support from grass-roots workers to fight against feudal kings and the Panchayat regime, must understand that there is no longer a need for political affiliation of unions. Unions should be independent of political colour and focus not only on protecting the rights of workers, but also on ensuring that they contribute to larger issues like productivity and efficiency, so that the growth of the enterprise would benefit the workforce.

The rights of the labourer are protected well under the current legislation but employers are left to fend for themselves. Economic reforms taking place without reform in labour laws, will not give incentive to current investors to continue investing, let alone attract foreign investors. One of the key labour reforms in Malaysia in 1995, allowed employment contracts to be entered into freely by employers and employees. The lead article of the Malaysian Labour Act states, 'Every employee must be given a written contract of employment which states the terms and conditions of the employment, including the notice period required to terminate it.' This is a good example of a legal framework for the market that gives freedom to employers, workers and unions to work out mutually satisfactory working relationships that suit their own needs. The role of government then, is limited to providing a legal system that respects and enforces the contracts freely entered into by employers, workers, and their representatives.[5]

Labour legislation should also ensure that there are proper mechanisms and designated government agencies to regulate enterprises. Enterprises that do not adhere to existing labour laws should not be allowed to go scot-free and they should be penalized severely if they are not even following basic requirements like providing appointment letters, holiday benefits, and defined hours of work. The government needs to push to bring more enterprises under the net of legal structures not only so that the rights of the worker are protected, but also so that the government can monitor tax collections against payment of salaries.

Aid Donors and Wealth Creation

Multilateral, bilateral and international donors have a big role to play in facilitating Nepal's transformation into a capitalist welfare state and in the alleviation of poverty through wealth creation. The issues and the shortcomings of the Nepali aid architecture have been discussed in Chapter 5; this part will focus on the reform prescription.

Aid should be in the business of putting itself out of business rather than finding newer modes of engagement. Like the transformation we are seeking in the mindsets of the government and the private sector, a serious makeover is called for in the thinking of the donor world. There has to be a departure from project-oriented studies to action. Nepal perhaps competes with African nations for highest per capita reports produced by aid agencies. If we do a back-of-the-envelope calculation, 1500 agencies active in Nepal producing an average of ten reports a year would mean 15,000 reports a year and a staggering 300,000 reports in the past twenty-odd years.

Aid targets should be assessed by the number of sustainable interventions completed rather than by the number of interventions planned. A recommendation in a paper published by Institute of State Effectiveness in April 2007 sums up most of what Nepal needs to do:

> Adopt state building as the overarching framework for aid delivery, based on a double-compact between donors and the government, and the government and the Nepali people; improve coordination through shared analysis, selectivity of labour, pooled funding and joint programs; and assist the private sector through support for innovative mechanisms to attract significant international and national capital in line with economic priorities.[6]

It is essential that donors make an effort to coordinate activity amongst themselves. The coming together of the World Bank, Asian Development Bank and Department for International Development (DFID), UK, to work on a common strategy for 2009–11, is a welcome sign and more agencies should join the bandwagon. Along with this, governance, management and financial structures within the development community need improvement. This means public disclosure of receipts and expenditure that is as good as, if not better than that provided by publicly traded companies. An amount of USD 10 million per annum needs to be fixed as the minimum amount of financial aid that can be offered by the donors. Transparency in procurement processes, in the hiring of staff and in contracting service providers is also a must. Finally, a code of ethics must be defined and strictly adhered to, be it rules relating to travel, hotel stay utilization, conferences, seminars, allowances or other rules that are generally governed by employment contracts and organization rules. It is also important that all money provided by donors be regulated through the government treasury, thereby giving no leeway to individual donor countries or institutions to bypass the government.

Further, privately managed philanthropic funds should become a reality in Nepal, where donors, especially non-governmental organizations, as well as multilateral and bilateral aid agencies, would have the choice of giving money to such funds, as this will ensure that the overheads of managing the money are minimized. A good example of the donor's dollar walking the longest mile is A Room to Read, an education initiative started by John Wood, who left a Senior Executive's position in Microsoft to start this not-for-profit organization.[7] It began in Nepal and now operates in four countries, with just 10 per cent overheads in contrast to the 25 per cent to 30 per cent overheads of many international INGOs.

Leveraging Community Based Organizations

One of the biggest achievements of Nepal over the past two decades has been the emergence of a plethora of grass-roots organizations that have helped in the transformation of livelihoods, such as the community forest user groups that have a combined strength of 1.2 million households,[8] managing Rs 1 billion without supervision.[9] While the urban centres were reeling under sixty hours of power cuts every week in February 2009, many of Nepal's villages were enjoying twenty-four-hour electricity from the micro-hydro-projects they have built. In areas where state utility is absent, communities are paying market prices to ensure there is an uninterrupted supply of electricity. The challenge is in working with communities whose expectations have increased significantly, partly because of politicians who tend to promise everything under the sun while not delivering.

The key strengths we need to pick up from the community-based organizations would be their understanding of local skills and networks, local innovation and thought processes and their desire to be part of the process of unleashing Nepal's potential. The government, aid agencies, NGOs and private enterprises need to harness these strengths collectively and not compete with each other in doing so.

The strengths of rural Nepal are substantial. While no specific studies are available, one can observe that a large number of female nurses working in the United States come from different parts of Chitwan; a large number of restaurant workers, be it in Japan or in the US, come from Kaski and Baglung; and a large section of successful professionals and entrepreneurs in Nepal came to Kathmandu after spending their formative years in the villages. The drive to succeed of people from outside Kathmandu, is observed to be stronger than that of most of Kathmandu inhabitants, who perhaps were more fortunate when they started out.

Nepal's experimentation with decentralization began with Dr Harka Gurung, social thinker and former minister during the Panchayat era, who propagated the concept of regional planning. By 1997, with the enactment of the Local Self Governance Act, it seemed that Nepal was really in a process of rapid decentralization. However, Prime Minister Sher Bahadur Deuba's decision to dissolve the District Development Centre and Village Development Centre in 2002, which was supported by the parliament, stalled the process of political decentralization. The growth and strengthening of community-based organizations that was made possible by these local governance bodies was squandered. The political euphoria of the removal of the king in 2008 again pushed the agenda of federalism, with Nepal being declared a Federal Democratic Republic by the constituent assembly before the constitution writing process could decide the contours of federalism. Federalism prescribes the division of the country by creating another level of political boundaries within the country and delimiting the areas of authority and responsibility of the federated states, the federal government and the common list between the states and the federal government. In contrast, decentralization devolves the authority to collect revenue and determine expenditure within the existing political and administrative structures. Rather than embarking on the journey of federalism, Nepal would perhaps have been better off had it pursued a decentralization agenda. Nepal at this juncture is not prepared to deal with the complexities of resource allocation and expenditure for a federated state, but is aware of the practices of a decentralized state and what can make it work.

The structure of the federated state and the modality of resource-sharing between the federal, state, district and village governments is still unknown. Until these aspects of governance become clear, there is the danger that community expectations will hinder the implementation of development as well as investment projects which predominantly benefit those outside a local community. The construction of many hydropower projects has been suspended due to communities continuously adding items to their laundry list of demands that can range from free electricity to free school and hospitals to employment guarantees. When they make such demands, the communities need to be given a good explanation of the advantages of forgoing their stake in the land, not in the sense of an ideological sacrifice for the country but in comparison to the annual productivity and income generated from the land. Given the demand for electricity and the exporting potential that any big hydropower project would generate, the income-generating benefits from a large project versus smaller micro-hydro projects are substantial. In such cases, transparency on part of the big projects is critical. This allows for the development of trust and a mutually beneficially relation between them. It is also important to bear in mind that the as per current provision of laws, a portion of the revenues that the government gets from these projects is required to be channelized directly into the districts and villages. Thus, even without federalism, equitable distribution of revenues from such projects can take place.

Forging Partnerships

By the end of 2012, the overuse and abuse of the phrase 'public–private partnerships' (PPPs) by the CPN (Maoists) converted an apt development tool for Nepal into political sloganeering. It is important to highlight the fact that the state-owned enterprises set up during the Panchayat government's rule between 1960 and 1990 were also models of public–private partnership. However, these enterprises were led by the public sector rather than by the private sector and to a large extent have been failures. The Maoists should take heed of previous failures and realize that all previous governments in Nepal sought to establish enterprises with the best of intentions for the nation. However, intentions alone are not sufficient and when they back an enterprise that is structurally unsound, failure is inevitable as is evident from the fact of state-owned enterprises that survived on taxpayers' contributions and the practice of employing party cadres. The failed socialist model in which state intervention is interpreted as a partnership with the people can no longer work or be accepted based only on ideological principles. Sale of petroleum products cannot remain the agenda of the government-owned Nepal Oil Corporation (NOC), as people are facing serious problems of irregular supply, poor quality and a price that is not linked to global markets, in addition to having to pay as tax payers to fund the losses resulting from the inefficiency of the NOC.

The only way to ensure a strong and successful capitalist welfare state is by building partnerships and also making them work. The challenge of delivering welfare can only be taken up through partnerships which provide the opportunity to uniquely tailor solutions to existing problems. At the centre of a capitalist welfare state, there are three major tasks—large infrastructure projects, social service delivery and sustainable micro-enterprises. Each of these can be led by only one player in the economy; for instance, the private sector could fund large infrastructure projects, the government could take on the task of social service delivery and the aid agencies could help communities to establish sustainable micro-enterprises. However, based on Nepal's previous unsuccessful experiences as shown in chapters 3 to 6 in comparison to the success stories from around the world, it is clear that best way to tackle each of these tasks is through a partnership involving all three sectors of the economy, but led by the sector most suited to the task. Based on the needs and the tasks, such partnerships could be modified and new modalities created to accommodate the coming together of different forms of private enterprises, government agencies, aid agencies, I/NGOs and community-based organizations.

For large infrastructure projects, partnerships involving all sectors of the economy are critical, but given the need for efficiency, private enterprises should be given the lead for conducting exploratory activities and investing, while the other players act as facilitators in this process. For instance, in the case of hydropower plants, the government can provide access to water resources under an agreement with the private sector and thereby encourage investment. The communities can participate in building better social service delivery mechanisms for themselves through the revenue earnings for which aid agencies/I/NGOs can act as facilitators. Different models of participation can be envisaged, wherein members of the communities at the project site are provided ownership in the project against the sale of land to the project. Further, to promote local businesses, a start-up subsidy or reduced tariff can be provided to micro-enterprises to facilitate the first year of operation.

Basic social service delivery, on the other hand, would have to be through government or community-led partnership between public and private players. Although the onus of the operations falls upon the government, for the sake of better delivery and efficiency it could contract these services out to private sector organizations or NGOs. For example, a community-owned school could be managed by a private school management company or even an NGO. The donor community can play a significant role in ensuring the sustainability of these partnerships by supporting them in the initial launching period and making the school sustainable in the long run. The government and donor community could also partner together for instituting teacher training and curriculum development programmes to ensure that a high quality of education is being provided. Private sector companies can be involved in a wide variety of services related to the educational sector, including the timely and error-free printing of textbooks, providing uniforms, stationery and sports equipment, sponsoring events and competitions and providing scholarships.

The fundamental principle is that all economic activity is interconnected and interlinked. In such an interlinked world, forging partnerships is not a luxury but a necessity. Partnerships have to be formed to develop micro-enterprise and sustainable self-employment opportunities. The key to doing business is to make sure that those possessing competencies and skills are self-employed. A cluster of self-employed people can form the backbone of a large business enterprise. For instance, milk cooperatives or tea cooperatives can feed into large private milk or tea processing plants. The donors can help in building such capacities and establishing sustainable partnerships. The role of the donor agencies as facilitators is critical, for without communication and understanding, no partnership can stand the test of time.

The dimension of the community has to be added to gradually grow the concept of PPP to Public Private Community Partnership (PPCP) as the inclusion of the community dimension is key to the success of partnerships. For partnerships to succeed, it is important to ensure separation of ownership, control and regulation. The partnership model itself should separate the three. An example of this is a school where the ownership may be vested with communities, while NGOs and private sector players can take on the management and regulation role. Thinking like enterprises, these partnerships should ensure that revenues meet expenses and that surpluses are intelligently reinvested. The best enterprise management modalities for sustainability, risk management and growth have to be adopted in all sectors of the economy to make the best use of limited resources and to maximize value addition. The basic principle remains getting more bang for your buck while operating in a sustainable and ethically acceptable way.

∾

In conclusion, for a country like Nepal, which suffers from acute poverty, the best way to address this problem is through the generation of wealth while ensuring equitable distribution. The model to follow for making this a reality is that of a capitalist welfare state. Success hinges on the active involvement of all sectors of society. To ensure that an entrepreneur and business-friendly environment is created, reforms in land, tax, labour, capital markets, the financial sector and fiscal policy have to be carried out. The government needs to bring about the necessary reforms, the private sector needs to take up the challenge of embracing reforms, donors need to facilitate the process of accelerating reforms and citizens needs to work together to create a Nepal with a sustainable, vibrant and inclusive economy.

10

SCALING UP

Success in most projects (other than TV news anchoring) depends on how well ideas are implemented, rather than on how well they are presented. The Maoist-led government that came to power in September 2008 has been unable to break free from the well tried and tested model of excessive posturing and promising without delivery. Nepali governments, new and old, have specialized in churning out promises, rather than focusing on action. The unleashing of Nepal's potential is completely dependent on the conversion of national pastimes like lip service, speeches, conferences, and reports into tangible, grounded and earthly actions. A country of nearly thirty million people, the world's forty-third largest population, definitely demands much more than hollow words and unimaginative implementation.

To the relief of some and appallingly for others, the key areas of economic focus have not changed much in the past sixty years. Agro-based industries, hydropower, and tourism remain the key sectors for the economy. The only addition to that would be the service sector, where Nepal is engaged in providing services through its migrant workforce outside Nepal, as it has been historically, from the mercenary *lahure*, to farm workers and domestic helpers in India, to the recent surge of workers heading towards the Middle East and Southeast Asian countries. Hydropower consultants are still consulting and re-writing reports on the same rivers that have not produced electricity for the past thirty years while a once energy-sufficient nation is mired in power cuts that effectively make the national electric utility a convenient power back-up. The lack of implementation, its complete sacrifice to the gods of lip service every single day, is best displayed in the government's complete failure in providing the most basic facilities of electricity and water to its capital city.

If the government especially after 1990 was a failure, the private sector was plagued with a lack of ambition, fear and protectionism. When the name of the game was scale and that too scaling upwards, most Nepali businesses were sadly found wanting. Historically, Nepali businesses have never pursued scale, perhaps complacent in the fact that Nepal already possessed the world's highest peak. The vision of the feudal rulers of the country was limited to their palatial abodes, while for the common Nepali, it did not go beyond their hamlet or courtyard. A classic example of myopia is the gratitude and pride the Nepali government oozed when it received a Japanese aid grant for the building of a single lane highway in the 1990s, at a time when the South Asian region was already moving to six-lane highways and airports that got too crowded before they were even commissioned. The prescriptions that follow are an attempt to prioritize the necessity of scaling up in four key areas: agriculture, hydropower, tourism and infrastructure. Nepal must be benchmarked against Malaysia, a country with a similar population, which had a GDP two and a half times that of Nepal in 1950 but whose GDP was sixteen times that of Nepal by 2012.

Leveraging Agriculture

Nepal's diverse geography, which features high-altitude mountains, plains, rainforests and desert areas, boasts a vast biodiversity that can be harnessed for commercial purposes. As far as comparative advantage is concerned, there has been much talk about Nepal's riches in medicinal plants and mountain herbs. Nepal has over 700 medicinal plant species, out of which 300 have been tested in laboratories for their medicinal properties.[1] Commercial cultivation of these herbal and medicinal plants, extracting their medical value, processing them and marketing them, are critical areas which the country and populace have not been able to take advantage of, even though they have excellent local and traditional knowledge. Instead, primary produce is carted away to create huge profits for middlemen in India and in the West. The national economy can also start to take advantage of cash crops like tea, cardamom, ginger, vegetable seed, coffee and so on, which would provide farmers with more income per hectare than traditional crops. The end goal is to maximize the net gains per hectare, per worker. For instance, experiments have shown how better agricultural practices can yield seven tonnes of maize per hectare against the average Nepali yield of two tonnes. The value addition per agricultural worker for Nepal is just USD 240 compared to USD 6680 for Malaysia, which indicates that the potential for growth in agriculture is tremendous.[2] Tapping these shortfalls in production is the first step towards value addition.

Agricultural practices need to incorporate new irrigation techniques, which should be extensively used to reduce dependency on the monsoon. Farmer cooperatives should establish direct links with producers and buyers, rather than going through intermediaries. Indeed, there will be no sustainable gains from an agricultural turnaround if the benefits do not reach the farmer level. A welfare state can only exist if agriculture can assume the form of business rather than being a mere source of subsistence. Assuming that 60 per cent of workers are still engaged in agriculture, just a dollar more per worker through better productivity in agriculture per year means an addition of USD twenty million to the national GDP. The additions can be substantially greater if Nepal takes advantage of its unique geological location and structure, which is Nepal's comparative advantage. Prabhakar Rana, Chairman Emeritus of the Soaltee Group, which is involved in the tobacco and tea business, points out that Nepal, being in the same latitude as Egypt and Ethiopia, should be engaged in cut flower cultivation as well as in flower extraction for fragrance products, which is big business in the aforementioned countries. These are high-value agricultural products, he explains, 'Nepali farmers cannot improve their living standards by just growing rice and lentils.' Dr Baburam Bhattarai, current finance minister, emphasizes that by commercializing agriculture, unemployment in the agriculture sector can be reduced by 25 per cent to 30 per cent.

Only the agricultural sector can have the necessary multiplier effect to reduce poverty significantly. The key again, is the creation of a tailor-made partnership between the private sector, government and local communities of farmers and a legal and institutional framework that can deliver scale. Fragmented land can never deliver economies of scale; therefore, it becomes important for large-scale land pooling to take place, be it in the form of corporations or cooperatives. As discussed in the previous chapter, land reform is critical to the success of the agricultural sector. Further, the technology used has to be cutting edge. In these ways, the sector has to be made attractive for large international companies to invest, transfer their technology and operate factories for the processing and packaging of agricultural products. Finally, the agricultural workers or the owners of land should be able to link their fate to the success of the business and at the same time earn decent wages for the labour they provide. For this, there have to be contemporary contract farming laws that can ensure that the buyer of agricultural products from farm cooperatives or companies, has the legal right to access the goods that have been contracted for.

This whole partnership mechanism can be illustrated for a product like coffee. Farmers can come together and pool together large tracts of land to cultivate coffee. An international or national coffee company can then provide the necessary technical inputs to get the best crops. The farmers, farm cooperatives and companies can, along with the international company, establish a factory to process the coffee and package it. The international company, through strong agreements, must be able to bind the producers of agriculture products to commit them towards timely delivery and quality standards, thus creating partnership confidence for buyers and not allowing for any slip ups in the contracted commitment. This simple structure can be replicated to create effective partnerships between farmers, farm workers and agro-commodities businesses for large-scale transformations in the agricultural sector. In the long run, retails outlets like Starbucks that specialize in the selling of Nepali coffee and sweets, are not unattainable dreams.

Making Hydropower Happen

From the time Rana Prime Minister Juddha Shumsher got a 5KW hydro power plant built in 1911 to light up his palace Singha Durbar,[3] the talk about Nepal's hydropower potential has never ceased. The undeniable fact is that hydropower is the best alternative to provide peaking power (power at times of highest demand), since unlike fossil fuel-driven energy sources, water can be stored and power generated according to demand. Its cost, compared to other forms of energy, is much lower, both financially as well as ecologically. Prabhakar Rana, great grandson of Juddha Shumsher and pioneer of the Bhote Koshi power project, laments the fact that despite the tremendous energy potential in Nepal, during the Panchayat days we chose to go around the world with begging bowls for aid money instead of developing our own energy resources. There is tremendous demand for energy in India and it is estimated that the current demand gap of 40,000 MW in north India alone will rise to 150,000 MW by 2030. Nepal's total supply stands at 700 MW at the end of 2008 and the net demand of 800 MW is based on sufficiency rather than actual need. In Malaysia, with a similar population to that of Nepal, the total power capacity installed and consumed currently produces and consumes is 22,000 MW. Nepal's annual per capita of consumption of electricity is among the lowest ten in the world. Bangladesh's per capita annual consumption is two and half times greater than Nepal's, India's is eight times greater and Sri Lanka's is six times greater. This means that if Nepal's consumption was on a par with that of Bangladesh, then the consumption would have been 1700 MW and if it was on a par with India, then the demand would have been 4200 MW of electricity.[4]

The latent demand for electricity is not considered; people are willing to pay for electricity as demonstrated in places where community projects are charging Rs 15 per unit. The substitution of the expensive LPG with electricity for cooking and exploring the railway system in place of expensive road transportation can give rise to huge demand. With a decrease in the prices of white goods and many other intelligent devices running on the available electricity, the demand can be very high.

We need to ensure that the opportunity in the hydropower sector is not squandered, as it was when a few self-styled consultants with donors' interests at heart, wrote self-serving reports about why the private sector should not be allowed to develop hydropower projects in Nepal, which sadly for the Nepali consumer, has meant no private sector involvement in power—and a staggering sixteen hours without power every day.

Nepal has the potential to run a bulk of its commercial as well as household needs on hydropower. By the end of 2012, with global oil prices hovering at around USD 100 per barrel, it cost Rs 35 to produce a unit of electricity using a diesel or furnace oil plant whereas hydropower, at its most expensive, is sold at Rs 8 a unit. More pertinently, household cooking costs far more when using Liquefied Petroleum Gas (LPG) rather than hydroelectricity sold at commercial rates. Likewise, the transportation cost per tonne per kilometre using a diesel vehicle is higher than for electric trains, even when factoring in the higher initial investment costs. This should act as an encouragement for innovations like three-wheeler electric vehicles for urban transportation while cable cars for mass transportation should be motivated to scale up their reach.

Hydropower can be made a reality if the government gets its act together. In December 2008, more than 250 licences (for plants with a capacity of above 10 MW), amounting to more than 50,000 MW of electricity, were pending approval at the Department of Electricity.[5] Forty-seven Power Purchase Agreements between the government-owned Nepal Electricity Authority (NEA), currently the only authorized buyer of power, and privately owned independent power producers, for sale of a total of 300 MW of electricity, are also pending execution.[6] It is clear that the government needs to expedite the unbundling of the Nepal

Electricity Authority (NEA), the monolith state monopoly, and allow generation, transmission, trading and distribution to be conducted by different agencies in the public and private sector domains. Till now, with the NEA controlling all these activities, it has led to a Catch-22 situation—the government pushes NEA to meet the growing demand, but NEA does not have the capacity to sustain more purchases, while large international developers are unsure about NEA's financial credibility and thus do not invest in large domestic projects. It is important that NEA just maintains the transmission business while private sector players enter into the field of generation, forming distribution companies with local municipalities to ensure that supply is based on demand rather than the other way around.

Similarly, there has to be a framework for the trading of power between Nepal and India. The Power Trade Agreements with India need to be implemented, allowing for Nepali power traders to link with Indian trading companies. A Nepali power trading company should be able to import power from or export power to an Indian power company using the NEA's transmission lines. With a latent demand in Nepal and a ready market in India, it is also time for the government to ponder the option of merchant plants, where the developer takes the risk of starting power generation projects without a definitive long-term power purchase agreement with the NEA. At present Nepali legislation does not allow for the development of power plants without a prior agreement with NEA on its purchasing contract from the new plant. Instead of selling power to the NEA through long-term contracts, power producers should be able to sell their power to power traders who in turn will sell it to the power distribution companies or consumers of large quantities of power.

The approach to hydropower development should shift from fulfilling a poorly estimated demand to creating adequate supply, which will convert latent demand into real demand. For instance, as a policy, no household in Kathmandu can get the three-phase connection required to run most electrical appliances. No one in the government, the private sector, aid agencies or consultancies has even looked at Nepal's latent domestic demand figures for power. Any large scale energy-dependent steel, aluminium, cement or fertilizer plant will not decide to set up in Nepal unless they are sure that power has moved from PowerPoint presentations to the transmission lines. For long-term gains from its hydropower potential, Nepal has to create energy markets that trade energy as explained above, instead of locking firms into long-term power purchase agreements with the financially inept NEA.

Hydropower energy pricing should be directly linked to oil prices, which means that when oil prices go up, prices of hydropower generated energy also go up, as for every hydropower plant not built, a fossil fuel plant has to be installed. Nepal, having the highest potential in the world in the hydropower sector, will have to take the lead in pushing the cause of energy markets that link hydropower energy prices to global petroleum prices, so that every time the oil prices go up, Nepal benefits through increased prices in hydropower energy sales.

The management of community expectations from hydropower projects along with social and physical environments needs to be taken as a priority. Communities cannot take projects as a blank cheque to fulfil their wish list and create impediments at any point in time for their selfish gains. The stoppage of construction work at hydropower project sites has become common headline material. It is important that hydropower projects become catalysts for the economic development of the communities living around such project sites, since a natural resource that is actually owned by the communities is being used by the project. The ownership of the community through free shares has to be non-negotiable, but beyond this, enterprises that are investing in power plants should be free from political and community interference in the operation and management of the plants. Innovative ways of providing long-term social security to the community can be put in place at the time of project negotiations. For instance, 100 per cent household studies can be done and children eligible for free education identified. The power companies can issue vouchers that can be cashed by the parents each year to get their children an education.

Apart from donor interests arguing against private involvement in hydropower and the impediments created by communities with high expectations, the prevalence of strong nationalist sentiment against the sale of electricity to India has also hindered the development of hydropower projects. Such nationalist sentiments against the export of hydropower need to be re-examined from an economic perspective. If fish as a by-product of water can be freely traded across the border, then why can't hydropower? While the sale of hydroelectricity to an energy-hungry India would change Nepal's fortunes, former Finance Minister Dr Ram Sharan Mahat expresses caution: 'The future also depends on relations with India. India will be a huge potential market for energy but that depends on the political relation with India. We need to develop appropriate relations.' It is important that energy sales between India and Nepal not be made a political issue, but assessed according to the economics of the deal where private power generation and trading companies get into transactions regulated by the laws of the respective governments.

Finally, there are a host of laws, regulations and institutional changes that are required to be able to attract global players in the hydropower sector. For instance, enterprises in Nepal are not credit rated by any of the international credit rating agencies which is one of the key facts deterring international investors. Nepal needs to have a credit rating system for its enterprises which will attract foreign investors and give them confidence. Similarly, there are many measures related to risk management, insurance, mutual fund laws, construction-related laws and third party liability-related laws that need to be enacted by the government. As an example, any large-scale project comes with requirements of large amounts of financing along with higher levels of risks, as risks and returns go hand-in-hand. Yet, no Nepali insurance company has the capacity to take on insurance of such large risks be it related to construction or third party liability. Therefore laws should be amended allowing foreign insurance companies to operate in Nepal. Similarly, there is not much competency within the country, in handling the financing of large scale projects, which often involve many times the paid-up capital of local banks. Unfortunately, hydropower, after roads and ports, is regarded as one of the riskiest investments anywhere, as investors, including the banks, have no assets (other than turbines) to take away and sell, in case the project hits a snag. This makes accurate appraisals of the projects critical, ensuring that investments would not be gobbled up without any results. These appraisal and monitoring capacities have to be created, which would mean opening up the consulting, legal, accounting and service sectors for foreign companies. The more foreign companies operate in Nepal, as in the example of the hotel industry discussed in earlier chapters, the more Nepalis will benefit from the transfer of knowledge. Eventually, this could help build up a large world-class Nepali support service industry comprising legal, consulting, risk management, financial management and project management services.

Nepal needs to replicate the success of Bhote Koshi and Khimti where successive governments continued to facilitate the process of licensing, construction and ensured that the projects completed in time. Successive governments also facilitated the transfer of technology and foreign capital investment in both shares and in loans. The bureaucracy also took these projects as projects of national importance and expedited processes, while the promoters too, worked tirelessly to ensure that he projects came online and started paying off over a period of time.

Unleashing Tourism

Tourism, unlike hydropower, can deliver an impact in a short period of time but requires partnerships of a different kind. In contrast to hydropower that requires building large physical infrastructure by investing huge amounts of money, tourism as an industry requires softer issues to be addressed with of course a good amount of investment. The future of tourism in Nepal requires a tremendous transformation of mindset, again with regard to scale. Consultants Arun Anand and Rahul Sen of Alchemy Social Infrastructure in Delhi, India were involved in the branding exercise of the Nepal Tourism Board in 2006 and provided a thought provoking 10:10:10 strategy for Nepal. This meant making Nepal one of the top ten destinations in the world attracting ten million tourists in ten years. This means the entire country needs to gear up to be able to attract and manage numbers that double every year. It is worth noting that Malaysia had tourist arrivals numbering 70,000 in 1970, when arrivals in Nepal were two-thirds of that figure at 46,000, but by 2012, when Nepal received 800,000 visitors, Malaysia recorded arrivals numbering 25 million tourists.[7] At 2012 prices, a twenty-fold increase in Nepal's numbers would mean an increase in earnings of USD 9 billion, 50 per cent of Nepal's 2012 GDP.

Quality has to go hand-in-hand with quantity and in a service industry, this means large investments in people. The key perceived comparative advantage of a Nepali is his or her smile and that forms the fundamental of the tourism business. The smile would have to be accompanied by state of the art training in delivering services. A large number of Nepali youth can be given vocational training in hospitality and travel management and employed in different jobs in this industry. Nepal needs to rediscover premium segments of its past, which would significantly increase its earnings per tourist in the top segment. Nepal till the early 1990s saw tourists who were not only willing to pay close to USD 200 dollars per room but who demanded dinners to be arranged at exotic locations paying USD 125 per meal and who did not mind chartering planes and helicopters to explore the country.

In addition, the Nepal tourism industry must shift its focus to the close to 2.5 billion people north and south of its border. Nepal needs to pursue an open sky policy that will connect cities in India and China with those in Nepal without restricting the number of flights or seats as is currently the case. Flights from Shanghai in China to Mumbai in India should be able to stop over in Kathmandu, which is currently not possible. More hotels need to be built to cater to the distinct tastes of the Indians and the Chinese. The investors for such airports and hotels can come from China and India too. Chinese outbound tourists are estimated at 50 million in 2010 and expected to double to 100 million in 2020.[8] Similarly, Indian tourists outbound are expected to number 50 million in 2020. All this means Nepal has access to immediate markets of 150 million tourists in 2020—just 10 per cent of these markets would be mean 15 million tourists in 2020!

There are more than ten Indian cities within an hour's flight from Kathmandu or Pokhara with a population of more than two million each. As Kanak Mani Dixit, editor of the magazine *Himal South Asian* points out, 'with the affluence of the people close to the Nepali border, the natural tendency of flying to or driving up to Nepal will increase and we have not even looked at those numbers.' Nepal also needs to find more reasons for a Chinese tourist to fly to Nepal, whether because it is closer than Macau, or because of the availability of spiritual tourism products for individuals born after the one child policy, who were pampered by six individuals and who now have the stressful task of taking care of six dependents! Nepal needs to work on more destinations for tourists to visit, ensure better urban planning to conserve our heritage, and develop innovative products, through home-stay programmes, eco-tourism or heli-skiing facilities. Enough money has been poured into the writing of reports, just a few need implementation to change the tourism landscape.

Nepal needs a tremendous amount of knowledge transfer in the tourism business. The successful experiment of the opening up the hotel sector to multinational players needs to now be replicated for international and domestic airlines, the travel and transportation business, guest services as well as other allied services. The protectionist role of the state is over and Nepali firms will need to partner with foreign firms to compete in the marketplace. Prabhakar Rana, Chairman Emeritus, Soaltee Hotel Limited, points out that global players like Thomas Cook and Kuoni dominated the Indian market soon after India finally decided to open up the tourism sector. Nepal needs to think out of the box. If Japan wants to take Lumbini on a fifty-year lease and develop a tourist paradise, we should allow that to happen. Look at what would have happened if we had given Pokhara on a similar lease thirty years back when the Japanese made such an offer; we would only have twenty years of lease left and the entire development done by the Japanese would have been ours. Similarly, Madhukar Rana, former finance minister, says that when Maldives is looking for land on long-term lease as a social security for its island residents against the submergence of the island, Nepal should try its best to woo them with a township they could lease. We could also learn from them what constitutes a successful tourist destination.

It is also important to have a paradigm shift when it comes to thinking about tourism. Products should be developed for domestic tourists. Some successful initiatives like the Manakamana Cable Car demonstrate that if one can target domestic tourists, it is possible to do very well. If even a tenth of the Nepali population starts travelling, it will be more than three times the international tourist arrivals. Successive research has shown that Nepali travellers and tourists spend more money on food and beverage compared to international tourists.

Infrastructure Mantra

The development of infrastructure in Nepal should have three fundamental purposes. First, to be able to resume infrastructure development that was not only stalled due to the ten-year Maoist conflict but also significantly destroyed by it. Second, to provide better facilities to citizens and take advantage of the economic opportunities that arise out of infrastructure development. Finally, to be able to create employment, which has become one of the fundamental buffers against future conflicts. Infrastructure development encompasses two distinct categories of interrelated development projects—transportation, comprising urban mass transportation, roads, railways, airports and waterways—and urban or rural infrastructure that encompasses housing, water, sanitation and communication. It is important to realize that various kinds of urban infrastructure tend to develop along the route of roads, both for convenience and safety measures. It is therefore necessary for a good partnership to develop among all sections of the infrastructure development project.

With a history of land being always owned by the rulers and never privately held till the 1950s and even later, infrastructure development in Nepal was seen as another set of favours that the rulers could bestow upon the populace. Therefore, the building of roads depended on who owned vehicles and airports were built close to hunting reserves. The trend continued during the Panchayat period between 1960 and 1990 and also post-1990 during multiparty rule; therefore, a dirt track became a blacktopped road in any alley where a minister decided to rent a house in Kathmandu Valley. The areas around the palace or ministers' residences received uninterrupted electricity and water supply. This is feudalism at its core and bears no resemblance to the democratic governance for the people that politicians continue to promise in eloquent speeches. The way in which infrastructure investments are made has to undergo a transformation whereby they are based on demand rather than at the discretion of the provider.

Infrastructure building will have to be preceded by a planning process in which the country is zoned based on population, resources and the economics of potential. The current spree of 'bulldozer terrorism' of building roads recklessly, without thinking about sustainability or environmental impact, can be fatal in the long run. Correspondingly, the expressways connecting Kathmandu with the Indian border should have land pooling plans that provide for the option of creating satellite towns along the expressway. The landowners would be more than happy to provide their land in return for developed land in a satellite township, thereby easing the entire process of land acquisition for the developer. Road linkages should be decided by assessing the size of the population that will benefit from the linkages as well as the potential of transporting resources to and from the points where roads are being proposed.

Nepal in 2008 has a road density of 0.65 km per 1000 people and 6 km per 100 sq km of land, the lowest figures in Asia on both counts. The building of highways, district roads and village roads will provide on the one hand, market access to producers and on the other, will accelerate social service delivery of education and health. The building of roads, however, should not be done in isolation but in sync with water, sewer, telecommunication cabling and electricity transmission structuring, especially in the flatland areas. Given the geological challenges, a distinct approach will be required for infrastructure development in the hills and mid-hills.

It is estimated that for Nepal to maintain a growth rate of even 5 per cent per annum, infrastructure investment till 2020 would have to be to the tune of USD 20 billion per annum.[9] It is important to have a holistic approach towards infrastructure—all infrastructure development should also be channelized through a federal infrastructure development agency that has the requisite authority to receive money from the treasury and grants from donors. This body can work in partnership with private sector companies to build, develop and maintain infrastructure. Concessionaires who are given the rights for developing infrastructure projects should be allowed to issue long-term bonds for infrastructure development and the government should provide tax benefits and rebates as its contribution.

Establishing the fundamental building blocks and foundations of a capitalist welfare state will require not only conducive government policies and a willing donor community, but a competent private sector leading the transformation and scaling up of enterprise and vision. Private enterprises that will take the risks involved in hydropower development, enterprises willing to develop different models in agriculture and entrepreneurs who would want to start the next innovative trekking route or eco-tourism programme, are the need of the day. The key requirement would not be just financial but also the availability of human resources with the knowledge and knowhow to lead the transformation. The success of the action will depend upon creating a pool of skilled people who will be able to take on different roles from planning to execution.

11

NEPALI YOUTH: AN ENGINE OF PRODUCTIVITY AND CHANGE

There is little room for doubt in questioning Nepal's integration into the global economy. Whether Nepal and the Nepali government like it or not, Nepal is already well immersed into the global economy. This immersion has largely happened haphazardly, unconsciously and opportunistically. Nepal must now develop a growing awareness of itself and its relative placement in the global economy, by setting a path and direction for its engagement with globalization.

Lacking a strong industrial and manufacturing base, the Nepali people will be best served if the nation capitalizes on its comparative advantages in the hospitality industry, tourism, a large pool of youth and its geographic and geological advantages in agriculture. This chapter follows from the previous chapter and talks about how Nepal can capitalize upon these comparative advantages, a task which that can only fully be realized if the infrastructural needs of the country discussed in the previous chapter are addressed.

Linking Youth to Services

Around six million people in Nepal are part of the rising generation of Nepali youth. In a country where political leaders in their mid-fifties still get referred to as youth leaders, it is important to define youth in the Nepali context. For the sake of clarity and to facilitate the analysis in this chapter, a youth is an individual in the age group of eighteen to thirty-five. With population growth rates well above 2 per cent for the past two decades, this segment of Nepali society is expected to grow to eight million by the year 2020 and to ten million by 2025.[1] Surprisingly this can be a source of comparative advantage, when one places it within a global context. The proportion of able workers entering the workforce is significantly declining in the Western world. Nepal has the opportunity to capitalize upon this shortfall and provide skilled workers for the global hospitality industry.

There is a popular saying in Nepal that claims that the youth are the future of the country. However, for the youth in almost every facet of Nepali society, the future never comes. This is most prominently displayed in the political leadership of the country, where the young are rarely given a voice and politicians in their fifties and sixties are still referred to as youth leaders. During the 1960s, leaders in all spheres of life were redefining Nepali society as Nepal emerged out of isolation. Since the early 1990s, the youth have gradually unshackled themselves from an overbearingly traditional and patriarchal Nepali society which demands unquestioned loyalty and respect towards their elders and seniors. A strong factor in this change is the growing disillusionment among the youth about the ability of the previous generation to secure their future. This was most vividly displayed during Jana Andolan II, the popular non-violent pro-democracy agitation of 2006, when the youth led the movement and challenged the most prominent symbol of traditional Nepali society, the monarchy. Two contradictory aspects of the power of the youth were displayed there: one, their participation in the violent People's War and the other, their capacity for non-violent popular protest.

For Nepal, the rise of the youth signals both opportunities and dangers. The discussions that follow are aimed at identifying the primary means through with Nepal can capitalize upon the rise of the youth grant them opportunities to engage themselves and prevent them from ever considering violence as a means to any end. I will first make a case for the three pillars or necessary conditions for the youth to engage constructively with the global economy—one, education, two, a value system or moral code, and three, information, communication and technology (ICT). With a firm base resting on these three pillars, we can then discuss how skilled Nepali youth can move up the service value chain in certain niche areas. Specialization and improved skills means more entrepreneurship along with better work opportunities at home and abroad. With so many Nepali youth seeking work abroad, a movement from unskilled to even semi-skilled tasks would mean a dramatic increase in overseas worker remittances to Nepal. Critically, these remittances need to be channelled towards investments in wealth creating projects. Without this drive to invest in productive assets, remittances will not necessarily facilitate the unleashing of the Nepali economy.

Given the prominence of the youth population in Nepal, at present and in the future, it is the youth who shall have to take the initiative to establish a modern capitalist welfare state. If Nepal is to tap its comparative advantage in possessing a young population and leverage its position to maximize its economic gains and ensure prosperity, it shall be the youth that have to carry it out. Only the present generation of youth have a base comprising the three pillars discussed earlier; older generations lack this base and thus, the ability and flexibility to adjust to an ever changing and dynamic global economy. For the youth to carry on with their tasks the leaders of the nation have to accept that their primary contribution to the nation must be the creation of an environment where the youth can fully express their potential. Nepal, in the years between Jana Andolan II in 2006 and the establishment of a new constitution in the unknown near future, stands astride a great divide; it has the opportunity to capitalize upon its position as decision makers and leaders or stands to face an increasingly disgruntled mass of youth who lack the space to express themselves.

The Power of Education

Historically, education has been a political tool in Nepal, be it the kings leveraging the knowledge of the Brahmins, the Rana rulers discouraging educational institutions, or the Maoists, during the insurgency, denying children access to education. It is perhaps this knowledge of the power of education among the ruling elite that has made it a highly politicized and contentious sector. The educational sector has completely been infiltrated by political hardliners and most government-run institutions function as indoctrination centres for various political groups. This dates back to 1940s, when educational institutes were used by political parties as centres of anti-Rana activity. This was followed in the 1950s by the establishment of political party-affiliated student wings which contested student union elections. Constituting the lower level cadres for political parties, the student-wing organizations became testing grounds for political leaders, from where they eventually made it up the ranks into the party hierarchy.

The politicization of the educational sector did not end with the students, but gnawed its way into the hearts of the administrative staff and teachers. This resulted in the formation of one of Nepal's strongest unions, the much-vaunted teachers' union. In rural Nepal, a teacher and a politician become synonymous as the job of the teacher was the one at the bottom of the job pyramid. People who could not become doctors or engineers or take up jobs at government offices and private companies were left only with the job of a teacher. During their college days, many had spent a great deal of time in student politics, which likely left them bereft of the academic qualifications that might have allowed a wider set of job options. They chose to keep in touch with their political masters and the most suitable job then became teaching, because it came with the advantages of a flexible work schedule, the opportunity to indoctrinate students and access to parents and other communities around the school.

The challenge now is to make a departure from the above-mentioned opportunistic and self-serving attitude to the youth, on the part of political leaders. An Indian example explains a lot; while non-retiring student leaders in the Indian state of West Bengal made a fiasco of the education system there, the non-political enterprising youths of Karnataka helped Bangalore become the second Silicon Valley. The one-point agenda therefore should be to free student unions and teacher unions from any political affiliation by allowing students and teachers to group within a particular school or college in the form of clubs or committees but do away with the system of elections to the these unions. The political parties should do away with the practice of affiliating these student and teacher unions, as the days when they were needed to wage proxy political battles in an autocratic state are gone, Nepal having emerged decisively as a democratic republic. Politics should involve the youth but not through student unions.

The shift from a paper and degree-oriented education system to a quality-based educational system would require not only a shift in government policies but also changes in the mindsets of people. When the bulk of employers were government and quasi-government firms, the 'piece of paper' approach to educational qualifications worked, but with the presence of more private firms and self-employment opportunities both of which share the fundamentals of efficiency and competition, education cannot be merely symbolic. In the past, a piece of paper that identified an individual as having a bachelors degree in archaeology would allow him to sit through the civil service exams. By looking over old questions and memorizing answers, he could secure adequate marks and pulling some strings could easily make it into the department of archaeology. He could then spend the rest of his days contributing little to nothing to the proper documentation and preservation of Nepal's archaeological history as long as he scraped out a few reports, drank a lot of tea and maintained cordial relations with everyone. It is safe to say that such practices should never have been and can no longer can be tolerated.

The need of the time is to hire the best person for the task. There can be no time allocated for dilly-dallying at the local tea shop when deadlines are looming. What is required are people well educated not just in churning out reports but in actually understanding and resolving problems and becoming solution providers. Education has to be pursued to gain knowledge and not degrees; therefore, the entire education system needs be transformed to deliver knowledge. A student of archaeology must be trained to understand and appreciate Nepal's cultural history, rather than to be a clerk who produces reports. He or she must be able to relate the past with the present and analyse facets of present-day Nepali society based on its past. He or she must be believe in the preservation of archaeological remains and have valid rational reasons for working towards this end. His or her job can no longer be one of obeying orders from above but working as part of a team that believes in documentation and preservation through innovative means that ensure conservation in practice as well as on paper. This can be best done by encouraging progressive and liberal educational practices that meet international standards and do not just teach a student to read but to understand and analyse as well. What is needed is an education that makes students think rather than obey. Such a standard can be achieved if private universities, international accreditation programmes that allow Nepali institutions to deliver internationally valid degrees, e-learning and continuing education are encouraged in Nepal. The biggest boon for Nepal in bringing about this change has been a rapidly improving communication network—far-flung areas that were never connected to the mainstream in Nepal are now connected through community radio and even mobile phones. This shift from the physical classrooms to virtual classrooms will open up education to a larger population.

A primary problem with education has always been its reach. In most cases it has been unsuccessful in reaching the poorest of the poor. This has resulted both from acute poverty and limitations within the educational system. Often, the system has been dominated by upper-class elites which have made it hard for lower castes to participate. In other cases there simply have not been enough teachers and infrastructure to reach all potential students. The use of communication technologies can go a long way in addressing the barriers of insufficient teachers and caste discrepancies. However, the problems of poverty and infrastructure still can pose significant barriers. Later in this chapter, I will discuss success stories of the use of information and communication technologies in promoting and spreading education in Nepal.

Education: Beyond Public versus Private

The educational modality to be followed in Nepal's educational system has been a subject of much debate. Arguments about whether education should be in the private domain or in the public domain, have been going on for the past few decades. More recently, there has been an increasing number of people who have argued for a more collaborative effort through community ownership, government regulation and private management. The general belief is that private schools cost more than their public counterparts but deliver better quality students. This perception has been created by the way both public and private educational systems developed in Nepal. Private education in Nepal started at a time when teachers were limited and public schools taught in Nepali. Private schools were able to pay employees more than public schools, draw the best teachers and provide an English language-based education. This placed the graduates from private schools at an advantage in comparison to their public school counterparts, helping develop the aura of quality around a private school education. However, with a boom in the private education business after the 1990s, the conflagration of private schools, lacking government regulation, has consumed the quality and excellence of education they once were known for.

Although there are still some private schools that provide quality education, most are beyond the reach of even middle-income families. Public schools on the other hand are well known for their inability to deliver quality education and their constant politicization. The solution to Nepal's educational woes might not be in the selection of one of these pre-existing modalities but in the realization of each domain's strengths and weaknesses, carefully walking the middle path. The government should do as much as it can to deliver primary and secondary education. The private sector can make investments for the development of education infrastructure in the form of specialized higher educational institutions. Kathmandu University, Manipal and other similar private higher education institutions are examples of private sector successes in tertiary education. Nepali students are in Ivy League universities in the US and in good universities in Europe and Asia mostly because of productivity-oriented private education. The government, for whom investment in specialized higher education is difficult, should remain a strong regulator of quality and fairness in private institutions. The primary difficulty for the government remains a limited educational budget and a consistently increasing demand for education. It will be important to get private educational institutions under strict governance codes so that it can be ensured that they just profit and do not profiteer.

It is important to acknowledge that the private and public institutions that dominate Nepal's educational landscape are only two of many options for the future. The recent popular initiative of community-owned schools seeks to take the middle path between these two modalities and has been adopted by the government to some extent. A community-owned school follows the belief that if the local community owns the school where its children go to study, then the parents will ensure that it is run at the best of its ability. While owned by the community, such schools can have an independent management team that is answerable to a board consisting of parents and senior management team members. Already 3300 schools have been handed over by the government to the communities.

A school in Balaju, on the outskirts of Kathmandu Valley, that was handed over to the community for management, is proud not only of its clean toilets, good library, neat and clean classrooms and computers, but also of the fact that all of its students have passed each year in the SLC exams. Students from private schools are switching to this school due to its superior education and facilities. For instance, parents demanded the same textbooks that are used in private schools and the management happily met their demands, thus providing a vivid example of how the onus of quality education has shifted from the school management to the communities themselves, for the betterment of the future of their children.[2]

The success of community ownership of schools needs quicker replication and private institutions which can take these schools on contract or under mentoring plans should be encouraged and supported. The success of community schools lies in the model they follow—separation of ownership and management, the ownership remaining with the community while the management is professional. This brings about an improvement in overall administration as well as a system of checks and balances. Replications of this model of community ownership and professional management can improve student intake, retention as well as the overall quality of education.

English, English and English

The English language has firmly established itself as the lingua franca of the world in the twenty-first century. Its popularity and use expanded with the fortunes of the British empire in the eighteenth, nineteenth and twentieth centuries and the prominence of the United States in the global economy from the nineteenth century onwards. Although imposed as a colonial language among the British colonies, it has become the language of choice in all global affairs. The status of the English language in the world once led *The Economist* to state that English had 'impregnably established itself as the world standard language: an intrinsic part of the global communications revolution'.[3] English is the working language of international organizations and conferences, scientific publications, international banking, economic affairs, trade, mass media, tourism, tertiary education and international laws. Future innovations in information, communications and technology will use the English language more extensively. With over a billion people who speak English as their first or second language, its dominance as the language of a globalized world is assured.

Nepal needs to embark on the project of producing people who communicate well in English, apart from Nepali and the many local languages and dialects. The challenge will be to create an education system that recognizes a multi-language platform in contrast to the one-language policy adopted during the Panchayat regime. The economic ascent of Singapore in the latter part of the twentieth century and the emergence of India as a global power in the beginning of the twenty-first century have one thing in common—an English language education system that does not compromise on other ethnic or regional languages. In the age of machines—the late nineteenth and early twentieth century—technology, such as gramophones and cars, could be adopted by anyone, without specific language ability. Today, however, adapting to technical innovation requires a strong understanding of the English language, embedded as it is in the software and operations of things from newer models of vehicles and global positioning systems to biotech engineering. To expect future Apple iPods and diagnostic software for printers and cars to be in a language other than English for the Nepal market, is a bit unrealistic.

Nepal's historical linkages with the British empire have already established English as the primary diplomatic language that Nepali diplomats use. Further, the incorporation of English language within the educational system has also been of some help in integrating Nepal into the global economy. Now the Nepali government needs to capitalize upon these conditions and ensure that all Nepali students who graduate from any educational institution in Nepal are proficient in English. This will be a considerable advantage whether Nepali students seek to go abroad for higher education or enter the national or international job markets. By knowing the English language, Nepali workers in particular will come already equipped with an invaluable skill, which not only allows for easier communications the world over, but also can be a valuable means through which new skills are acquired. Further, the knowledge of English lets you read more about your own culture and heritage since a bulk of information on Nepali culture, society, religion and heritage is in English.

The Importance of a Workable Value System

Do the youth of Nepal have the progressive and future-oriented value system that is needed to unleash Nepal's full potential? Ten years of conflict between Maoists and the state have created a widespread, if unarticulated belief that violence is an accepted means to power. The impunity granted to those guilty of committing grave crimes of violence has almost certainly influenced the values of the Nepali youth. The creation of militant youth groups by various political parties in 2008, in response to the Young Communist League (YCL) of the CPN (Maoist), has meant that we have a significant population of youth who are willing to take the law into their hands at any time. This stark disregard for the rule of law by political parties from whose ranks we elect the supposed leaders and securers of law has frightening consequences.

If the conflict corroded trust, the post-conflict scenario has eroded what remained of trust to the bare bone. The entire value system of the country, once built upon a strong sense of mutual and societal trust, has crumbled. Nepalis don't trust each other any more, as can be seen when people feel uncomfortable talking to a fellow passenger on a bus or striking up a conversation in a highway tea stall. Dr Jagadish Pokhrel, former vice chairman of the National Planning Commission remarks, 'The impact of conflict has been that the fear factor rules the mind and trust has been wiped out. The most negative effect of the conflict has been the damaging of trust.' One of the major cornerstones of our success in tourism till the mid-1990s was Nepal's identity as a peaceful country with peaceful people. Many stories of the strong value system amongst the Nepali people were written in many travelogues. It is time again to go back to being identified with peace, which means developing a future generation that shuns violence and develops a culture of tolerance.

While many positive values in individuals have been inculcated through religious practices in Nepal, it is important to find newer ways of engaging youths positively. This could be done through the cultivation of hobbies as part of education early in childhood. The inborn talent many youth have for music and the arts needs to be honed. It is important also to improve our image globally about our perception of life and the value of life. The fact of impunity for those who have committed grave crimes is as much a contributor to a negative international image as is the sheer apathy often displayed in Nepal, to people injured in road accidents.

Ramping Up Technology and Communication

The success of Jana Andolan II, the popular agitation of April 2006, was assured by the mass participation of youth, with the help of FM Radio channels and mobile text messaging to spread the non-violent democratic spirit. Young people knew where the major rallies were happening and where a show of strength was required. The young have adapted technology in certain areas like producing world class music videos like the band Mt. 8848's *Rat Gujarna*. With the spread of television and the Internet, the band's video was viewed by Nepali youth both in Nepal and abroad via You Tube. For the first time, Nepali youth, whether in Kanchanpur in western Nepal, Kalimpong in India, Kathmandu or Kansas City in the USA, could identify with a common culture that was truly Nepali and modern.

We are yet to fully harness the power of technology and communication towards the project of integrating Nepal, but some important steps have been made. One of the greatest successes of Nepal has been community radio, with over 300 FM channels transmitting programmes from different parts of the country. With cheap Chinese radios available for less than a dollar, far greater numbers have access to the flow of information. These radios have been utilized effectively by many organizations to disseminate education and information.

A good example of the effective use of information and communication technology in Nepal is 2007 Magsaysay Award winner Mahabir Pun's efforts in rural Nepal. Using old obsolete computers collected from a variety of donors and utilizing the power of wireless communication technology in the rural hills of Nepal, Mahabir Pun has set up a communication network in an area that previously did not know computers. This technology has allowed villagers to use the Internet as a means for communication, quickly replacing the limited conventional telephones being issued by the state-owned Telecom Corporation. Mahabir's use of technology has also impacted other industries in his area, most importantly health and education. Through a video link, doctors in Pokhara are examining patients through Internet conferencing programmes while schools can be run by virtual professors. Mahabir was able to implement his wireless technology and tech-savvy rural industry at a time when the use of wireless technology by private individuals or companies was illegal in Nepal. The quick popularity of Pun's initiative and his growing fame, allowed him to dictate a change of policy by the government. The government should learn from this experience and realize that many of its laws could be restricting the kinds of entrepreneurship that could benefit large numbers of people.

Nepal also needs to further efforts like those carried out by Madan Puraskar Library, Nepal's oldest library, on Free Open Source Software and build virtual Nepali communities that exchange data and computer programmes in Nepali. Madan Puraskar Library is seeking to establish a digital database of all of its physical records, books and photographs. The library is also carrying out an initiative to develop Nepali language-based software and create a platform for uploading on to the web in Nepali. The embracing of English will have to be supplemented by more software in Nepali and other ethnic languages, since more information made available in those languages will open up more vistas. The power of technology is made vivid if one follows a track of Google trends on Nepali language hits or the dramatic increase in Nepali language content on Wikipedia. Both these trends reveal that Nepali people are increasingly engaging with the Internet in the Nepali language and that technology is facilitating this.

Similarly, with the population of youth being the biggest consumers of government services, e-governance has to become a reality, enabling young people to pay taxes, get university transcripts or even vote for elections online. The youth, who have grown up with the Internet, cell phones, ATM cards, music downloads and portable music players, have to be serviced in a different way. Nepal is fortunate to have the world's hardware superpower to its north and a software superpower to its south; we need to leverage this geographical advantage to the fullest.

As the cost of installing voting machines throughout the country is very expensive, it might be more feasible to devise a mechanism allowing individuals to vote through a mobile phone. Mobile software can be created to ensure a secure transaction wherein the identity of the voter would be unique and not duplicated. Nepal can become the first country to allow voting through SMS on mobile phones as a way of enhancing the participation of youth in democratic processes.

The emergence of social media has led to an expansion in reach. With over 2 million Nepalis signed on to Facebook, the way information is shared or distributed has changed. A jewellery store that has a Facebook page that provides daily information on gold prices and posts pictures of jewellery has over 37,000 followers, more than what any English-language traditional media can boast of. The voting of Anuradha Koirala and Pushpa Basnet as CNN Heroes for 2011 and 2012 and the votes garnered by Miss Nepal in the Miss World contest through Facebook shows the power of social media. The 'likes' for social celebrities on Facebook went up to as many as 131,000 in January 2013. Apolitical activist groups emerged that offered to paint temples or create pressure groups for key issues facing Nepali society.

Hi-gration: Moving Up the Value Chain through Education

An estimated 500,000 skilled and unskilled job seekers entered the job market in 2012 and it is estimated that there will be substantial increases in this number, due to a decreasing inclination among the youth to become farm workers.[4] With a greater number of people gaining access to education, many more Nepali youths are attempting and passing the School Leaving Certificate (SLC) Exams. The SLC exams have historically stood as an iron gate between children passing 10th grade and moving on to higher education. Better access to education and greater access to better quality education has decreased the relevance of the antiquated SLC exams. In March 2012 nearly 500,000 students sat for this exam, which means that even if half of them pass, Nepal faces the challenge of providing higher education opportunities for those who pass and vocational training or other inputs for those who fail, so that they can get into the job market. Historically, the Nepali people have been venturing out of the country into different service industries, becoming mercenaries, guards, cleaners and house helpers. In contrast, the proportion of migrant entrepreneurs has always been very small. It has also been observed that Nepalis who go to India return only after reaching the age of retirement or getting to the stage where they cannot work due to old age. In India, Nepalis have become synonymous with guards, known as *durbans*, and domestic help, known as *kanchas* and *kanchis*. It is imperative that the large numbers of Nepali youth who cannot pursue a tertiary education get better vocational training so that there is a tangible value addition to their skill set, that will result in significant increases in earnings. For instance, the slightest addition of value would mean that the ubiquitous *kancha* can upgrade through language and other skills to become a butler and the *kanchi* can upgrade to become a nanny.

Nepali workers cannot move up the value chain and Nepali industries cannot move up the labour supply chain with sub-standard workers. The private sector and government both must cooperate in increasing the skills and capacities of workers. The private sector should realize that the training of workers to go abroad or work here can be a profitable venture. Entrepreneurs must explore profitability models in training and placing skilled workers while the government has to start establishing more transparent, credible and stringent educational qualifications and standards that are independent from the universities. The development sector can contribute towards the upgradation of worker skills by discouraging militant labour and running awareness campaigns on the dangers of continued business closures among workers. The workers must realize that labour unions are institutions for ensuring proper working conditions, preventing discrimination and protecting the rights of workers, rather than a means of coercion. They should be politically unaffiliated, allowing workers, if they choose, to vote for the political parties that best promote business and employment rather than mere ideology or the opportunity to join politics.

Given India's proximity and the growth that country is seeing, it will remain the biggest job market for Nepali migrant workers for the foreseeable future. With an increase in wages in India, many opportunities for Nepali workers will open up in the growing retail business, hospitality, financial services industry and outsourcing industry. Further, with the significant growth of the affluent class in India, there is going to be a very high demand for many kinds of skilled people, be they trained domestic help or drivers who double up as multi-skilled assistants. Given the proximity, cultural similarity and working conditions in India, these options would be far better and closer to home for migrant Nepali workers, than living in labour camps in faraway Malaysia or the Middle East. For Nepal to fully benefit from and tap the growth its southern neighbour is experiencing, a coherent and strategic partnership between the private, public and development sectors must be struck to harness the potential of the Nepali youth and match them with the future demands of the job markets.

Global Hospitality Service Providers

In the global arena, the hospitality and tourism sector should continue to be the focus of Nepali workers. Nepal's historical reputation as a tourist paradise, its plethora of lodges, hotels and restaurants and the friendly nature of the Nepali people, make this sector an obvious choice. In 2005, the deposed Thai Prime Minister Thaksin Shinawatra announced the 'Thai Kitchen to the World' project that basically aimed at making Thai food enter all the kitchens of the world. Similarly, Nepal needs to be embarking on a project to ensure that Nepalis become the hospitality and tourism service people anywhere in the world. Nepalis should be seen in every nook and corner of the world in hotels staffing at all levels, operating restaurants and working in them, running catering services or specialty eating places. With the other important aim of continuous improvement and learning, a waiter or a room attendant in Dubai can work towards becoming the General Manager of the hotel. A worker who starts working at the bottom of the pyramid in a hotel in the Middle East would be earning about USD 300 per month but the General Manager of the hotel would be earning anything between USD 6000 to USD 10,000. The dream would be to have Nepalis become synonymous with the hospitality industry globally, perhaps in the next twenty-five years; similar to the way Gujarati Patels belonging to the state of Gujarat in India are immediately associated with motels in the United States.

The other sector Nepal needs to seriously pursue as a destination for migrant labour is nursing and care to people living in rehabilitation centres and old age homes overseas. With the ageing population rapidly increasing in the twenty-first century, it is estimated that the number of people above the age of eighty would rise to 379 million worldwide in 2050. Of this, about 147 million would live in India and China.[5] Nepal can build on the already prevalent perception that it produces good nurses and care providers and churn out thousands of such people. Further, Nepal can build sanatoriums, rehabilitation centres and assisted care centres, taking advantage of its favourable climate. Planes could be chartered to bring patients into Nepal, as it would be far cheaper to provide assisted care services in Nepal as compared to Japan, Europe or North America. In this regard, Nepal still has the potential to become the care capital of the world.

The onus of developing the hospitality industry is on the private sector, which should nevertheless realize that it cannot do this alone. It needs the support and active participation of the government and the development sector. The government and development sector must target and tackle the militancy of labour. The private sector must learn to invest in its human resources. Without a skilled and well-trained workforce that knows what level of service is required and demanded in today's globalized world, the hospitality sector cannot compete internationally. In hospitality projects related to health and rehabilitation, government and development agencies can play an active role. Partnerships can be developed where an international and affluent clientele subsidize the treatment of those in need. Development agencies can also actively support rehabilitation programmes under a similar model of subsidization, while adding their own expertise in the technical aspects of the projects.

Glo-Yuva: From Rock Concerts to Global Youth Icons

When one watches Nepali youths swaying to music at a peace concert in the tourist district in downtown Thamel, one wonders what can be done to tap this infectious energy of 50,000 people. The CPN (Maoist) did their bit in trying to woo the youth, which led to a conflict where more than 13,000 people died. One hopes that the Nepali youth have seen the folly of violence and the power of a non-violent movement. They appear to be attuned to changes in the global economic and political landscape and are increasingly aware of the false dreams that political leaders have been selling to the Nepali people. They also are increasingly motivated and dedicated towards building and doing rather than talking and preaching, as they observe the failures of the generations before them. Coffee shops like Himalayan Java, restaurant chains like Roadhouse Café, hotel management schools like Silver Mountain, IT companies like Yomari and school supply companies like Lotus Enterprises all demonstrate the energy and zeal of the Nepali youth.

Nepali youth also need to think beyond the ordinary options and begin to dream of becoming global icons in specific fields—music and football immediately suggest themselves. There are opportunities to train young Nepalis to play club football in different parts of the world. This just requires entrepreneurs to take the risks, invest in players and make them successful footballers. Nepali youth need to visualize a Nepali team ready to make it to the World Cup. A sport today is a business and not a hobby. Good talent always attracts good sports management companies and investors who are willing to risk their investments on the future of potential players. Similarly, Nepali singers, musicians, DJs, RJs and music video producers could make themselves known as the best entertainment solution providers in any part of the world. Just as a large number of Filipino migrant workers, designated by the Philippines as Overseas Foreign Workers (OFW), work overseas as performing artistes, there are tremendous opportunities for the Nepali youth to get into the global entertainment industry. It is important to recall that Nepali musicians like Louis Banks from the hills of Darjeeling in India were the most popular performers on the Indian hotel circuit in the 1960s and 1970s and were also quite visible in the Bombay (now Mumbai) film music industry. Prabal Gurung, a youth who aspired to lead in the global fashion world shot to fame with Michelle Obama and other celebrities donning his designs. He became a global icon whom young Nepalis wanted to emulate and be associated with. The honing and nurturing of millions of Glo-Yuva, Nepali youths with a global mindset, will shape the future of Nepal.

Aside from education, the youth have to be provided training in the arts and art appreciation. Without such cultured and balanced growth, youth in Nepal stand to lose out on a lot of social skills, worldly knowledge and perspectives that are expressed through the arts and literature. For this, the development of cultural centres where the youth can experience and learn the arts is critical. Such centres have to be created in partnership between the government and the private sector. The bilateral aid agencies can also help, by sharing the cultural histories of their countries with the Nepali youth.

Building an Economy around Remittance

In 2012, the overseas workers' remittance to Nepal was estimated at USD 3 billion, which is 16 per cent of Nepal's GDP of USD 18 billion. The World Bank's Migration and Remittances Fact Book of 2012 places Nepal sixth in the world in terms of migrant worker remittance to GDP ratio. All over the world, people from countries with lesser opportunities are migrating to countries with better opportunities. Nepal needs to accept the reality that remittances from overseas workers will remain the backbone of the economy for the foreseeable future. A country with a relatively high population density for the landmass available can surely afford this reliance on remittance through the exporting of the labour force. Therefore, it is important to work out strategies to ensure a significant increase in the average remittance per person, to address this segment distinctively, just as the Philippines does, in giving its migrant workers the special status of Overseas Foreign Workers (OFW). Nepal too, should extend special services to *bipalis* (unskilled and semi-skilled migrant labour) and also divert a greater proportion of remittances into wealth-generating projects rather non-productive assets like land and houses. This deployment of remittances in wealth-generating investment opportunities will benefit the *bipali* as well as Nepal.

A separate government agency needs to be created that will be a one-stop shop providing services to the *bipalis* overseas, regulating the people involved in the migrant labour business as well as those in the business of transferring remittances. By becoming a data warehouse, such an agency could also utilize this data to conduct socio-economic and nationwide surveys. The official recognition of *bipali*s as a distinct segment of Nepali society and their recognition as a major revenue source, will bring them dignity. The proposed agency's measures could range from providing separate and better facilities for *bipali*s at the airport to the fast track processing of requests, questions, queries and visa applications at the embassies of the countries *bipali*s work in. Similarly, it would be important to create a ministry that would both interface with foreign embassies on issues of concern to *bipali*s and regulate industries and services that are built around the phenomenon of migrant labour—including consulting agencies, manpower agencies and worker welfare organizations.

With the *bipali*s being considered a separate segment, they have to be provided distinctive treatment vis-à-vis investment opportunities as well as incentives. For instance, a tax break for an Infrastructure Mutual Fund that takes exclusively *bipali* money can help in channelizing the billions that Nepal desperately needs to finance infrastructure rehabilitation and development. Allowing banks the leeway to provide preferential treatment in terms of products and services to *bipali*s will help in the productive use of remittances which are currently getting invested in unproductive sectors. For instance, when India initially allowed non-resident Indians (NRIs) to maintain their money in the currency of remittance and provided additional percentages of interest, it not only attracted NRI money, but also moved money away from an informal mode of money transfer like *hundi*, that is very prevalent among Indian migrant workers in the Middle East and Southeast Asia. Different financial instruments can be created based on hedging the future earnings of the *bipali*s, thereby providing much needed cash to their families as well as to the financial system in Nepal. For example, if a worker had a three-year binding employment stipulating his salary, that document could serve as collateral to borrow money, thereby eliminating the need to borrow money from the informal sector at exorbitant rates of interest. Withdrawing a portion of one's future earnings which have been hedged by insurance products, would provide upfront cash to fund education and debt payments.

From *Bipalis* to Non-resident Nepalis (NRN)

While earlier on in this chapter, we discussed how moving up the value chain will result in an increased remittance per person, a distinction has to be made between the remittances that would flow back to the country and the investment that the unskilled or semi-skilled *bipali* who graduates to become a skilled, professional NRN (non-resident Nepali) would make. For instance, in Qatar, individuals who went in as workers have now, over a period of time become subcontractors who supply labour, thereby moving up the value chain significantly. They would like to be referred to as NRNs and not *bipalis*. The conversion is more visible in developed countries like the US and UK, where migrant workers who leave as students graduate to become NRNs. The biggest incentive for a student to graduate would be the hope graduation offers of becoming an NRN. NRNs could transform the economy of Nepal. As Dr Jagadish Chandra Pokhrel, former vice chairman of the National Planning Commission emphasizes, 'Let the diaspora expand, not only physically into many countries but also mentally. Look at the Chinese and Indian diaspora, they have been responsible in bringing about the accelerated growth through remittances and investments, it needs to be replicated in Nepal also.' This also means that the government needs to bring about the necessary legislation that allows Nepalis with Nepali passports to invest outside Nepal and grants Nepalis in specific countries dual citizenship.

When a migrant worker leaves Nepal he or she is so occupied with thoughts of how to repay the heavy loan taken from the agent that little attention is devoted to how the earnings left over after loan repayment will be used. There exists tremendous business opportunity to manage the wallets of the migrant workers. This would mean services ranging from providing loans to secure the job, to conducting the remittance transaction, to managing the remittance once it gets into Nepal. Remittance money is often used to buy land, housing or to make other investments, but there is the opportunity to create financial tools, such as loans in Nepal against future foreign earnings, that would better aid the education and health of the families at home.

☙

Gagan Thapa, a prominent youth leader of the Nepali Congress, discussed with this author the limited scope of genuine youth participation in political parties. He explains that party structures are too rigid to allow the majority of cadre to climb the ranks. Party constitutions are skewed towards the leadership, which, in turn, is restricted to few people. This frustrates the rank and file cadre of the party. The Nepali youth have never got their due; in politics it took them ages to make themselves known, in bureaucracy they remained in the lower rungs since accelerated programmes for advancement do not exist, in the private sector the lack of professionalism has meant that age rules over competence. Young entrepreneurs are in a fix, whether they come from a business family or not—if they do, seniors in the family are not willing to risk their money, if they don't, there are no funds for them to access. Therefore, working for someone else becomes the obvious option.

The more productivity per youth Nepal can generate, the faster and quicker it will grow. If every youth in Nepal betters her or his productivity by just ten dollars a month, we are talking about a monthly increase in productivity of 120 dollars per youth, that is USD 720 million per year, a nearly 7 per cent increase in our GDP. The future lies in not leaving the youth to fend for themselves, but in being able to harness their energy and skill to create a productive work force in Nepal. This means planning their migration, ensuring that they move up the value chain and productively harnessing their remittances for the betterment of both their immediate families and the nation. For this, private, public and development sectors must form a strategic partnership, to ensure that youth in Nepal are being provided with the necessary training and skills so that when they enter the market, their skills are in demand. Youth entrepreneurial initiatives should also be supported and encouraged. It is imperative that the youth in Nepal are given a medium of expression, that they do not perceive themselves to be neglected, that they see a future if they work and dedicate themselves to a cause.

12

REDEFINING NEPAL'S
ECONOMIC BORDERS

The pursuit of capitalism requires distinguishing between political and economic boundaries. The realities of today's flat and globalized world must be engaged with from the perspective of maximizing economic returns to the nation. The political actors of every nation in the world must realize that in this globalized world every country must expand beyond its political boundaries. With the help of information and communication technologies, the entire political and economic landscape of the world is changing. Nepal's political leadership and its citizens must take part in this process of globalization; there is no other viable alternative. However, we must do so on our own terms, knowing our limits, our goals and our vision for Nepal fifty years into the future.

The first steps towards a globalized Nepal are a globalized Nepali political leadership and citizenry. As Dr Jagadish Chandra Pokhrel, former vice chairperson of the National Planning Commission puts it, 'We as Nepali people must give up this perspective of Nepal as being a landlocked country or a yam between two hard rocks,* and instead see Nepal as a beautiful and diverse country

---

*A popular idiom which refers to Nepal being pressured by India to its south and China to its north.

situated between two large, friendly countries which are growing rapidly.' No yam, no rocks, no sense of being squeezed. Thinking positive has positive effects not only in individual lives but also for national identities. For such effects to manifest, Nepal must no longer fear the changes that globalization will inevitably bring about. We must acknowledge change but accept it on our own terms, thus being able to command change rather than passively ceding to its demands.

Decades of cold war and the strenuous ties between China and India have made us myopic in our assessment of Nepal's potential. Till the Nepal–India Trade and Transit Treaty of 1960, Nepal functioned more like an Indian economic principality. Both India and Nepal have viewed Nepal's economic pursuits, be they trade, selling electricity, or seeking open transit links through Bangladesh, from a political perspective rather than from the point of view of what benefits either country could derive from them. India reacts to goods from Nepal with headlines asserting that Nepal's imports are killing Indian industry, even though the total imports from Nepal make up less than a percentage of India's total imports.[1] It is unfortunate that while Indian companies have gone global and multinational companies operate in India, Nepal is still viewed with suspicion. India has looked at Nepal in terms of how it could become a hub for Pakistan's Inter-Services Intelligence (ISI) operations and whether or not it should have strong linkages with China and the US. Instead, India could think about how Nepal's vast water, energy, biodiversity and human resources could be useful to India's economic growth.

The Political Border and Economic Border

The time has now come to unleash the Nepal economy beyond its political boundaries. Nepal must redefine its economic boundaries and understand the vast markets that it has access to. We need to understand that we are positioned like Canada is; only, we have a southern market population that is one and a half times the size of the entire population of the United States. If we take the population of the Indian states of Uttar Pradesh at 200 million, Bihar at 103 million, Uttarakhand at 10 million, West Bengal at 91 million and of Assam and other North Eastern States at 47 million,[2] we are talking about a region that comprises 450 million people, a population one and a half times that of the United States. This is not counting the domestic population of Nepal as the forty-third most populous nation in the world. To put the size of the market into perspective, if the bordering state of Uttar Pradesh in India were a country, then it would be the sixth most populous country in the world. In addition to the Indian states around Nepal, the proximity of Nepal's eastern borders with Bangladesh also places it in an ideal location to tap the 150 million people living there. The combined GDP of the above Indian states in 2012 was USD 320 billion.[3] Bangladesh had a GDP of USD 111 billion.[4] So far we have not even considered our northern neighbour China, but even if we just consider Tibet, we have a market of 3 million people and a GDP close to USD 10 billion.

Nepal has a GDP of just USD 18 billion, but lies in close proximity to China, India and Bangladesh—an economic bloc consisting of 600 million people and a combined GDP of nearly half a trillion dollars. Nepal is at the centre of this entire economic bloc. If we look at our comparative advantages vis-à-vis India as a nation, there are stark differences and Nepal will always fall short. However, if we look at the regions collectively, in the way mentioned above, Nepal still has the opportunity and comparative advantage to becoming a driving economic force in the region.

As Kanak Mani Dixit, editor of *Himal South Asian*, puts it, 'Between the open borders of Nepal's Terai and the inner Terai of India you have one of the most populous regions of the world, with the geo-physical advantage of an east-west highway.' We need to shed our ideas about Nepal being a small country between two large countries and instead see Nepal as a country with the potential of becoming an economic nexus between the countries that surround it. Along with cashing in on the population dividend, the quicker we get into changing our perception of our economic boundaries, the more we will benefit from the pursuit of rapid economic growth. The open border must also be used to our advantage and never thought of as a safety valve for Nepal. Kanak

Dixit remarks that the very fact that we are not closing the border indicates that we are far from any economic or social progress—we have never thought that one day we will have to close it to restrict entry into our prosperous land! Instead we have always interpreted the open border as a safety valve and not as a great opportunity.

Landlocked versus Land Linked

As a country, Nepal needs to overcome the much used and abused misconception of being a landlocked country. Nepal needs to understand its geographic location and familiarize itself with its own terrain. Kathmandu is closer to a seaport than Delhi is—it lies a mere 800 km from Kolkata compared to Delhi, which is 1490 km from Kolkata. Similarly, if we look at the industrial belt of Birgunj, in the border area of Nepal, the distance to the markets of Delhi is a mere 780 kilometres. If Nepal was to establish a Special Economic Zone (SEZ) in Mahendranagar, a border city in far western Nepal, the SEZ would be as close to Delhi as Delhi is to the Indian city of Jaipur. It would be closer to Delhi than are the Indian cities of Kanpur, Lucknow and Allahabad. The markets of northeast India can be more easily serviced by the Nepali border towns of Birgunj, Jogbani or Kakarvitta in the east than they would be by the geographically more distant northern Indian states. What can be ascertained from this geographic analysis is that Nepal is ideally situated to serve as a trading and manufacturing nexus for most of north India.

For a country that exports over a million workers to its southern neighbour, the geographical assets Nepal possesses should have been self evident. However, as Dr Jagadish Pokhrel, former vice chairman of National Planning Commission puts it, 'we suffer from a tremendous inferiority complex.' Nepal has used the excuse of being landlocked as a veil for its inefficiencies. By focusing on what is lacking rather that on what it possesses, Nepal has also lost out on innovation and productivity. The blame, however, has to be shared equally by Nepal and India—both governments have exclusively viewed each other through the prism of politics. The lack of an economic viewpoint has cost both countries dearly and has impacted the growth of Nepal as well as the Indian states that border the country. The first step towards the creation of a more prosperous region would be for both countries to view India–Nepal relations through an economic lens, in order to meet the needs of people on the ground with work and employment.

Similarly, in the north, Lhasa, capital of the Tibetan Autonomous Region of China, is soon to be a mere 770 km rail journey from the border town of Khasa in Tibet, just across the Nepali border. With the completion of China's rail link to the border town of Khasa expected by 2013,[5] it would mean that only 900 km separate Kathmandu from Lhasa and a mere 1100 km separate Lhasa from the Indian border town of Raxaul. Knowing this, Nepal can either continue discussing the impact of such a rail link in conferences and talk about the geopolitical issues it would raise, or it can take advantage of its unique position. Nepal already has a broad gauge railway connecting the Indian border town of Raxaul to Jogbani in Nepal; it should now explore the possibility of a rail link from Khasa in Tibet to Raxual in India. A rail link through Nepal would ensure that Nepal becomes an active member in this trade route and can re-establish its role as an entrepot for goods between India and China. Further, along its railway lines and highways, Nepal should be actively seeking to establish world-class entertainment centres and Special Economic Zones where the usual trade barriers are lowered, so that it can fully take advantage of a rail linkage between the two fastest growing and most populous economies in the world.

The movement should not be limited to goods alone but should be extended to facilitate the movement of people in world-class electric trains. Tibet received over seven million foreign tourists in 2012 including 300,000 foreign tourists and a small fraction of those tourists either gō through Nepal or come to Nepal afterwards. Here is more great potential to be unleashed. Similarly, Nepal could have world-class gaming and entertainment centres as Macau does and draw a substantial number of tourists from China. In 2007, Macau received twenty-seven million tourists out of which the majority of visitors were from mainland China. Nepal has the opportunity to draw a small fraction of this movement into Nepal by capitalizing upon its hospitality and gaming industry. The future of Nepal lies in integration and linkages of various kinds with 'Chindia', a term coined by Indian politician Jairam Ramesh and made famous by a book of the same title.[6] No other country has such an opportunity of being linked to the two economic superpowers of the twenty-first century.

Opportunities in Regionalization

One of the most lucrative prospects for Nepal will be to become a part of a South Asian economic bloc, which could be a reality by year 2025. Further, it is to look at this bloc from the perspective of East South Asia, West South Asia, North South Asia and South South Asia. The onus of forming such a bloc is upon India—the merits of such an economic bloc far outweigh any demerits. The bloc would probably include Afghanistan and Myanmar in addition to the existing SAARC member signatories of the South Asian Free Trade Area (SAFTA). For Nepal, the emergence of the economic bloc should mean the possibility of entering into a Schengen-type visa arrangement amongst the South Asian countries leading to an increase in the free movement of people for work and leisure within the region. The unleashing of the service industry will necessitate such free movement of people within the region. For Nepal, as a country that will be creating skilled people for the market, this will be essential.

Another benefit will be from an integrated currency currently touted as the 'Rupa' that can perhaps become a reality along the lines of the Euro. The Euro changed the fortunes of East European countries more than it changed the integrated markets of western Europe. Nepal can ride on the purchasing power of a unified currency thereby eliminating the discussions on fixed and floating exchange rates as well as convertibility and non-convertibility. A common currency will spur investments in Nepal as well as integrate the markets. For instance, for hydropower plants, the whole issue of the currency in which the tariff is fixed and the risks involved in financing power plants due to exchange rate changes, would be overcome. The greatest benefit Nepal could reap would be the linkages that would develop between the financial markets in the region. This would allow a Nepali firm to raise funds in the region by listing itself in one among the Mumbai, Dhaka, Colombo or Karachi stock exchanges and riding the economic growth of that region. Similarly, regional companies can be listed in Nepal and investment avenues opened. The movement of a unified currency across different bourses has undreamt of possibilities for Nepal and the region at large.

The Bay of Bengal Initiative for Multi-sectoral Technical and Economic Co-operation (BIMSTEC) is another economic bloc which is beginning to take shape—it tries to develop linkages between the largely Southeast Asian ASEAN and the largely South Asian SAARC countries. BIMSTEC includes seven members and covers thirteen sectors of cooperation. Given that the composition of BIMSTEC is similar to SAARC, with Pakistan substituted by Thailand and the Maldives by Myanmar, politically, it may get a quicker push, given the historically uneasy relationship between India and Pakistan. Here again, Nepal has a tremendous opportunity to leverage this cooperation and play a proactive role in making the best of the alliance. Nepal missed an opportunity during the meeting in 2007 to become a proactive leader for the tourism sector within BIMSTEC as it had not done enough homework, but it still has not lost the opportunity to catch up.

Regional Private Wealth Centre

One of the major items of business news in 1996 was a plan to legalize the establishment of Offshore Financial Service Centre (OFC) in Nepal, which, however, never saw the light of day. While the government in 1999 passed an enabling legislation in this regard, the issue remained as a much featured item in each year's budget speech until the Maoist-led government decided to drop the issue altogether from the 2008–09 budget. Mauritius, a country in the Indian Ocean, increased its per capita income from just over USD 200 in 1968 to over USD 16,000 in 2012 largely by becoming an offshore financial centre with the income from offshore financial services forming 10 per cent of its GDP. The success story of

Switzerland, which previously was a global centre for offshore financial services, and the more recent success of Caribbean offshore services provide a sound example of how such a service industry can contribute towards tremendous growth in Nepal. The objective is not to create a tax haven but to provide a hub that delivers world-class financial services.

While Collins and Associates, a Boston-based consulting firm, along with Harvard Law School, recommended in a 1996 report the establishment of a financial services centre in Nepal fundamentally based on time zone considerations, that issue has become insignificant with the advent of new kinds of communication technology. The issue of OFCs must therefore be looked at again from the perspective of the growing population of people requiring such services in India and China. With millionaires increasing in number in both the countries, it is but natural that they look for OFCs to park their money. OFCs were initially formed mainly as a tool for tax avoidance but are now based more on the market credibility of the OFC. Nepal has the two most critical and important elements of an OFC: first, it has its market of investors, the estimated two million millionaires living in the region; second, it is already a tourist destination like all the other OFCs. Therefore, Nepal can move towards the concept of Special Financial Zones that would be physical spaces, while also being home to virtual spaces that are OFCs. These would be regulated under separate sets of legislation wherein the operations, foreign exchange laws and monetary regulations could be different from what prevails in the rest of the country.

Nepal Is Where Nepalis Are

Another mindset change that is required is to stop talking about brain drain and leverage the presence and network of Nepalis globally. There is an increasing number of non-resident Nepali (NRN) communities being established all around the world. The quicker these Nepali workers move up the economic ladder in the countries they have made their home, the more chances Nepal has of receiving higher levels of investment. Even in India, the initial

Foreign Direct Investment that came into the country was mostly from non-resident Indians (NRIs), it was only much later that multinational corporations started queuing up to get into India. Further, it was because Indians were at the helm of global companies that investments began to flow into India. Apart from improving India's brand image, they were able to direct more investments from their multinational companies into India, encouraging other successful NRIs and multinationals in general to also invest in India.

In South Asia, the development of all the countries has taken place because of internal growth supplemented by remittances and investments from the diaspora. Out of the total USD 46 billion in remittances that flows into South Asia, the USD 2 billion Nepal receives is the lowest amongst the South Asian countries. The diaspora creates a demand for goods and services that provides large business potential for local companies. These range from staple food products of the region to traditional apparel to home furnishings. There are home furnishing stores in Delhi where one can order curtains for US window sizes. Similarly, with many NRNs buying Nepali textile products, the potential for such enterprises is going to be enormous.

Global Education and Health Care Centres

The creation of world-class education and health care institutes in Nepal would be one of the best uses of the gifts nature has endowed the country with. Nepal does not have the best global business school or a world class school of design, but it definitely has the opportunity to establish some of the best global liberal arts universities, institutions for the study of bio-diversity, climate change, ecology, music, theatre, film-making and animation. With the hospitality sector being a major revenue generator, it becomes necessary for it to be the focus of the educational system as well. A high quality of service in the hospitality sector can be ensured when Nepal has some of the best hotel management, tourism and travel institutions in world.

In the case of the health sector, there could be alternative medicine and healing centres that meet international standards of quality and comfort. The health sector should be integrally linked with the hospitality sector and be able to provide a quality of service that one expects in a world class destination. Similarly, rehabilitation centres and sanatoriums could have institutions attached that can help train a large set of people in the assisted care business. Here again, the example of getting multinational companies like Manipal to run these businesses would make the skills acquired transnational as well as of international standard.

This would automatically lead to an education and health care-facilitated tourism business that would help promote quality tourism, thereby increasing the average revenue per tourist. This coupled with liberalized laws on property ownership by foreigners through long-term lease agreements would bring in a sizeable expatriate population that would invest in the local economy.

Brand Smile

One thing Nepal has to offer that is completely indigenous, human and heart-warming is its 'brand smile'. Nepalis living in the hills continue to smile even though they spend hours fetching water or firewood. This natural instinct has led to Nepalis finding good opportunities in the service sector, be it in health care, as airline flight attendants or restaurant stewards. The smile is not something that is taught to them; it comes on its own and the success of the tourism industry is often attributed to this phenomenon. Combining brand smile with skill development can create one of the foremost service sector workforces, especially bearing in mind that by 2030 out of the 40 million people in Nepal, 22 million will be under the age of twenty-five.

Brand Nepal

Nepal needs to dream and continue to pursue its dream. As Thomas L. Friedman notes about India in *The World is Flat*, 'India only twenty years ago, before the triple convergence, was known as a country of snake charmers, poor people, and Mother Teresa. Today its image has been recalibrated.'[7] Nepal needs to also recalibrate its image, from that of a small, poor country and a backpacker's destination to one that suggests invigorating prosperity, diversity and future-oriented youthful energy.

Brand Nepal needs to primarily be internalized, so that Nepalis are proud of their country, a task that essentially requires brand icons. In a country with a large youth population, sports stars, music stars and entrepreneurs provide those brand icons. India's transformation has been facilitated by brand icons like Bollywood stars, cricket stars and the large number of entrepreneurs who have made success a way of life.

Brand Nepal can also be delivered through products and services. High-value agriculture products can be used to brand Nepali identity as flowers do for the Netherlands and lately for Colombia. Tea, coffee, cardamom and various herbs could be made synonyms for Nepal, as cigars are for Cuba and cocoa for Ghana. This would require global marketing and advertising companies that have tremendous brand experience and it would require working at vast scales that Nepal is not currently used to.

Brand Nepal can also extend through its various products like handicrafts, handmade paper, home décor items and a range of apparel. Companies like Fabindia, a chain of popular lifestyle stores that sell the products of crafts people from different parts of India, have transformed the markets through brands that suggest social responsibility, rural wholesomeness and national inclusiveness, while also delivering world-class products. Such companies can be models for Mahaguthi and Dhukuti[8] and other handicraft retail outlets of Nepal.

The biggest brand for Nepal would be the identity of the Nepali youth that will take on the service sector of the world, be it in hospitality, retail or IT outsourcing. These omnipresent and talented youth with smiles that can win the world at hotels, restaurants, banks, shopping malls, cruises and hospitals in Nepal and all around the world, will be the future brand of Nepal. Already there are Nepali fashion designers who have made it to the front cover of *Vogue*, a Nepali working for NASA, and Nepali bands and artists that have captured international recognition. This is but the beginning, the youth of Nepal are just awakening and they should be able to chase their dreams. Once that happens, Nepal will be known for its efficient, effective and smiling workers and professionals, in sectors ranging from hospitality to art, from financial services to scientific research. This will be the country's brand and what Nepali people are identified with. The day this starts to happen, Nepal's potential will have been unleashed.

13

IN SEARCH OF UNLEASHING

Since the book was released, in October 2009, a lot of muck has passed under the Bagmati River. However, Gurcharan Das's foreword to the book remains relevant as Nepal votes for yet another constituent assembly after the last one was dissolved on 28 May 2010. In the past four years, over two million babies were born and five people became prime minister in Nepal, while Obama remained the President of the United States and Dr Manmohan Singh, the prime minister of India. In Nepal, over 100 people have had an opportunity to become a minister, increasing the number of our ex-ministers. Ram Chandra Poudel from the Nepali Congress earned the dubious distinction of losing seventeen elections to become the PM—the happiest in this debacle being his own party people. People who were studying for class twelve exams have finished their undergraduate studies—a good number of them outside Nepal—and some of those who were pursuing undergrad studies are either in graduate school or are working. Many potential youth leaders have lost their credibility to project themselves as vanguards for the youth, but continue to do so, depriving the hardworking and deserving youth of any real chance.

After the book was published, over 1000 contacts were added to my address book, since the management consulting and advisory business I work for continues to grow and consolidate. I delivered over a hundred talks and interacted with hundreds of people in the quest of providing a different set of lenses with which to view Nepal. When I talked outside Nepal, I continued to focus on just one thing—telling the story of unleashing Nepal's potential. *Unleashing Nepal* tries to provide a perspective on Nepal, which is currently identified with three Ms—mountains, massacres and Maoists.

The Business of Selling Uncertainty

The dissolution of the constituent assembly on 28 May 2012 led to a political impasse as a caretaker government continued to run the country. In March 2013, a government was formed solely for the purpose of holding elections; it was led by the chief justice of the Supreme Court and comprised former bureaucrats. Naysayers were quick to start making statements about how Nepal was on its way to becoming a failed state. The couple of hundred people in Kathmandu whose livelihood thrived on talking and writing about the pessimistic and fatalistic perspective continued to find new ways of getting consultancies to write papers or go on junkets. These people found new excuses to meet head of diplomatic missions, bilateral agencies and international NGOs (INGOs) to pitch for their NGOs or consulting businesses. Private sector associations used these meetings to discuss the grave state of the nation and to find avenues to fund their junkets in the name of investment promotion. Donors continued to find new missions that could come to Nepal and tried to use these so-called impasses to begin newer programmes that would keep many experts and consultants happy.

Personal Reflections

I was dubbed an ultra-optimist and a lot of questions were raised about the crux of *Unleashing Nepal*. What about political uncertainty? What about inclusive growth? What about the high levels of migration? What about labour problems? How can you say there are opportunities? However, the only answer I had was that in a country where four years ago we started our company, beed, with just a vision document, no clients, no definitive source of revenue, in the same country we have since serviced over sixty clients, kept a team of fifteen professionals afloat and strengthened our cash flow year after year. We won a global bid to manage a USD 14 million fund for the International Finance Corporation (IFC), the World Bank arm, while everyone was claiming that investors were shying away from Nepal. In my quest to work with a variety of clients I gained more insight into what happens in Nepal. I saw how governments function and sat at meetings with private sector entrepreneurs and development organizations, learning how people were reluctant to change the status quo. I had over fifty young Nepalis, educated in the best of institutes in the world, go through the beed experience. Interacting with these young minds, learning of their aspirations and their visions for the future of Nepal provided me with additional perspectives. As I interviewed a host of people for different positions, I was fortunate to get the view of over a hundred pairs of eyes regarding issues in Nepal. One of the key lessons I learned from these experiences was that in Nepal, problems lie not with managing financial resources but with managing human resources. I was thus prompted to explore the domain of people management, and completed the Columbia Coaching Certification Program from Columbia University, USA. Then, starting the beed leadership center, I made forays in the area of leadership development by conducting 'thinkshops' and one-on-one personal coaching. This provided me a fresh ray of hope about unleashing Nepal's potential, because, instead of merely throwing money on hardware, the focus has to be on mindware and humanware.

During these four years, I also had the opportunity not only to travel extensively within Nepal but also in Rwanda as beed had started working on assignments there. Travelling to other parts of Africa, I started to realize how fortunate Nepal is with its geography and topography. In addition, I made trips to India, Bhutan, Cambodia and Mongolia, exploring niche areas for business opportunities. Seeing the positive developments happening in these countries gave me the hope to benchmark Nepal against these nations, and reassured me of unleashing Nepal's potential. Speaking recently at the Global Private Equity Conference, I proposed a new theme of F2F (Fragile to Frontier). This is a move Nepal will make over the next ten years as we see the fragile countries of the past decade—Columbia, Peru and Liberia—move to become investment frontiers.

It is very difficult to say that Nepal is worse off than it was four years ago. In rural Nepal, people find that the agenda of political discourse is only for people in Kathmandu and some other cities. They are busy constructing new roads, new houses, buying motorcycles and talking about what schools their children should go to. The others, who remain fatalistic about Nepal, are busy pursuing options to go abroad. Those at home are busy receiving remittances from money transfer centres. Mobile phones and social media have provided new tools for the youth to indulge in, as they discover the world beyond Nepal and connect with a world that was closed to them for decades. Families feel closer as they connect through mobile phones and Skype, through which they are able to stay in touch with their near and dear ones. Grandparents in Kathmandu enjoy hearing their grandchildren speaking in Nepali on the Internet, something that could not have happened ten years ago. Despite all the perceptions of uncertainty fuelled by a media feeding negative political news to a news-hungry population, and a complete lack of analysis of Nepal's economic growth, Nepal did make big strides supported by the expansion of communication networks and building of road networks. Communities started empowering themselves by taking their own decisions, no longer waiting for the political masters in Kathmandu to make the move. The gross disposable income increased manifold, as did Nepal's performance in the Human Development Index.

Worse Could Have Happened!

Things could have surely gotten worse. No one was definite about what the Maoists would do in 2009, as their use of force had not ceased. The Maoist factional infighting could have become violent and killings could have taken place, as has often happened in the fight for leadership in other parts of the world. The former king who continues to surface now and then could have aroused a lot of religious sentiment by beginning a movement that would have made the situation chaotic. The heightening debate and volatile temper of people who wanted ethnicity-based federalism and those who opposed it could have led to violent clashes resulting in bloodshed. The intra- and inter-party fights between the Madhesi parties could have followed the pattern of fights in Bihar and Uttar Pradesh that would have not only led to bloodshed but also made the Terai a difficult place for hill-dwelling Nepalis to live in. The integration of the ex-Maoist combatants could have taken a prolonged route that was noticed in a few countries in Africa. But, whenever the situation seemed to be going out of hand, a sudden sense of order came in. The Maoists had begun to shut down Kathmandu in May 2010 by pressurizing the residents to house their cadres, who were coming in from all parts of the country. They also started a campaign of unprecedented extortion. In response, the citizens of the valley rose against them. Over a hundred thousand people poured into the Kathmandu Durbar Square in a silent cry of rebellion against the Maoist push.[1] This forced the Maoists to not only retreat but slowly move towards doing business through back-door means and to abandon their much-feared Young Communist League (YCL).

Change for the Better Continues

Despite the several setbacks on the political front, many issues that required a lot of political will did get pursued. The government formed Investment Board Nepal (informally known as Board of Investments or BOI) that recruited a former banker Radhesh Pant as its CEO. BOI has since survived the political turmoil. Roads in Kathmandu and Lalitpur have been widened despite opposition, and the Nepal Police have got their confidence back after they began to implement the stringent 'zero tolerance to alcohol' rule. No one thought that this would be workable for such a long time, but people actually started to consume less alcohol at parties as they were wary of being caught. Perhaps Kathmandu is the only city in South Asia where a woman traffic police officer can actually take on a potentially drunk male driver at ten o'clock at night. Women empowerment is an inbuilt feature of Nepali society, but it is unfortunately not understood by the report-belching agencies that continue to discover newer forms of gender discrimination for their own gain. Another development was that several corrupt leaders were put behind bars. This raised a lot of hope that corruption will be noticed and punished. The judiciary delivered some landmark judgements and a few of the government watchdog agencies actually tried to prove that they could not only bark but also bite.

These four years have been eventful. People in Nepal have begun to realize that Nepal is not a small country, that it is in fact bigger than Denmark, Switzerland and Israel put together. It has a population close to 30 million, which is nearly the same as the population of Canada, the second largest country in the world. They know now that the problems Nepal is facing are not problems of a small nation but problems of a big country. Nepal has expanded in the minds of the people as the discourse on ethnicity has made people realize the complicated nature of Nepali society and the expanse of its geography. Suddenly, Kathmandu has started to look like a city that houses power-hungry people who do not want to let go of the control that they have enjoyed over the land and the people 300 km to the east and 700 km to the west of Kathmandu. In the following sections, we will examine what factors have had a bearing on Nepal's future and the unleashing of its potential.

Politics Is Power. Period.

The Unified Communist Party of Nepal (Maoist), earlier known as the Communist Party of Nepal (Maoist), raised the hopes and expectations of a lot of people and managed to become the largest party in the constituent assembly. But it slowly started to act just like any other political party, interested purely in staying in power. It continued to stall the proceedings of the constituent assembly and used all the means possible, from street protests and bandhs, to get to positions of power; and it clung on once it got there. As more stories emerged in the press of the collusion between businesses and this party, more people got convinced that the lives of 15,000 Nepalis were sacrificed in the party's quest for power.

The charisma of Pushpa Kamal Dahal soon started to fade as he was perceived to be on par with the likes of Ram Chandra Poudel, Madhav Kumar Nepal or Jhala Nath Khanal. His son's antics reminded Nepalis of the former crown prince Paras, as he, his son and the party became a punching bag for the growing vernacular media in Nepal and the many cut-and-paste tabloids that get published in Doha, Kuala Lumpur, Mumbai or New York. The party managed to siphon off money from the state allotment for ex-combatants and tried to take control of the trusts that the royal family had created to manage the holy temple of Pashupati and Buddha's birthplace, Lumbini, and the National Trust for Nature Conservation (NTNC). For instance, a very successful conservation programme—the Annapurna Conservation Area Project (ACAP), under the NTNC, which collects entry fee from trekkers—was converted into an autonomous body in January 2012 to ensure that the party could have control over the revenue.[2] It became an acceptable fact in Nepali lives that any tendering for government or quasi-government organizations would be rigged in favour of the party's cadres, be it for collection of tourist tax in Patan or contracts to build or break anything. With more cash flowing into the war chest of this erstwhile extortionist party, it started working with willing business people in real estate, and rumours of the party investing in banks, media houses and hospitals slowly started to be assumed as fact. Business people who were about to default on bank loans were provided informal credit, which not only earned the business people and the party some interest but also stemmed the sliding of the real estate prices that they were heavily invested in. Cadres who used to travel via public transport were suddenly seen driving expensive SUVs and making it through cocktail circuits. From being part of an underground revolution, they moved into the dizzy social life of the Kathmandu elite and were introduced to expensive whisky and wine and gourmet restaurants. The leaders started to juggle between Mao's *Red Book* during the day and Red Label whisky at night. The ideology of communism that they had been indoctrinated with had taught them about equality, and so they started becoming equals of the upper class of Kathmandu. This led to bitter infighting that finally resulted in the party's split. The common terms being used were 'Cash Maoist', for the UCPN, and 'Dash Maoist', or those whose hopes have been dashed, for the splinter group, the Communist Party of Nepal (Maoist), which did not get its share of booty.

In March 2010, the Nepali Congress lost Girija Prasad Koirala, its autocratic leader, and was saddled with managing the party under democratic norms. This party too had its share of infighting and could not produce anything substantial or spectacular in terms of vision, agenda or a means of going ahead. Its economic agenda continues to be socialistic. Therefore it cannot be distinguished from the competing communist parties, due to which the common Nepali people are unable to figure out whether it has anything different to offer. As it stayed away from power, the clout it had carried with the people slowly waned, and its struggle to validate its existence became ever harder.

The Communist Party of Nepal (Unified Marxist-Leninist), or CPN (UML), functioned as Nepal's largest NGO, with plans and programmes well drawn-up for it to survive. As in the past, it continued to use the opportunities of being in power to fill up its war chest and to engage in antics that had defined its tenure in power over the last twenty years. It extended its grip over the development business as its cadres gained control of development projects through any means possible. When the Multi-Stakeholder Forestry Programme (MSFP), a joint project funded by Switzerland, the UK and Finland, was put to bid and the CPN (UML)-backed groups lost, they used all their clout to get the bids cancelled.[3]

The last four years also saw the Madhesi parties from Terai becoming an important part of national politics. With the president and vice president both from the Madhes and the key position of deputy prime minster being constantly occupied by a representative of one of the many Madhesi fronts and parties, the voice of the Madhes was finally heard in the capital. However, the tendency to factionalize, intra-party squabbles and constant splits similar to the regional parties in Bihar and Uttar Pradesh in India eroded the efficacy of this newfound voice. According to Vijay Kant Karna, Madhes intellectual and former ambassador to Denmark, there are twenty-six Madhesi parties of which only nine are registered with the Election Commission.

These four years also saw an emerging space for right-wing politics as Kamal Thapa continued his solo crusade for the restoration of constitutional monarchy. If his party tows the line of the Bharatiya Janata Party (BJP) in India by embracing a Hindu agenda, dumping the idea of constitutional monarchy and getting the ex-king involved as a patron, then this voice will be one that cannot be ignored in the future, and will also be able to attract a lot of votes of the people who are frustrated with the current parties and political set-up.

Because of the never-ending political quagmire people could not wait for the situation to improve, and continued to pursue their lives and businesses, taking into consideration that in Nepal the only constant in the past sixty years has been instability. Not once, in the post-1950 history of Nepal, have Nepalis felt a sense of stability for longer than four years.

Equidistance Policy Prevails

Each successive political party in Nepal tried to woo both the Chinese and Indian governments, continuing the play-them-against-each-other policy, which has been practised for over sixty years. From the time that Nepal had to take sides during the heightening of tensions between India and China in the early 1960s, which led to the 1962 war, it has practised the politics of equidistance. It has kept both the neighbours happy, while at the same time trying to play one against the other to seek favours. However, it is still a bumpy ride, as even though the government tries to please both India and China, it never loses an opportunity to blame them for the problems of the country. Nepal holds India responsible for every political mishap and India holds China responsible for every political mishap that India is unable to read. China has begun to pursue a hands-off policy and has allowed the Indian diplomacy, intelligence agencies, security apparatus and South Block bureaucracy tow their separate lines rather than push for a cohesive Indian approach towards Nepal.

Instead of looking into what should happen in 2050, the Indo-Nepal relationship is continuously seen from the lens of the 1950 Nepal–India Treaty of Peace and Friendship. With the rise of India's position in global geopolitics, no Indian Foreign Service (IFS) officer wants to become a Nepal specialist, so the job becomes the pastime of retired officials. The irony is that in India you will not become a Nepal expert till you retire and are above sixty years of age. In Nepal, too, you will not graduate from being a youth leader to a mainstream leader till you are sixty. How will these people, many of whom many will never live till 2050, actually decide on a futuristic policy? The people concerned with security just see Nepal through the viewpoint of fake currency and as a potential playground for Pakistan's ISI. For Nepalis who interact frequently with India, that is the people on the border, India has not changed. They have not seen, and perhaps will not see, the developments of Gurgaon, Bangalore or Hyderabad. For them India is what they see when they cross the border. For instance, the eastern border town of Naxalbari, the gateway for many Nepalis into India, has physically remained the same for the past thirty years. Neither the physical space nor the attitude of the people manning the border has changed. This vision of non-transformation of India, which many Nepalis witness, helps fuel their anti-India nationalism. At crucial moments, political parties take advantage of this sentiment and whip it up, whether by continuously blaming India for meddling in the internal affairs of the country or telling their cadres how Nepal will be gobbled up like Sikkim or treated as a protectorate like Bhutan. China continues to influence Nepalis in day-to-day life rather than through politics by maintaining that Nepali politicians should work with India for future stability. Confucius Institute, a Chinese NGO that started operations in Nepal through Kathmandu University in 2007, offers Mandarin language classes at very low rates. Volunteers from this institute travel to different parts of Nepal to teach Mandarin to primary school students for free. The Chinese also have a programme in Nepali on FM radio, which translates and broadcasts news as seen through the Chinese perspective. Similarly, they use different institutes to propagate different agendas. For instance, the Asia Pacific Exchange & Cooperation Foundation has created a USD 3 billion development project in Lumbini[4] and, among others, have Pushpa Kamal Dahal, the Maoist chairman, as their main crusader. As evidenced by the multitude of high-level visits by Chinese officials to Nepal in the past four years, including a visit by Premier Wen Jiabao in 2012, it is very clear that China has a deep interest in Nepal, even though Nepalis seem to underestimate it.

Nepal does not realize that India and China will not fight over dominance in Nepal as they eye trade volumes with each other of up to USD 100 billion by 2015.[5] Both countries will not want to put their relationship into jeopardy for the sake of Nepal. Just as the US does good business with China but never loses an opportunity to bring up the Tibet issue, India will try to further its business with China but never spare a chance to blame China for anything that happens in Nepal which it does not understand. It is for Nepal to decide how it needs to redefine its relationship with its neighbours that are the two fastest-growing economies of the world from the perspective of economic growth and development.

Reforms Suffer

Economic reforms suffered the most because of the absence of a distinct political force. When governments did not have the mandate to even present budgets for a full fiscal year, discussing reforms became a priority that they could avoid. The high politicization of the appointment of bureaucrats and the auctioning of positions by political parties made short-term gains the main agenda. People who bought the positions were more interested in making money to recover the money they had paid rather than in working on policy issues. The risk-taking ability of the bureaucracy was drastically reduced as their tenure in their positions was uncertain. The frequent transfers of staff every time the government changed further marred the vision of the already myopic Nepalis. They were unable to see beyond the immediate future and it hindered their ability to care about political reform. The absence of a stable government meant that the government worked through interim plans devised by donors who themselves were operating under timelines shorter than the usual three or five years. Some of the key reforms, as mentioned in Chapter 9 of the book including land reform, labour reform, financial sector reform, capital market reform, were therefore stalled.

Since most of the government appointees were either communist ideologues or left-of-centre thinkers, the policies they pursued and propagated were anti-capitalist, anti-free-market, and revolved around governmental controls and equitable distribution. Therefore, Nepal Rastra Bank, the Central Bank of Nepal, became more engaged in capping CEO salaries and controlling interest rates, rather than in working on other value-adding policies such as enabling online transactions. Despite this, the private sector had such low credibility that the disillusionment with it helped the successive governments get away with their anti-free-market policies.

Rather than trying to reform the financial services sector, successive governments encouraged cooperatives that had little accountability or regulation. Despite hundreds of them going bust and disappearing, the government continued to support them in an attempt to be seen as a propagator of socialistic policies and against market-oriented capitalism.

Despite the suspect promises of bringing 10,000 to 20,000 MW of electrical power to Nepal,[6] the country continued to be a hydro-rich yet electricity-deprived country. The state-run NEA started to mean No Electricity Authority. The duration of power cuts increased to twenty hours in peak winter season in 2012, and there are no signs of improvement till 2020.

Inflation continued unabated as petroleum prices soared from Rs 78 in 2008 to Rs 125 in December 2012, an increase of 60 per cent.[7] The spiralling effect of increased fuel costs could be seen in the increase of other product and service prices. The government continued to increase its taxes as the prices of petroleum products escalated and the import of gold and vehicles kept growing. Added to that, the Nepali rupee depreciated against the dollar, following the slide of the Indian rupee.

Private Sector: Improved Activity Low Credibility

The four years did see sizeable increase in domestic investments despite the fluid political conditions. KFC and Pizza Hut entered Nepal along with franchises for many India-based coffee shops and restaurants. Bhat-Bhateni Supermarket added four more outlets, with more than half a million square feet of space. Lifestyle brands like the home-grown Sherpa Adventure Gear started making a mark along with stores like Tara Oriental. More cement factories opened and more companies were acquired. Much activity was seen in the property development sector, but stalled as the interest rates climbed and speculative demand reduced. People started exploring the agriculture markets, and new areas of investment in technology-related businesses emerged. Private educational institutions and health-care facilities mushroomed across Nepal, because the government was neither able to provide proper facilities nor regulate the private ones. Outsourcing companies, from security to cleaning to human resources to accounting to IT burgeoned. The telecom service company Ncell, which began operations after acquiring Mero Mobile in March 2010, crossed the 10 million mark by May 2013.[8] With tourism looking to pick up, existing hotels started renovating and new hotels started to be built. Since 2010, all hotels that were in the red slowly started to report profits. The fact that a hotel like Temple Tree in Pokhara could make a mark for itself within first year of operation shows that there is space for good products and services in Nepal.

In Nepal, businesses have generally performed well. After reviewing the statistics of firms who made their data available, most performing firms grew compounded at minimum 20 per cent per annum.[9] However, no one wants to tell a success story. When one meets a business person, he will always have sob stories about how things are not going well and would not share that he had just upgraded his vehicle or bought a new apartment. This negative discourse on Nepal's progress has increased the perception of there being no economic development.

Despite the increased economic activity, business and profitability, the credibility of the private sector plummeted. More business people started being seen in newspapers for bank defaults and auction notices, and the list of people blacklisted due to defaults on their loans increased. The list of value added tax (VAT) evaders included many prominent business people and organizations. When Rameshwor Khanal resigned as finance secretary on the dispute with the finance minister on making the VAT evaders list public,[10] everyone showed concern apart from the business community. Similarly, the business community opposed the government's decision to make Know Your Customer (KYC) norms mandatory under the anti-money laundering laws.

Business associations increasingly started to be used as a means to further individual agendas. People who did not have good meeting rooms in their own offices suddenly found spaces for free at these various association premises. With donors focused on working with such associations, money for junkets became easy to come by, and association positions became lucrative as they entailed the benefits of travel and hospitality. People who led the associations continued to find opportunities for themselves as they got to hobnob with the politicians.

The lackadaisical attitude of the business associations did not improve and they failed to bring in a sense of professionalism. They did not hand over the management of associations to the professionals; instead, these were run by political leaders who canvassed and spent the donors' money on election after election. The rivalry between various factions within the associations as well as with other associations continued. For instance, a powerful programme of the Nepal Business Forum (NBF), sponsored by the International Finance Corporation (IFC), lost a lot of time on deciding on the location of the secretariat, as the FNCCI and the Confederation of Nepalese Industries (CNI) continued to fight rather than cooperate.

The objectives of the average business person continued to be status and power rather than taking the business to the next level. During the past four years, many more business people became consuls general of countries ranging from Malta to Togo, increasing the number to over thirty. With special blue licence plates on their vehicles, and special treatment at airports, they felt a great sense of arrival. The ultimate goal of the Nepali entrepreneur was to pull out a multifold business card that carried the list of institutions he was affiliated with, to drive a blue-number-plated vehicle, get felicitation notices printed in newspapers and constantly be covered by the print media and television.

Tourism: The Only Low-Hanging Fruit

The number of tourists increased from 500,277 in 2008[11] to 800,000 in 2012.[12] In contrast, the same number of Nepalis flew in and out of Kathmandu, many as tourists to other countries. The arrivals continued to be dominated by Indians. Among Indians, Nepal gets more visitors coming overland from Tier II and Tier III cities because Nepal has stopped marketing itself in Tier I cities. Chinese tourists started to come in droves, and we will see their numbers increasing in the years to come. In China, as the Chinese people are questioning communism, they are finding it easier to seek solace in Buddhism, which they see as a way of life. More Chinese, therefore, want to visit Nepal as it is the birthplace of Buddha.[13] The handicraft cottage industry is becoming completely dependent on these tourists. This is happening despite any major government intervention.

Everyone realized that state or other interventions in tourism would not work since in Nepal, tourism has always been led by entrepreneurs. Therefore, programmes like Nepal Tourism Year 2011 were a disaster. Money was spent in running advertisements in Nepali and spending a good chunk of the budget on a lavish programme at the stadium watched only by Nepalis on television. The initiative, led by people from the private sector, generated only column centimetres and sound bites for the local media. Outside Nepal, there was little.

Nepal Airlines continues to be the national mascot for mockery because Qatar Airways tops the list as Nepal's national airline, flying in four flights each day from Doha since 2012. Other airlines have started their daily second flight, and more are to follow suit. As a positive trend, however, from twenty-three international airlines flying over 15,000 flights annually into Kathmandu in

2008, twenty-seven airlines started flying 23,000 flights annually by 2012.

The potential of domestic tourism is suddenly becoming visible as Nepalis have started to show more interest in exploring and appreciating their own country. With motorbikes and vehicles at their disposal, nuclear families are discovering Nepal apart from religious purposes. Hotels that cater to only domestic travellers are springing up, and packages are being developed for this new emerging Nepali traveller.

However, the labour union continues to play spoilsport as they use their age-old tactic of pressurizing the owners of the hotels at the critical juncture of high occupancy. Hotel owners also have not really invested much in management staff, and former union workers who are promoted as managers cannot defend the management position. While prices of lodging have gone up, service has not improved because the investment in hospitality training has been minimal. And, while the numbers of tourists are growing, the yield per traveller is not increasing substantially.

The potential for tourism will depend on redefining the way Nepal looks at the entire sector. Instead of focusing on arriving at the magic number of one million tourists, as it has been doing for the past two decades, it should look at how to tap domestic tourists. One-tenth of the Nepali population stands at three million. That is three times the elusive one million.

Development Business Flourishes

As Nepal had no space for conflict resolution specialists, a new set of 'parachute consultants' specializing in post-conflict countries started to land. They could use the post-conflict lens on everything from constructing fender to gender. From long-term programmes, everyone started shifting to shorter and interim programmes whose failure would not remain in anyone's memory for long.

Like the labour in Nepal, which would rather pursue the position of a union leader than work well, and a business person who would aspire to be the head of an association rather than grow his business, development practitioners started to place more value on meeting political leaders and senior bureaucrats than actually going about the business of development. More consultative meetings were held and more missions arrived at times of pleasant weather in Kathmandu than ever before.

More INGOs were registered in the past four years and more aid poured in. In the absence of institutional knowledge within the organizations, interventions that had failed in the past began to be made again, be it funding the near-bankrupt and corrupt state electricity utility to undertake construction of new power projects or funding business associations for conducting programmes that they were incapable of carrying through.

The consulting rates have not changed over the past years as more and more retired bureaucrats become the easy choice to hire; they work for lower rates, so reports are mostly written under the same budgets as before. And there is a paradox when donors find those very retirees delivering solutions that they were not able to come up with when they were in power.

Nepal needs to continue to explore a long-term policy in working with the donors. For instance, an amount of USD 10 million per annum can be fixed as the minimum amount of financial aid that donors must offer in order to work in Nepal. Also, necessary regulations can be passed to ensure that all agencies working with public money make their financials public by putting it up on their websites. The benefits government officials have received—like offers to go on junkets or getting top-up salaries or a vehicle and staff for projects—should be made public. People in the bureaucracy are reluctant to raise issues against the donors as they know they will be employed by them post-retirement. They should mend their self-seeking ways and start questioning the conduct of these institutions. The discourse now needs to shift from need assessments to accountability and responsibility.

Remittances: The Saviour

Remittances from the *bipali*s increased from USD 2.5 billion in 2008 to close to USD 4 billion in 2012—an increase of 60 per cent as 1200 Nepalis on average started to leave Nepal each day.[14] The remittances continue to provide the money that is keeping the rural households running and the national economy afloat. The trend accelerated as job opportunities were limited to union politics, and people were averse to living in a country where everyone had a fatalistic view of Nepal. However, these remittances were not channelled towards development of infrastructure or investment because the government was neither able to figure out its own strategy nor did it have the courage to open up the sector for private banks to create fund instruments to channelize this money. Rather than trying to develop programmes that would put remittance money to good use, the donor projects continued to focus on studying ethnicity, inequality, gender and social disorder and issues of remittance, thereby continuously giving the world a very negative impression of Nepal. Remittances changed the history, geography and society of rural Nepal because the offices of money-transfer firms have now become the iconic address used as a reference point in villages and towns. The future unleashing of Nepal will hinge on how this big chunk of money can be put into productive use, such as building infrastructure, creation of jobs and entrepreneurial development.

The Unseen Transformation

Nepalis suffer from Mass Alzheimer's and people tend to forget many things very easily. The ten years of insurgency leaving 15,000 people dead has already been forgotten, as has the fact that at that time it was almost impossible to travel within Nepal due to several blockades put up by the state as well as the insurgents. The Maoists had actually threatened to capture many places, many times, but still we were very happy to invite them as chief guests at our functions and show off how close we were to the same folks we once protested against. For the forgiving, resilient and forgetful Nepalis, life moved on.

If you stand at a street junction in Kathmandu for ten minutes and observe the traffic and people, suddenly you wonder where all these women driving cars and bikes came from. You notice that there are no barefooted Nepalis nor people clad in tattered clothing.

You then realize that perhaps the poster boys and girls of poverty projects are slowly vanishing. You start seeing teenagers sporting South Korean fashion, emulating the stars they watch on Korean soap operas. Walk and drive around and see the numerous party palaces, day-care centres and beauty salons that have opened not only in Kathmandu and major cities but even in smaller towns. The collages of signage seek the attention of the customer, who now has some money to spend.

More fine dining restaurants have opened in Kathmandu Valley and different types of cafés have blossomed in other cities and towns. Restaurants that were opened to cater only to tourists and expatriates now focus more energy on targeting local clientele. In a small one-square-kilometre area christened Jhamel (Thamel in Jhamsikhel), Patan, more than fifty restaurants have opened in the past four years. Similarly, eating places, party palaces to host social functions and jewellery stores opened at a rapid pace. In the New Road area of Kathmandu, there are more than 100 jewellery stores selling gold jewellery and diamonds, and have started becoming a rage. The more the prices of gold increased, the more the number of jewellery stores went up, and more people bought gold and jewellery, making everyone wonder where the money was coming from.

At the same time, the social and political analysis being done in the media dwindled, giving way to advertorials such as interviews, products launches and celebrity photographs. Taking advantage of people willing to see themselves in the media, ECS Media group successfully launched several magazines leveraging on the hunger of the people for easy publicity. More broad sheets were added and traditional media houses did not mind making good money publishing shallow weeklies with sleazy pictures. Radio stations continued to expand; in January 2013, the government decided to stop issuing licenses as 475 licences had been already issued, and 375 of them were in operation.[15] Between January 2008 and May 2013, twenty more licences for television channels were issued in addition to the existing ten, despite long hours of power cuts; but, only a couple of channels were news-free channels.[16]

International events started to take place in Nepal; Bryan Adams came and performed, as did MLTR. Literary festivals attracting international writers and speakers took place, putting Nepal on the South Asian literary map; bestseller authors started to discover the fan following they enjoyed in Nepal. Narayan Wagle became the first Nepali writer to cross the 50,000-copies-sold market with his debut novel, *Palpasa Café*, and more writers got signed to write in Nepali and English. Jazzmandu, a music festival, became a permanent feature in the international music itinerary. Kathmandu International Arts Festival made its debut in 2012. Additionally, the Indian embassy started to bring in more Indian artists to Nepal, and other embassies too started to support initiatives that promoted arts and culture.

Glo-Yuva: Global Youth Emerging

Prabal Gurung, who went to New York and started his fashion career, hit the headlines as Michelle Obama wore his dress in 2009. After that he has been a rave in the fashion world, inspiring many more Nepali youth to take on the global stage. The Nepali cricket team, after winning the Division 4 matches, is now poised to play at the World Cup in 2015. Nepali footballer Rohit Chand signed for an Indonesian club and Anil Gurung signed in for the Chelsea reserve team. Suma Tharu, who wrote and sang about the sufferings of Kamlari, the bonded labour, found the spotlight as she was recognized by the then US Secretary of State Hillary Clinton in the Women in the World Summit 2012. Pushpa Basnet, the founder of Early Childhood Development Center was named CNN Hero 2012.

The number of Nepalis returning after their studies abroad is increasing and they are testing their skills in start-up companies and new social organizations. Platforms like Entrepreneur for You started successfully, showcasing entrepreneurs and providing opportunities to interact with them. Incubation centres like Biruwa Ventures were formed and companies like CloudFactory, a crowdsourcing company, started hiring in hundreds. The conversation has started to move from complaining to viewing Nepal as a land of opportunity and a place to demonstrate something. More people have started realizing the value of a life that is not so taxing. They are realizing the value of being in the same city as your parents and having a social security net that vouchers cannot buy. The emergence of India and China also made people wonder whether they should be to the east or the west of the GMT. Young people started to realize that perhaps it is better to start something in Nepal itself, where they would know the business environment, understand the markets and have some lead time before the competitors. If one walks into a café filled with young Nepali returnee professionals or visits a company like Incessant Rain Studios, an animation company that caters to clients like Disney, one can see the power of unleashing Nepal's potential, first-hand. It is the energy, enthusiasm and the non-defeatist sense of hope that people have that keeps it going.

IT Moves: Social Media

In September 2011, three Nepali not-for-profits—Nyaya Health, Help Nepal Network and Grassroot Movement in Nepal (GMIN)—won a USD 100,000 award each from the Chase Community Giving programme. The award was given for the most number of votes garnered on their Facebook pages. Similarly, Anuradha Koirala in 2010 and Pushpa Basnet in 2012 were voted CNN Heroes based on social media votes. Social media began the transformation in Nepal that traditional media may have taken many years to accomplish.

Facebook users grew to two million users by 2012, and more people joined Twitter and other social networking sites. On Facebook, female users constituted up to 31 per cent of the users, showing that the digital divide between men and women was reducing.[17] Apps released in US, Japan or Korea began to find their way to Nepal the same day of their release. The usage of social media, crowdsourcing and leveraging YouTube videos changed the lives of many. When Google launched Google+, Nepal became the fourth-largest user country in the first week of the launch itself.[18]

The Nepali youth is keeping up with the developments on the Internet at a similar pace as in the region, if not globally. In the past four years, people learnt cloud computing as they oscillated between Dropbox, SkyDrive and Google Drive. From just communicating on Skype, suddenly WhatsApp, Viber and many more options became available. Ncell introduced Blackberry on the go only to take on stiff competition from Android phones. When Samsung launched its Galaxy S III phone model, the phones were available in the Nepal market just a few weeks after the global launch.

The gaming business has grown as well, with both the young and the not-so-young getting hooked on to online games. Online chatting has changed parenting responsibilities and schools are not being able to respond to the pace of change the students are being exposed to. Teens may find, with gadgets replacing human interaction, that conversing with other human beings sometimes becomes a problem.

Waiting for the Unleashing

The last four years could not have been more eventful. Nepal moves into yet another phase of electing a new constituent assembly, deciding on its federal structure, its form of government and the legal structures for economic empowerment. There are change agents who are working relentlessly in their own fields, outside the glare of the media and the public, and they will slowly start showing results. If one Dr Ram Shrestha of Dhulikhel Hospital could transform a two-room hospital into an institution including schools, a medical college and multi-disciplinary hospital that deals with KG (kindergarten) to PG (postgraduate) students in a span of just fifteen years, many more people can spearhead such transformation and at the same time make such initiatives sustainable in the long run.

We will know Nepal has unleashed its potential when the discourse on Nepal outside shifts from being the land of three Ms (Maoists, massacres and mountains) to that of three Ss—smile, service and success.

NOTES

Author's Prologue

1. 'World Population Prospects, the 2010 Revision', United Nations, Department of Economic and Social Affairs, http://esa.un.org/unpd/wpp/Sorting-Tables/tab-sorting_population.htm (accessed September 2012).
2. Kanak Dixit and Shastri Ramachandran, *State of Nepal* (Himal Books, 2001).
3. Manjushree Thapa, *Forget Kathmandu* (Penguin Viking, 2005).
4. Gurcharan Das, *India Unbound* (Penguin Viking, 1999).
5. Thomas L. Friedman, *The World Is Flat* (Penguin Books, 2006), p. 561.

1. Isolation, Isolation and Isolation

1. M.C. Regmi, *An Economic History of Nepal 1768–1846* (Adroit Publishers, 1972).
2. D.S. Kansakar Hilker, *Syamukapu* (Vajra Publications, 2005).
3. Prithvi Narayan Shah, *Divya Upadesh*, (Nepal, HMG of Nepal, Ministry of Information and Communication, Information Department, 2003).
4. Ludwig F. Stiller, *The Rise of the House of Gorkha: A Study in the Unification of Nepal* (Human Resource Development Centre, 1995), pp. 242–43.
5. M.C. Regmi, *Kings and Political Leaders of The Gorkhali Empire* (Orient Longman, 1995), pp. 12–14.
6. Perceval Landon, *History of Nepal, Vol. I* (Adarsha Enterprises, 2001), p. 132.
7. Sanjeev Upreti, *Mimicry, Masculinity, Strategy* (Kathmandu, 2007) 3.
8. Deepak Gyawali, 'Yam Between Bhot and Mughal' in *State of Nepal*, ed. Kanak Dixit and Shastri Ramachandaran (Himal Books, 2005), p. 212.

9. Ram Sharan Mahat, *In Defense of Democracy* (Adroit Publishers, 2005), p. 45.
10. Dor Bahadur Bista, *Fatalism and Development* (Orient Longman, 1991), p. 94.

2. Mixed Economy of the 1950s—Confused Results

1. Library of Congress, 'A Country Study: Nepal', http://lcweb2.loc.gov/frd/cs/nptoc.html (accessed January 2009).
2. Library of Congress, 'A Country Study: Nepal', http://lcweb2.loc.gov/frd/cs/nptoc.html (accessed January 2009).

3. The People's Movement of 1990: Emergence and Squander

1. Compiled from Ministry of Finance, Economic Survey (Ministry of Finance, 1994).
2. Compiled from records at the Nepal Stock Exchange and details provided by Standard Chartered Bank, Nepal.
3. Sujeev Shakya, *Making Private Sector an Engine for Growth* (DFID, 2008).
4. Sujeev Shakya, 'Rs 15,000,000,000: That Is How Much the Maoist Strike Has Cost the Country So Far', *Nepali Times*, Issue 501, 7–13 May 2010.
5. 'Khetan Group Sells Cash Cow to Foreign Partner', *The Kathmandu Post*, 10 November 2010, available at http://www.ekantipur.com/the-kathmandu-post/2010/11/10/money/khetan-group-sells-cash-cow-to-foreign-partner/214685/.
6. 'Nepse Starts First Day of FY with a Bang', *The Kathmandu Post*, 17 July 2011, available at http://www.ekantipur.com/the-kathmandu-post/2011/07/17/money/nepse-starts-first-day-of-fy-with-a-bang/224129.html.
7. Tourism Malaysia 'Tourism Malaysia Corporate Media Centre', http://www.tourism.gov.my/corporate/mediacentre.asp (accessed January 2009)
8. Compiled from Trading Economics, http://www.tradingeconomics.com/nepal/gdp (accessed May 2013).
9. Compiled from Trading Economics, http://www.tradingeconomics.com/malaysia/gdp (accessed May 2013).

4. Disappointing Private Sector

1. Sujeev Shakya, *Making Private Sector an Engine for Growth* (DFID, 2008).
2. Government of Nepal, *Statistical Year Book of Nepal* (Central Bureau of Statistics, 2003).

3. Sujeev Shakya, *Making Private Sector an Engine for Growth* (DFID, 2008).
4. John Welpton, *A History of Nepal* (Cambridge University Press, 2005).
5. *The Himalayan Times*, 'Power par blow to adulterators', 15 December 2008.
6. My Sansar, '*Kantipur Futne Bhayo*', (Kantipur Will Split), http://www.mysansar.com/2008/07/2857.html.

5. The Business of Development

1. Truman Library, Truman, Harry S., Inaugural speech of 1949, http://www.trumanlibrary.org/calendar/viewpapers.php?pid=1030 (accessed January 2009).
2. The author served on the board of Rupantaran from 2010 to 2012.
3. Eugene Bramer Mihalay, *Foreign Aid and Politics in Nepal: A Case Study* (2002).
4. United Nations, *Asian Regional Team for Employment Promotion Report* (UN, 1974).
5. 'Experts flay tardy pace of financial sector reforms', *The Kathmandu Post*, 2 April 2004.
6. Government of Nepal, *Foreign Aid Policy* 2002, http://www.mof.gov.np/facd/policies/pdf/foreignaid.pdf (accessed January 2009).
7. United Nations, 'Millennium Development Goals', http://www.un.org/millenniumgoals/, (accessed January 2009).

6. Governance Woes

1. Sujeev Shakya, *Role of Private Sector in Governance* (Swiss Development Co-operation, 2002).
2. Institute of International Education, http://www.iie.org/Who-We-Are/News-and-vents/Press-Center/Press-Releases/2011/2011-11-14-Open-Doors-International-Students (accessed January 2013).
3. '15,000 Nepal teachers have fake degrees', *The Hindustan Times, Delhi, India*, http://chautari.wnso.org/forums/index.php?showtopic=1051 (accessed January 2009).
4. United Nations Data, http://data.un.org/Data.aspx?d=PopDiv&f=variableID:77 (accessed January 2009).

7. Conflictonomics

1. Deepak Thapa and Bandita Sijapati, *A Kingdom Under Siege* (The Printhouse, 2003).
2. Crisis Group Asia Report No. 104, 'Nepal's Maoists: Their Aims, Structure and Strategy', 2005, p. 8.

3. Human Rights Watch, *Children in the Ranks: The Maoists' Use of Child Soldiers in Nepal* (2007), p. 2.

4. Jo Becker, *Child Recruitment in Burma, Sri Lanka and Nepal* (Human Rights Watch, 2007), p. 6.

5. Human Rights Watch, *Children in the Ranks: The Maoists' Use of Child Soldiers in Nepal* (2007), p. 3.

6. Ram Sharan Mahat, *In Defense of Democracy*, (Adroit Publishers, 2005).

7. Kedar Subedi, *Suraksha bina ko suraksha karcha, Himal Khabarpatrika*, 13–27 February 2005.

8. Ujir Magar, *Nepal Weekly*, year 4, number 29, 2006.

9. 'Interview with Chairman Prachanda', *Maoist Information Bulletin—4*, 15 September 2003, Communist Party of Nepal (Maoist) via http://www.cpnm.org/new/English/documents/information_bulletin-4.htm, (accessed January 2009).

10. Kedar Subedi, '*Suraksha Bina Ko Suraksha Karcha*', *Himal Khabarpatrika*, 13–27 February 2005.

11. Bhaskar Gautam, Purna Basnet and Chiran Manandhar. *Mauwadi Virodh: Sashatra Sangharsh Ko Avadhi* (Martin Chautari, 2007).

12. Ibid.

13. Ibid.

14. UNHCR, *UNHCR Nepal Factsheet*, UNHCR, November 2008, http://www.un.org.np/unhcr/docfile/2008-12-16-unhcr-nepal-factsheet.pdf (accessed January 2009).

15. Government of West Bengal, India, *West Bengal Industrial Policy* (1978).

16. Keshar Kumar Lamgade, *Nepal's Exodus for Foreign Employment, Nepali Monitor*, Feb 2008, http://www.nepalmonitor.com/2008/02/nepals_exodus_for_foreign_employment_.html (accessed January 2009).

8. Emergence of the Remittance Economy

1. Garden Court Chambers, 'The launch of The Gurkhas: The Forgotten Veterans', http://www.gardencourtchambers.co.uk/news/news_detail.cfm?iNewsID=230 (accessed January 2009).

2. Ibid.

3. C. Mishra, L.P. Uprety, T. Panday, '*Seasonal Agricultural Labour Migration from India*, (Centre for Nepal and Asian Studies, 2000).

4. Raju Bhattrai, 'Open borders, closed citizenships: Nepali labor migrants in Delhi' (Institute of Social Studies, 2007), p. 3.

9. Alleviating Poverty, Creating Wealth

1. Martin Ravallion, Shaohua Chen and Prem Sangraula, *Update on Dollar a Day*, (World Bank, August 2008).
2. Gates Foundation, 'Grants Overview', Bill and Melinda Gates Foundation, http://www.gatesfoundation.org/grants/Pages/overview.aspx.
3. The name of the Act in Nepali: *Bidesh Ma Lagani Garna Pratibanda Gareko Ain*, literally translated, means prohibition on Nepalis investing in foreign countries.
4. The World Bank in *The Doing Business Report 2009* (World Bank, 2009) ranks Nepal 111 out of 181 countries.
5. World Bank, *Nepal Trade and Competitiveness Study*, (World Bank, 2003), p. 71.
6. Institute for State Effectiveness, 2007 (ISE), *Nepal—The Emerging Order*, (ISE, April 2007), p. 12.
7. John Wood, *Leaving Microsoft to Change the World*, (HarperCollins, US, 2006).
8. Department of Forestry, 'Achievements', http://www.dof.gov.np/achievements.
9. Rajendra K.C., Aasha Khattri, '*Contribution of Community Forestry in Reducing Rural Poverty in Nepal*', http://www.tropentag.de/2008/abstracts/full/147.pdf.

10. Scaling Up

1. Sujeev Shakya, *Private Sector Assessment* (ADB, 2004).
2. Computed from CIA World Fact Book, Nepal, https://www.cia.gov/library/publications/the-world-factbook/print/np.html (accessed January 2009).
3. Ramesh C. Arya, '*Boot Experiences in Nepal—Recent Practices*' in Hydropower in the New Millennium ed. Bjørn Honningsvåg, Grethe Holm Midttomme, K. Repp (Taylor & Francis, 2001), p. 3.
4. Computations are based on International Energy Agency (IEA) figures—Statistics Division, http://www.iea.org, 2007.
5. Data computed from Department of Electricity Development, 'Licenses', http://www.doed.gov.np (accessed December 2008).
6. Bijay Man Sherchan, *Hydropower Development in Nepal—Developers' Dilemma*, http://nepaliperspectives.blogspot.com/2008/08/hydropower-development-in-nepal.html, 2008.
7. Nepal data computed from Nepal Tourism Board, http://www.welcomenepal.com and Malaysia data from Malaysia Tourism Board http://www.tourism.gov.my/.

8. Computed based on reports of Pacific Asia Travel Association (www.pata.org) and Vision 2020 Reports of World Trade Organizations (www.world-tourism.org).
9. Gautam, Kul Chandra, 'How To Avoid Nepal's Descent Into A Failed State' (Nepal, 2004).

11. Nepali Youth: An Engine of Productivity and Change

1. Computed from 2007 Nepal Population Projection Reports, Central Bureau of Statistics, Nepal.
2. Anjali Subedi, 'Community School Progresses, Invites Maoist Resistance', *The Kathmandu Post*, 31 July 2007.
3. 'Language and Electronics: The Coming Global Tongue', *The Economist*, 21 December 1996, pp. 37–39.
4. Helvetas Nepal, 'F Skill', http://www.helvetasnepal.org.np/fskill.htm.
5. United Nations, Department of Economic and Social Affairs, Population Division, 'World Population Increasing, 1950–2050' (UN, 2002).

12. Redefining Nepal's Economic Borders

1. In 2007-08, imports from Nepal constituted 0.25 per cent of the total imports, Government of India, Department of Commerce, Export Import Data Bank, Import—Country-wise, http://commerce.nic.in/eidb/icnt.asp.
2. Computed from current records of the Census of India—Office of the Registrar General and Census Commissioner India, http://www.censusindia.gov.in.
3. Computed from Government of India, Ministry of Statistics and Program Implementation, http://mospi.nic.in/6_gsdp_cur_9394ser.htm (accessed January 2009).
4. World Bank, Development Data, 'Bangladesh At a Glance', http://devdata.worldbank.org/AAG/bgd_aag.pdf (accessed January 2009).
5. Sudha Ramachandran, 'Nepal To Get China Raillink', *Asia Times*, 15 May 2008.
6. Pete Engardio, *Chindia* (Tata McGraw Hill, India, 2008).
7. Thomas L. Friedman, *The World Is Flat* (Penguin, Books, 2006), p. 561.
8. Mahaguthi and Dhukuti are popular retail outlets owned by not-for-profits. They sell Nepali handicrafts and products produced by local artisans.

13. In Search of Unleashing

1. 'Maoists Withdraw Strike', in The Brief, *Nepali Times* online blog, 7 May 2010, http://www.nepalitimes.com/blogs/thebrief/2010/05/07/strike-withdrawn/.

2. Hum Gurung, 'Saving Annapurna', *The Kathmandu Post*, 24 December 2012, available at http://www.ekantipur.com/the-kathmandu-post/2012/12/24/oped/saving-annapurna/243286.html.

3. This author was on the board of Rupantaran Nepal, the organization that had won the bid.

4. Yubaraj Ghimire, 'Prachanda Gets China NGO Help for Lumbini', *The Indian Express*, 8 November 2012, Kathmandu, http://www.indianexpress.com/news/prachanda-gets-china-ngo-help-for-lumbini/1028349/.

5. Dillip Kumar Satapathy, 'India-China Bilateral Trade Projected at $100 bn by 2015', *Business Standard*, 15 April 2013, Bhubaneshwar, http://www.business-standard.com/article/economy-policy/india-china-bilateral-trade-projected-at-100-bn-by-2015-113041500358_1.html.

6. 'Prachanda: Time to Go for a Fresh Start', *The Hindu*, 17 September 2008, http://www.hindu.com/2008/09/17/stories/2008091760871200.htm. See also, 'Harsh Reality Outweighs Tall Claims', *The Kathmandu Post*, 30 August 2012, available at http://www.ekantipur.com/the-kathmandu-post/2012/08/29/top-story/harsh-reality-outweighs-tall-claims/238970.html.

7. All prices computed from Nepal Oil Corporation statistics, available at http://www.nepaloil.com.np/main/?opt1=sellingprice&opt2=previoussellingprice (accessed May 2013).

8. Ramesh Shrestha, 'Ncell Clinches No 1 spot from Nepal Telecom', *The Kathmandu Post*, 4 May 2013, available at http://www.ekantipur.com/the-kathmandu-post/2011/05/04/money/ncell-clinches-no-1-spot-from-nepal-telecom/221341.html.

9. Data from Nepal Economic Forum analysis.

10. 'Civil Servants Protest Khanal's Resignation', eKantipur.com, 30 March 2011, http://www.ekantipur.com/2011/03/30/capital/civil-servants-protest-khanals-resignation/331722.html.

11. Compiled from *Nepal Tourism Statistics 2011: Annual Statistical Report*, Ministry of Culture, Tourism and Civil Aviation, Government of Nepal, https://docs.google.com/viewer?url=http%3A%2F%2Fwww.tourism.gov.np%2Fuploaded%2Ffullpage.pdf.

12. Number of tourists arriving by air was 595,262 in 2011–12, according

to data in 'Current Macroeconomic Situation of Nepal', NRB.org, http://www.nrb.org.np/ofg/current_macroeconomic/Current_ Macroeconomic_Situation_(English)—2069-05_Text_(Based_on_ Annual_Data_of_2068-69).pdf.

13. 'More Chinese Tourists Coming to Visit Nepal', *People's Daily Online*, 21 August 2011, http://english.peopledaily.com.cn/90883/ 7575210.html.

14. 'Current Macroeconomic Situation of Nepal'.

15. 'Government Suspends Issuance of Radio License', *Republica*, 10 January 2013, http://www.myrepublica.com/portal/ index.php?action=news_details&news_id=48000. See list of licences, Ministry of Information and Communication, Government of Nepal, https://docs.google.com/viewer?url=http%3A%2F% 2Fwww.moic.gov.np%2Fpdf%2Ffm-list-2069-10-25.pdf (accessed May 2013).

16. List of licences, Ministry of Information and Communication, Government of Nepal, https://docs.google.com/viewer?url= http%3A%2F%2Fwww.moic.gov.np%2Fpdf%2Ftv-list- 2069-11-20.pdf (accessed May 2013).

17. 'Asia Marketing Research, Internet Usage, Population Statistics and Facebook Information', Internet World Stats.com, http:// www.internetworldstats.com/asia.htm.

18. Leplan, 'India, Nepal and Sri Lanka Among Top 5 Nations with Maximum Google Plus Users', Buzzom.com, 13 July 2011, http:// www.buzzom.com/2011/07/india-nepal-and-sri-lanka-among-top-5- nations-with-maximum-google-plus-users/.

INDEX